T0093538

Secure Data Management for Online Learning Applications

With the increasing use of e-learning, technology has not only revolution-ized the way businesses operate but has also impacted learning processes in the education sector. E-Learning is slowly replacing traditional methods of teaching and security in e-learning is an important issue in the educational context. With this book, you will be familiarized with the theoretical frame-works, technical methodologies, information security, and empirical research findings in the field to protect your computers and information from threats. *Secure Data Management for Online Learning Applications* will keep you interested and involved throughout.

Secure Data Management for Online Learning Applications

Edited by
L. Jegatha Deborah
P. Vijayakumar
Brij B. Gupta
Danilo Pelusi

CRC Press
Taylor & Francis Group
Boca Raton London New York

CRC Press is an imprint of the
Taylor & Francis Group, an **informa** business

First edition published 2023
by CRC Press
6000 Broken Sound Parkway NW, Suite 300, Boca Raton, FL 33487-2742

and by CRC Press
4 Park Square, Milton Park, Abingdon, Oxon, OX14 4RN

CRC Press is an imprint of Taylor & Francis Group, LLC

Library of Congress Cataloging-in-Publication Data
Names: Deborah, L. Jegatha, editor. | Vijayakumar, P., editor. | Gupta,
Brij, 1982- editor. | Pelusi, Danilo, editor.
Title: Secure data management for online learning applications / edited by:
L. Jegatha Deborah, P. Vijayakumar, Brij B.Gupta and Danilo Pelusi.
Description: First Edition. | Boca Raton ; London : CRC Press, 2023. |
Includes bibliographical references and index.
Identifiers: LCCN 2022047445 (print) | LCCN 2022047446 (ebook) | ISBN
9781032206424 (Hardback) | ISBN 9781032206431 (Paperback) | ISBN
9781003264538 (eBook)
Subjects: LCSH: Distance education--Computer-assisted
instruction--Management. | Computer networks--Security
measures--Computer programs. | Educational technology--Access control.
Classification: LCC LC5803.C65 S435 2023 (print) | LCC LC5803.C65 (ebook)
| DDC 371.33/4--dc23/eng/20221003
LC record available at https://lccn.loc.gov/2022047445
LC ebook record available at https://lccn.loc.gov/2022047446

ISBN: 978-1-032-20642-4 (hbk)
ISBN: 978-1-032-20643-1 (pbk)
ISBN: 978-1-003-26453-8 (ebk)

DOI: 10.1201/9781003264538

Typeset in Sabon
by SPi Technologies India Pvt Ltd (Straive)

Dedicated to my husband and children for their constant support during the course of this book.

L. Jegatha Deborah

Dedicated to my wife and children for their constant support during the course of this book.

P. Vijayakumar

Dedicated to my wife Varsha Gupta for her constant support during the course of this book.

Brij B. Gupta

Dedicated to my wife and children for their constant support during the course of this book.

Danilo Pelusi

Contents

Preface

As technology advances and user experience improves, so too does the popularity of online education, which has been proven to be a successful method of learning and offers a number of different benefits when compared with traditional education. Online teaching and learning refers to education that takes place over the internet. A significant number of colleges in the US and abroad are moving from the traditional face-to-face classes into fully online, web-based courses. Online education, often called distance education or web-based education, is currently the latest, and most popular form of distance education. It has recently become an integral part of many university programs. With the pandemic nearing no visible end, it is understood that educators, both in schools and colleges, will continue to rely on online learning. In the era of digitalization that we live in, cyber security incidences have reached unprecedented heights, and online learning needs to be secured from hackers.

Chapter 1: The topic of safe online evaluation of students' learning is covered as e-learning gradually replaces traditional classroom settings. Online education and learning have become major topics in regard to cyber security. Without the utilization of digital infrastructure, e-learning, which uses electronic technologies to provide knowledge and skills, is not conceivable. As e-learning spreads and more people enroll in online classes, safety and security have grown to be a significant issue in the contemporary academic environment. The integrity of data, authentication, content retention, access management, and other crucial issues must all be taken into account. This chapter focuses on using online services as learning and teaching platforms and discusses how spending time on social networking sites affects students' performance and productivity.

Chapter 2: the internet or the web is essential to the full operation of online learning techniques. Despite all the advantages the internet offers for uninterruptible learning, it is inescapably the source of all security risks. Online learning environments are hence more vulnerable to cyber-attacks. Numerous well-known video conferencing and online learning platforms, such as Moodle and Google Classroom, among others, all have their share of security risks. The various security risks, mostly from outside intruders, that could directly or indirectly influence online learning systems include virus threats, hacker risks, SQL injection risks, brute force risks, and denial of service risks. ARP cache poisoning, IP spoofing, stack-smashing attacks, session hijacking, cross-site request forgery (CSRF), masquerade, cross-site scripting (XSS), and MITM attacks are additional security dangers. This chapter on the numerous hazards or vulnerabilities associated with online learning may surprise e-learning companies as they install security measures.

Chapter 3: The global pandemic had a significant impact on school education and higher education because educational institutions were forced to close. The use of web and mobile learning applications has increased dramatically in recent years as a result of the COVID pandemic. Online learning apps are consequently susceptible to all types of security attacks, according to the Open Web Application Security Project (OWASP). Network eavesdropping, user password guessing, spamming, tunneling, man-in-the-middle attacks, HTTP manipulation, cookie manipulation, cross-site scripting, information exposure, and more are common attacks in online learning. Both the teacher and the student are immediately impacted by these when they are conducted through an online learning environment. This chapter gives analysis of the risks associated with using online learning apps, their classification as risks, and their effect on end users. It also discusses several preventative and preventive steps that can be taken when using online learning tools.

Chapter 4: The framework in this chapter is intended to guarantee the privacy-preserving data storage of online course data, the identity authentication of online learning users based on evaluation of trustworthiness, and the sharing of various significant online learning data. First of all, while authenticating people, both their identity and their reliability are taken into account. The evaluation of a user's trustworthiness is made possible by cloud computing and is based on the user's many attributes. In order to achieve access-traceless storage and user privacy preservation, Oblivious Random Access Memory (ORAM) is used.

Chapter 5: Due to the COVID pandemic, classroom learning has become almost impossible, and online learning has become the usual for both professors and pupils. Though it cannot replace in-person instruction, online learning can help teachers connect with students on a more personal level and make lessons more engaging. The teacher and student must be present in a physical classroom when using the traditional blended model, which also makes use of digital resources for interaction, as explored in this chapter.

Chapter 6: These days, group communication is necessary and the number of groups is rising. This causes problems with distributed systems' scalability characteristics. The size of the key domain increases proportionally as the size of the group steadily increases. In a setting of group conversations, the size of the storage required to retain this big quantum of keys becomes a contentious issue. This problem is reflected in both new user registrations for the group and group member departures. Because the group key must be regenerated at these two events, key updating must be done at those times. The certificate authority (CA) is in charge of transferring the key in a secure manner. The very large ongoing challenge is applications based on multi-cast as well as multi-media key distribution.

Chapter 7: By incorporating visuals and animation in presentations, online learning facilitates quick and effective understanding. E-learning includes live readings from the agricultural and medical fields that are valuable for prediction and decision-making in real time, in addition to traditional classroom instruction. Keys are required to create encryption, envelopes, and encapsulations in the secure learning approaches presented here. Therefore, playing a significant part in creating effective, secure learning is crucial.

Chapter 8: This chapter provides information on integrity verification for e-learning settings and makes three attempts to address the problems with e-learning data integrity verification. The first is the development of a brand-new integrity verification system that makes use of elliptic curve cryptography's high level of security. The careful design of the protocol with less computationally intensive procedures to accommodate various devices is the second context. The third setting focuses on making public auditing techniques more defensible.

Chapter 9: The preferred method of learning is through e-learning recommendation systems. Personalized course learning materials based on each student's learning preferences are not without their limitations and security issues, even if both institutions and students welcome the use of technology in their educational processes. By adding data about the users and the material they are seeing, no-blockchain recommendation engines, such as collaborative and content-based filtering, may now better target their suggestions. This chapter addresses these concerns and improves the consistency, security, and quality of the recommendation system. There is no regard for the preferences of students, such as their preferred ways of learning, which will help to assure the accuracy and security of course learning materials.

Chapter 10: This chapter must test various presentation and meeting formats in order to investigate various options for sending data securely and quickly. The goal is to achieve high information performance efficiency for textual, multimedia, and secured transmission. Certain key management and distribution mechanisms can be used to ensure secure transmission. Currently, Zoom, Google Meet, Microsoft Teams, Cisco Screen Sharing, and Zoho Meeting are used to arrange online classes, teleconferencing, web conferencing, webinars, and screen or application sharing. These innovative solutions provide private link sharing in a safe way with participants or an audience. The chapter's goal is to describe several key management approaches that might be used to safeguard online teaching and learning environments.

Chapter 11: Online education has expanded quickly. It may be divided into many different categories, for instance, vocational training, evaluation and certification training, and primary and secondary education, which are all important aspects of education (Kindergarten through 12th grade). The popularity of massive open online courses (MOOCs) has increased significantly. Comparing the present forms and procedures to a digital internet that is freer and more open reveals several problems. An asymmetric encryption technique is used in blockchain cryptography to safeguard the data's integrity. Based on this idea, a certification system for learning outcomes might be created. The online education platform or issuing organization keeps track of student learning information. The data is encrypted using either the platform's or the company's private key. The encrypted digital certificates are then sent to the students and other network users.

Chapter 12: As the fourth industrial revolution takes hold, online education is expanding quickly (Industry 4.0). Teachers can effectively present their material to students by using a variety of online technologies. Furthermore, learners can access the material from any place and at any time. Online learning is thus advantageous to both students and teachers. Since sharing of content takes place online, a reliable system for sending information securely to organizations is needed.

Chapter 13 discusses web technology, which allows for the widespread availability and accessibility of user-generated information on the internet. This accessibility has made space for a paradigm shift in idea gathering that is simpler. We do not have time to stand about and gaze in our fast-paced world, which is perfect for a situation when we do not want to read each and every assessment of a good or service. Sentiment analysis is thus a necessary procedure that aids every producer and brand owner in weighing the advantages and disadvantages of both their own products and those of their rivals.

Acknowledgements

Many people have contributed greatly to this book, *Secure Data Management for Online Learning Applications*. We, the editors, would like to acknowledge all of them for their valuable help and generous ideas in improving the quality of this book. We convey our feelings of gratitude to all mentioned below. The first mention is the authors and reviewers of each chapter of this book. Without their expertise, constructive reviews and devoted effort, this comprehensive book would not be nearly as effective. The second mention is the CRC Press/Taylor & Francis Group staff, especially Gabriella Williams and her team for their constant encouragement, continuous assistance, and untiring support. Without their technical contributions, this book would not have been completed. The third mention are the editors' families for being the source of continuous love, unconditional support and prayers not only for this work, but in all other matters. Last but far from least, we express our heartfelt thanks to the Almighty for bestowing on us the courage to face the complexities of life and to complete this work.

March 2022
L. Jegatha Deborah
P. Vijayakumar
Brij B. Gupta
Danilo Pelusi

Editors' biographies

L. Jegatha Deborah has 15 years of experience in teaching and five years of experience in research. Her core research areas of interest include artificial intelligence, cognitive linguistics, key management in network security, and machine learning. She received her BE degree in computer science and engineering from Madurai Kamaraj University, Madurai, India in 2002, her ME degree in computer science and engineering from the Karunya Institute of Technology, Coimbatore, India in 2005, and her PhD degree in computer science and engineering from Anna University, Chennai, India in 2013. She is a life member of the ISTE professional body and is serving as a doctoral committee member for various universities such as VIT University and Sathyabama University. She is currently guiding four Doctoral of Philosophy scholars in various domains including online learning, intelligent transportation systems, key management for industrial Internet of Things (IoT) applications, and machine learning for autistic children. She has given many guest lectures at international conferences, seminars, and workshops in various domains such as data mining, neural networks, artificial intelligence, and intelligent tutoring systems. She has written many research papers published in reputed journals by IEEE, Elsevier, Springer, Wiley, Taylor & Francis, and Inderscience, among others. One of her research papers based on intelligent transportation systems was awarded "Best Paper" during a presentation for an international conference for Springer publishers. She is very interested in cognitive linguistics and has developed a model for learning management systems. She has also been a guest editor for special issues published by Elsevier, Inderscience and others. With regard to societal initiatives, she is an active member of the Youth Red Cross and also the program officer in a working institute. She has visited many countries for international conferences and for employment including Malaysia, the USA, and China, as well as west Africa.

P. Vijayakumar received his BE degree in computer science and engineering from Madurai Kamaraj University, Madurai, India in 2002, his ME degree in computer science and engineering from the Karunya Institute of Technology, Coimbatore, India in 2005, and his PhD degree in computer science and engineering from Anna University, Chennai, India in 2013. He is the former dean and currently an assistant professor with the Department of Computer Science and Engineering, University College of Engineering Tindivanam, Melpakkam, India, which is a constituent college of Anna University Chennai, India. He has seventeen years of teaching experience, and he has successfully guided four PhD candidates. He has also authored and co-authored more than 100 quality papers in various IEEE transactions/journals, ACM transactions, Elsevier, IET, Springer, Wiley, and IGI Global journals. He is serving as associate editor in many SCI indexed journals, namely *IEEE Transactions on Intelligent Transportation Systems (T-ITS)*, *International Journal of Communication Systems* (Wiley), *PLOS One*, *International Journal of Semantic Web and Information Systems* (IGI Global), and *Security and Communication Networks* (Wiley/Hindawi). Moreover, he is serving as an academic editor for the *International Journal of Organizational and Collective Intelligence* (IGI Global), *International Journal of Software Science and Computational Intelligence* (IGI Global), *International Journal of Cloud Applications and Computing* (IGI Global), *International Journal of Digital Strategy, Governance, and Business Transformation* (IGI Global), and *Security and Privacy*(Wiley). He is also serving as a technical committee member for the journal *Computer Communications* (Elsevier). Recently, he was elevated to the position of editor-in-chief for the journal *Cyber Security and Applications* (KeAi/Elsevier). Till now he has authored four books on various subjects relating to the department of computer science and engineering. He is a senior member of IEEE. He was also listed in the world's top 2% of scientists for citation impact during the calendar year 2020 by Stanford University.

Professor Brij B. Gupta is director of the International Center for AI and Cyber Security Research and Innovations, & Department of Computer Science and Information Engineering, Asia University, Taichung 413, Taiwan. In more than 17 years of professional experience, he has published over 500 papers in journals/conferences including 30 books and 10 patents with over 18,000 citations. He has received numerous national and international awards including the Canadian Commonwealth Scholarship (2009), the Faculty Research Fellowship Award (2017), MeitY, GoI, IEEE, GCCE outstanding and WIE paper awards and Best Faculty Award (2018 and 2019), NIT, KKR, respectively. Professor Gupta was recently elected for the 2022 Clarivate Web of Science Highly Cited Researchers in Computer Science list (the only researcher in computer science from Taiwan and India in this prestigious 2022 HCR list). He was also selected in the 2022, 2021 and 2020 Stanford University's ranking of the world's top 2% scientists. He is also a visiting/adjunct professor with several universities worldwide, an IEEE Senior Member (2017) and was selected as 2021 Distinguished Lecturer in IEEE CTSoc. Professor Gupta is also serving as Member-in-Large on the Board of Governors, IEEE Consumer Technology Society

(2022–2024). Professor Gupta leads IJSWIS, IJSSCI, STE, and IJCAC as Editor-in-Chief. Moreover, he is also serving as lead-editor of a Book Series with CRC and IET press. He also served as TPC member at more than 150 international conferences and as associate/guest editor of various journals and transactions. His research interests include information security, cyber physical systems, cloud computing, blockchain technologies, intrusion detection, AI, social media, and networking.

Danilo Pelusi received the degree in Physics from the University of Bologna (Italy) and the Ph.D. degree in Computational Astrophysics from the University of Teramo (Italy). He is an Associate Professor of Computer Science at the Department of Communication Sciences, University of Teramo. Editor of Springer, Elsevier and CRS books, and Associate Editor of IEEE Transactions on Emerging Topics in Computational Intelligence (2017-2020), IEEE Access (2018-present), IEEE Transactions on Neural Networks and Learning Systems (2022-present) and IEEE Transactions on Intelligent Transportation Systems (2022-present), he is Guest Editor for Elsevier, Springer, MDPI and Hindawi journals. Keynote speaker, Guest of Honor and Chair of IEEE conferences, he is inventor of international patents on Artificial Intelligence. World's 2% Top Scientist 2021, his research interests include Fuzzy Logic, Neural Networks, Information Theory, Machine Learning and Evolutionary Algorithms.

Contributors

S. Ambika
E.G.S. Pillay Engineering College
Nagapatinam, India

Jennifer Daffodils Amesh
The American College, Madurai,
    India

A.S. Anakath
E.G.S. Pillay Engineering College
Nagapatinam, India

S. Arunkumar
Nehru Institute of Engineering &
    Technology
Coimbatore, India

C. Beulah
Karunya Institute of Technology
    and Sciences
Coimbatore, India

S. Deepa Kanmani
Sri Krishna College of Engineering
    and Technology
Coimbatore, India

S. Geetha
Department of Geography
Government College for Women (A)
Kumbakonam, India

L. Jegatha Deborah
Department of Computer Science
    and Engineering
University College of Engineering
    Tindivanam
Tindivanam, India

V. Jeyalakshmi
College of Engineering Guindy
Anna University, Chennai, India

Adri Jovin John Joseph
Department of Information
    Technology
Sri Ramakrishna Institute of
    Technology
Coimbatore, India

R. Kannadasan
VIT University
Vellore, India

K.R. Karthick
Anna University Regional Campus
    Madurai
Keelakuilkudi, Madurai, India

R. Karthika
Department of Computer Science
    and Engineering
University College of Engineering
    Tindivanam
Tindivanam, India

Christalin Latha
Karunya Institute of Technology
    and Sciences
Coimbatore, India

Azees Maria
School of Computer Science and
    Engineering
VIT-AP University
Inavolu, Beside AP Secretariat,
    Amaravathi 522237, India

Marikkannan Mariappan
Department of Computer Science
    and Engineering
Government College of Engineering
Erode, India

S. Milton Ganesh
University College of Engineering
    Tindivanam
Tindivanam, India

K.S. Niraja
BVRIT Hyderabad College of
    Engineering for Women
Hyderabad, India

K. Nithya
Dr. M.G.R. Educational and
    Research Institute University
Chennai, India

Sujni Paul
Faculty Higher Colleges of
    Technology
Dubai, UAE

S. Rajakumar
University College of Engineering
    Ariyalur
Ariyalur, India

Rajan John
College of Computer Science and
    Information Technology
Jazan University, KSA

Arun Sekar Rajasekaran
Department of ECE
KPR Institute of Engineering and
    Technology
Coimbatore, India

S. Rajkumar
PSNA college of Engineering and
    Technology
Dindigul, India

S.C. Rajkumar
Department of Computer Science
    and Engineering
Anna University Regional Campus
    Madurai
Keelakuilkudi, Madurai, India

G. Ramesh
KLN College of Engineering and
    technology
Madurai, India

Dahlia Sam
Dr. M.G.R. Educational and
    Research Institute University
Chennai, India

J. Satheeshkumar
Anna University Regional Campus
    Madurai
Keelakuilkudi, Madurai, India

S. Senthilkumar
University College of Engineering
    Pattukkottai
Rajamadam, India

A. Shamila Ebenezer
Karunya Institute of Technology
    and Sciences
Coimbatore, India

Adlin Sheeba
St. Joseph's Institute of Technology
Chennai, India

Jian Shen
School of Information Science and
    Engineering
Zhejiang Sci-Tech University
Hangzhou, China

C. Sindhu
Department of Computing
    Technologies
SRM Institute of Science and
    Technology
Kattankulathur, India

Fahmina Taranum
Muffakham Jah College of
    Engineering and Technology
Osmania University
Hyderabad, India

B. Uma Maheswari
St. Joseph's College of Engineering
Chennai, India

G. Vadivu
Department of Data Science and
    Business Systems
SRM Institute of Science and
    Technology
Kattankulathur, India

S.V. Vijaya Karthik
SAP Consultant
Tata Consultancy Services
Bangalore, India

P. Vijayakumar
University College of Engineering
Tindivanam, India

Chen Wang
School of Information Science and
    Engineering
Zhejiang Sci-Tech University
Hangzhou, China

Huijie Yang
School of Computer and Software
Nanjing University of Information
    Science & Technology
Nanjing, China

Tianqi Zhou
School of Information Science and
    Engineering
Zhejiang Sci-Tech University
Hangzhou, China

Chapter 1

Secure online assessment of students using optimized deep learning techniques

S.V. Vijaya Karthik

Tata Consultancy Services, Bangalore, India

S. Arunkumar

Nehru Institute of Engineering & Technology, Coimbatore, India

CONTENTS

DOI: 10.1201/9781003264538-1

Nowadays, due to the current pandemic situation, education is slowly shifting ahead from conventional classroom environments and toward e-learning that is online education. When it comes to cybersecurity, online education and learning has emerged as a hot subject. E-learning, as a way of delivering information as well as skills via electronic methods, is impossible to do in the absence of the use of digital infrastructure. In alternate words, it is heavily reliant on online infrastructure for the exchange of thoughts and knowledge. Unfortunately, the network system is indeed a haven for intruders, hackers, and internet fraudsters. As the internet's influence extends to include ever-wider areas of education, learning, and public welfare, cyber-attacks are a key worry when it comes to the confidentiality, authenticity, and privacy of user data kept on a database domain controller. Safety and security have become a major problem in the current academic environment, as e-learning is becoming increasingly widespread, and many individuals are attending online classes. Numerous essential factors need to be considered, including integrity of data, authentication, content preservation, access management and so on. Approaches including encryption, network protocols and cryptography could be used to achieve data security. The internet's limitless expanse is referred to as cyberspace. Cyber security is the framework of regulations set in place to preserve cyberspace. Various investigations have shown the rising usage of e-learning platforms, which continues to expand; nevertheless, minimal consideration has been devoted to the problem of e-learning platform security in both education as well as research. In this chapter, a classification model for evaluating students' productivity via an online system via machine learning techniques is developed using the optimized DNN. The study concentrates on using online services as a learning and teaching platform and how students' productivity and performance are affected when they spend time on social media sites. With a plethora of digital sources, technologies might serve to strengthen the education system. Educators could use a wide range of applications or reliable online tools to enhance traditional teaching methods and engage pupils further. Digital lesson preparation, graduating software, plus online assessments could help educators conserve a huge amount of time. Cyber security provides digitalized data sets that can also be used for learning assessment, such as using paths to improve learning activity along with the atmosphere that students leave behind. There is emphasis on employing learning analytics in online information safety and security training to create a better proof-based systematic way for analyzing learning impacts and generating more effective learning. There is one thing that teachers, organizers, and digital company owners must keep in mind: the chapter's primary goal is to investigate all present techniques for data stealing which utilize cyber security learning. Initially, the data associated with e-learning is gathered from standard, publicly available database sources. From the gathered data sources, user-centric techniques such as, "learner support, teaching support, learning centers, and feedback" are specified. Further, the classification is done by the well- performing deep learning algorithm called Deep Neural Network (DNN), where the hidden neurons are tuned by the proposed Fitness-based Butterfly Optimization Algorithm (F-BOA) with the consideration of minimizing the insecure information ratio, thus called Modified Deep Neural Network (MDNN). This MDNN classifies the final output according to whether the data is secure or insecure. Finally, in order to evidence that the newly proposed F-BOA is better or not, it is contrasted with traditional metaheuristic-based as well as classifier algorithms in terms of various analyses that describe the superiority of the introduced F-BOA.

1.1 INTRODUCTION

E-learning enhances as well as enriches the education method by utilizing gadgets dependent on computing and software technologies. Virtual classrooms, digital collaboration, web-based learning, and computer-based learning are all examples of e-learning application fields and methods. The information can be accessed digitally through the web, CD-ROM, audio cassette, intranet, video cassette, satellite and DVD. E-learning is the term used to describe web-based learning and online courses, among others. As a result, a computer-based educational system might be described as an e-learning element because it does not need a continual connection with an instructor or other pupils. E-learning has a lot of advantages for firms, and is ideal for targeted and accurate corporate training. E-learning is a sort of correspondence course since the learners and the educator may be in different locations and the connectivity is primarily asynchronous. Because of emerging innovations in educational system growth and the necessity of constructing programs that can be accessed remotely, scientists and web software developers are becoming deeply focused on securing the data of e-learning platforms as well as authentication protocols. Meeting security and safety requirements in an e-education system is a complex challenge because the material, services, and private details must be safeguarded not just for outside entities, but also for internal entities, like administrators of the system. With a variety of online tools, technology may help improve education. To improve traditional teaching and increase student engagement, teachers can use a variety of applications or reliable online resources. Graduation software, online assessments, and virtual lesson preparation can help instructors save a lot of time. Machine learning (ML) algorithms are employed to find data structures or patterns that can help in decision-making. ML and decision-making depending on previous data and results are used to build existing behavioral traits. Some adjustments do need human assistance. Until today, ML is undoubtedly the most important AI subject. In the new training method, the ability to forecast student success is crucial.

Distance learning and e-learning are not the same thing. The physical separation of the learner from the teacher and the classroom is what differentiates distance education. E-learning, on the other hand, has always been a component of the classroom setting. The early usage of computers was intended to assist the teacher in the classroom. As more personal computers became available, several pioneering schools and universities began to investigate the notion of online classrooms. Distance education's early initiatives were impeded by opposition from fundamentalists in the teaching profession. Some used what they dubbed "educational philosophy" to argue that the educator was critical to the educational process. As a result of this opposition, early online degrees were inferior to regular degrees. This bias persisted even in the human resources divisions of big corporations. When deciding between two applicants who were otherwise equally competent, the conventional degree holder was given precedence. This has significantly altered in recent years. The capability to build virtual classrooms as well as the VLE has steadily smashed through opposition as e-learning technology has improved. The development of a new generation that has grown up with computers has aided this trend. It would not be shocking if the pendulum swings entirely in the next generation, with online degrees being the most highly regarded and sought. The conventional method of e-learning has been to utilize a VLE, which is software that is sometimes clunky and classy and is organized around courses, schedules, and assessment. This is a method that is much too often led by the demands of the institution instead of the needs of each individual learner. On the other hand, by integrating the usage of distinct but complementary tools and web services—including blogging, wikis, as well as other web applications—e-learning 2.0 supports the establishment of ad hoc learning societies by using a "little parts, loosely attached" strategy.

Higher education is increasingly exploring the use of computer systems as well as technologies to satisfy the requirements and demands of diversified learners who require more than conventional classroom-based courses. In modern course delivery techniques, face-to-face elements are being integrated with e-learning, webinars, and other online digital material. Since e-learning platforms allow for both asynchronous and synchronous interactions, it's vital to establish confidence and help involvement amongst learners. Asynchronous education is self-reliant and enables individuals to communicate knowledge or information without depending on the simultaneous involvement of other participants. Synchronous learning takes place in the real-time world, with all individuals participating simultaneously. During the last several years, e-learning has exploded in popularity [2]. WebCT, Moodle, and Blackboard are examples of e-learning systems that are varied and widely used. They are large and crowded, with a diverse set of entities and assets. Sharing of information, cooperation, collaboration, and connectivity are critical components of any e-learning system. After this, the information must be protected to guarantee its privacy, security, integrity, and accessibility. Data corruption, fake user authorization, and privacy risks are all key security problems in e-learning. Meanwhile, e-learning trends necessitate more interoperability of applications, studying atmosphere, and heterogeneous systems.

The current chapter's contribution is:

- To investigate all present techniques for data stealing which utilize cyber security learning through the optimized deep learning technique.
- To specify user-centric techniques such as, "learner support, teaching support, learning centers, and feedback."
- To perform classification by the well-performing deep learning algorithm, Deep Neural Network (DNN), where the hidden neurons are tuned with the consideration of minimizing the insecure information ratio, thus called the Modified Deep Neural Network (MDNN).
- To propose a novel optimization algorithm called Fitness-based Butterfly Optimization Algorithm (F-BOA) for enhancing the classification phase, and to compare with existing heuristic-based as well as classifier algorithms in terms of various analyses that describe the superiority of the introduced F-BOA.

The chapter is organized as follows. Section 1.1. provides a detailed introduction of online assessment methods. Section 1.2. deals with a detailed literature survey regarding the secure online assessment of students. Section 1.3. illustrates the proposed architectural model as well as the user-centric system in education. The employed process for the purpose of e-learning is given in Section 1.4, while Section 1.5 elaborates on cyber security in the field of education. Section 1.6 provides information about security threats, detection, and protection in distributed e-learning systems. The MDNN based on the proposed F-BOA is depicted in Section 1.7. The results and discussions are presented in Section 1.8, and finally, the conclusion of the chapter is given in Section 1.9.

1.2 LITERATURE SURVEY

1.2.1 Related works

In 2017, Núñez et al. [1] defined and analyzed the process of establishing a mini exclusive online program that fits the requirements for being offered as a big course. The beginning step was an online higher education program that had formerly been offered as Open Course Ware. Information from 112 enrolled students in four academic terms were evaluated in this study, during which time alterations were progressively introduced to transform the standard course into an open course. The results show that students' perceptions of resources and evaluations, as well as their general contentment, increased. New evaluation measures were developed and validated without sacrificing academic achievements. Although the technique had a positive influence on the final course's instructional design, some issues were discovered when the course was transformed into a massive course. The completed course provides useful input for future adjustments as well as a more successful student-centered strategy.

In 2021, Naveh and Bykhovsky [2] conducted a situational study of an online peer assessment (PA) deployment in a random processes course. Learners were asked to complete simulation tasks and then assess the work of their peers. The study used questionnaires to learn about the students' perceptions of the activity throughout the semester, as well as data from the course to learn about their behavior and academic achievement.

In 2005, Cleaver and Elbasyouni [3] in an introductory circuits class, utilized interactive online lessons as a supplement to traditional instructional delivery. Web-related constraints-passing techniques and cookies were used to track the pupils' online activities. Most students repeated the lessons enough times to obtain flawless marks, according to the writers.

In 2008, Farrow and King [4] assessed undergraduates who had studied Java for two terms using an online programming test. The benefits include that learners are evaluated on what they must accomplish in practice rather than on their academic knowledge, and the examiner's workload is significantly reduced. The type of question asked, and the outcomes of the test are both examined.

In 2020, J. S. Jeong and D. Gonzalez-Gomez [5] employed the Fuzzy-Decision-Making Trial and Evaluation Laboratory (F-DEMATEL) / Multi-Criteria Decision Analysis (MCDA) method to determine and analyze the most essential sustainability science education criteria in e-learning systems. To attain the intended goal, sustainability, science education, e-learning, and technology criteria were specified, allocated, weighted, and assessed in four categories. Within the scope of impact and assessment, the participatory F-DEMATEL technique was utilized to analyze 16 sub-criteria depending on the amount and computation of coefficients. Weighted Linear Combination (WLC) was used to collect the most important criteria, which were then examined utilizing risk assessment of six implementation strategies (A to F), and a skilled online survey was used to acquire the sub-criteria. According to the F-DEMATEL/MCDA study, the most significant criteria in durability and e-learning platforms in scientific education were sustainability characteristics (Approach A, 0.54 with 84% most probable and likely professional perception survey). It also demonstrated that environmental information was the most critical variable amongst sub-criteria (0.57 with 77% more likely and probable professional perception survey). Approach F obtained a 19% excellent expert evaluation since the major critical criteria were considered equally (0.25). As a consequence, fuzzy-operational and multi-decision evaluation, as well as a specialist poll, can be employed to determine the most essential sustainability science online-learning characteristics, which could then be utilized to create versatile and appropriate choice features.

Lawrence-Benedict et al. [6] investigated the conceptual as well as the administrative components of an online sport administration degree program from the standpoint of Community of Inquiry (CoI) in 2019. The researchers utilized adapted CoI concepts to evaluate qualitative and quantitative data from student departure surveys from an online professional graduate degree in sport management in order to improve the program's content, structure, and delivery. According to the quantitative statistics, students rated the program highly in almost all measured components of CoI. As per the qualitative data, learners had partaken in the three key areas of CoI such as coaching, cognitive, and social. The qualitative data supports the quantitative findings and demonstrates that the program adhered to CoI principles. As an outcome of the research, academic leaders and faculty were informed about aspects of CoI and the nature of holistic assessment of academic programs.

In 2014, Cukusic et al. [7] found that the advantages of online self-assessment examinations as a formative evaluation strategy were proven in one of the first-year UG programs. Students' accomplishments, such as examination results and pass rates, were contrasted throughout three centuries for the same topic, as well as against examination outcomes from other courses given during the same semester. According to the study, with the addition of online self-assessment, there was a reasonably noteworthy variance among the categories for half-semester exams and examination pass rates. A simulation model was used to mimic positive impacts on student achievement for the entire institution. The findings show that a little improvement in pass rates can have a big influence on overall success, specifically, lower dropout rates.

In 2019, Venter et al. [8] discovered that a particular training style made young South African women disproportionately vulnerable to cyber-attacks, regardless that in reality the group was mostly male. As a result, we feel that cryptography should be studied alongside the "3 Rs": delivering required skills at college level does not adequately prepare young South Africans for a future in which cyber security is essential. In order to guarantee that people have the skills they need when they need them, commencing teaching cyber security knowledge and consciousness in elementary school and incorporating it throughout the syllabus would close the gender gap in cyber security awareness.

Gürdür Broo et al. [9] investigated how these new traits would affect Cyber Physical systems (CPS) education and research by 2030, the United Nations' deadline for fulfilling the Sustainable Development Agenda. To do this, a trend identifying exercise to uncover possible key determinants was conducted, that might have a substantial impact on CPS research and education in the future. These elements were divided into 12 categories, four of which were certain (connectivity, electricity, data, and automation) and eight of which were uncertain (labor market, intelligence, higher education, data ethics, technology trust, sustainable development goals, technological development speed, and lifelong learning). Then, two of the eight uncertainties were identified and employed to generate a four-scenario scenario matrix. The two uncertainties—the so-called strategic uncertainty—were the achievement of sustainable development goals and the nature of technological growth. These two key uncertainties were considered in the scenarios due to their potential impact on CPS education and research.

Katsantonis et al. [10] proposed the Conceptual Framework for E-learning and Training (COFELET) ontology and COFELET in 2021. The COFELET ontology outlines fundamental aspects of such methods in order to use well-known cyber security threat assessment and modelling standards as a means of creating engaging teaching experiences. COFELET is a concept that may be used to construct and evaluate successful cyber security education and training initiatives. COFELET game life-cycle was proposed, a blueprint exhibiting the design elements and the sequence of steps for the production of COFELET compliance games, with the purpose of providing insights into how COFELET compliant ways may be generated (COFELET games). A COFELET ontology expansion was also suggested, which outlines the relevant components utilized in the development of the COFELET games' training and instructional components. Based on the life-cycle of a COFELET game and the enhanced COFELET ontology, a prototype hacking simulator COFELET game was developed and named HackLearn. A systematic extract of the HackLearn framework was provided, together with an assessment based on the Activity Theory Model for Serious Games (ATMSG) and a set of COFELET ontology object instances. Ultimately, HackLearn's game design was tested using a preliminary evaluation technique created for the assessment of innovative cyber security game-based learning methodologies. The outcomes of the review showed that HackLearn integrates a number of features of cyber security game-based learning methodologies, as well as reasons to be optimistic about the efficiency of the cyber security education and experience it will provide.

1.2.2 Review

The educational landscape has been transformed by open education. Massive open online courses (MOOCs) have emerged as the primary showcase for free educational resources, yet the rush to have a foothold in the movement has resulted in the rapid publishing of numerous courses of questionable quality. Table 1.1 depicts the merits and demerits of traditional online

Table 1.1 Features and challenges of traditional online assessment methods

Author [citation]	Methodology	Features	Challenges
Núñez et al. [1]	PBL	It provides a significant information source for making adjustments and future enhancement of several MOOCs.	Various contrasting studies are needed for the enhancement and usage of OER.
Naveh and Bykhovsky [2]	Peer assessment	The complexity of the PA implementation in the case of engineering education is described clearly.	It does not make different case studies for the identical settings.
Cleaver and Elbasyouni [3]	Web-based education	The problems are solved by the students in earlier attempts and are solved correctly in the final attempt.	It spends more time on each tutorial.
Farrow and King [4]	Automatic evaluation	It does not significantly disadvantage the students.	It does not propose various demanding question types for enhanced classes.
J. S. Jeong and D. Gonzalez-Gomez [5]	F-DEMATEL/MCDA	It handles the MCDA problem because of to pertinent and pliable features.	It does not return a meaningful difference.

(*Continued*)

Table 1.1 (Continued) Features and challenges of traditional online assessment methods

Author [citation]	Methodology	Features	Challenges
Lawrence-Benedict et al.[6]	CoI	The community is assessed over time by the quantitative instrument or element.	It does not strengthen the entire offerings through a robust online degree program.
Cukusic et al. [7]	Online self-assessment	Student success is reinforced by the formative assessment shift.	It does not generalize the studied group according to demographic, geographic, and social differences.
Venter et al. [8]	Gendered cyber crime	The current gender imbalances are removed in cyber security awareness.	Urgent requirement is not met to teach cyber security principles at an earlier stage.
Gürdür Broo et al. [9]	TAIDA framework	The CPS is addressed with respect to integrated and technological product development.	The access to learning platforms is not expanded.
Katsantonis et al [10]	COFELET	It is less expensive for generating novel scenarios.	It does not consider the multi-mode operations and multi-player support.

assessment methods. Problem-Based Learning (PBL) [1] provides a significant information source for making the adjustments and future enhancement of several MOOCs, but various contrasting studies are needed for the enhancement and usage of Open Educational Resources (OER). Peer assessment [2] clearly describes the complexity of the PA implementation in the case of engineering education. Still, it does not make different case studies for identical settings. Web-based education [3] solves the problems by the students in earlier attempts and is solved correctly in the final attempt. Yet, it spends more time on each tutorial. Automatic evaluation [4] does not significantly disadvantage the students. But it does not propose various demanding question types for enhanced classes. F-DEMATEL/MCDA [5] handles the Multi-Criteria Decision Analysis (MCDA) problem due to pertinent and pliable features. Still, it does not return a meaningful difference. CoI [6] assesses the community over time by the quantitative instrument or element. Yet, it does not strengthen the entire offerings through a robust online degree program.

Online self-assessment [7] reinforces the student's success by the formative assessment shift. But it does not generalize the studied group according to demographic, geographic, and social differences. Gendered cybercrime [8] removes the current gender imbalances in cyber security awareness. Still, the urgent requirement to teach cyber security principles in an earlier stage is not addressed. The Tracking Analyzing Imaging Deciding Acting (TAIDA) framework [9] addresses CPS with respect to integrated and technological product development. Yet, the access to learning platforms is not expanded. COFELET [10] is less expensive for generating novel scenarios. But multi-mode operations and multi-player support are not considered. Thus, it is necessary to introduce novel deep learning methods for protecting the online assessment of students from cyber hacking.

1.3 ARCHITECTURAL MODEL

1.3.1 Proposed architectural model and user-centric system in education

All higher academic institutions must be conscious of their obligations for the protection of academic and research data, and establish the appropriate precautions to ensure compliance with the Data Protection Act (DPA) in 1998. Most higher academic institutions would have distinct data and research management frameworks in place, as well as appropriate degrees of supervision. In addition, a variety of data management rules and procedures will be in place, with mistakes receiving relatively little attention. These characteristics make it difficult for corporate governance to appreciate the concerns while also comprehending the true requirement for a process framework to monitor, regulate, and reduce worker cyber security hazards. Ultimately, digital network safety is a shared accountability for the entire organization. By exchanging information with peers, the government, and others, network administrators and guardians may keep up to speed on risks and countermeasures. The importance of users' contributions to the safety and security of any of the network and related information cannot be overstated. They must be at the center of assessing the threats to information, understanding security goals, and, eventually, assuming responsibility for control implementation. The proposed architectural model is shown in Figure 1.1.

1.3.2 Support from learners

Learners should be provided with all necessary information prior to beginning their course so that they may make informed study selections and use all available tools and resources. Throughout the chapter, information

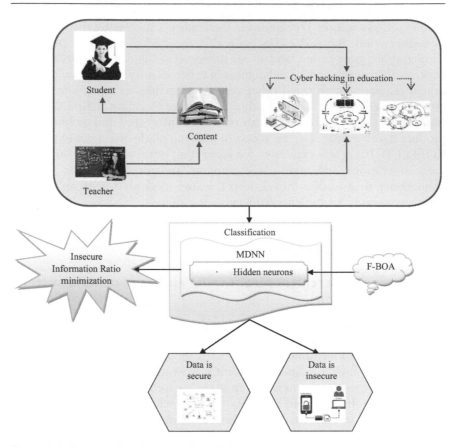

Figure 1.1 Proposed architectural model.

on various activities, research materials, evaluation methods, and other administrative support tools is offered. Learning Support System (LSS) is a class management application that includes attendance records, quizzes, schedules, and tasks. It is a class-based apprenticeship management system that students can use to strengthen their self-reliant studying abilities, as it encourages long-standing objectives, builds time-managing skills, increases learning autonomy, and improves self-assessment.

1.3.3 Support from teaching

Technical advisers, where theoretical and practical consultation will take place, tasks, practical programming, audio visual aid usage, teleconferences, interactive radio station services, and other details on university financing may be found here.

1.3.4 Centers of learning

Students can access technical assistance, rehabilitation services, homework submissions and evaluation, semester examinations, and also certain other common help.

1.3.5 Feedback

Instructor materials and students receive feedback on task replies.

$$X(t,d) = \frac{\left(1 + \log_2\left(o_{t,d}\right)\right) * \log_2\left(\frac{|M|}{t(d)}\right)}{\sqrt{\Sigma\left(\log_2\left(o_{t,d}\right)\right)^* } \log_2\left(\frac{|M|}{t(d)}\right)} \tag{1.1}$$

In Equation (1.1), each student t is linked with each topic d in lessons M with distinct vectors $t(d)$, $o_{t,d}$ is the association within the content and the student, $\log_2(o_{t,d})$ is the log-likelihood function of the content and the student, and $\log_2(o_{t,d})$ is the log-likelihood function of students and content. The weightage X of the learning process in pupils must be calculated. It is necessary to employ IT to choose, enroll, transfer, save, analyze, and present data accordance with the demands of the audience and the lab activity.

1.4 PROCESS UTILIZED FOR E-LEARNING

1.4.1 E-learning trends

Students can enter the digital classroom using a variety of digital gadgets as well as networks from a variety of places. To satisfy the demands for "know what" and "know how" training, e-learning technologies will supplant classroom training. Courseware or the digital classroom will gradually adapt to students' choices or requirements, whilst e-learning will enable more user customization. To put it another way, future e-learning apps will be intelligent and adaptable. Corporate education has evolved into knowledge management. In the digital economy, this is the overall tendency. Employee competencies are assets in knowledge management, and training increases their worth. This tendency has encouraged the creation of task-specific training rather than general training. Changes in company strategy directions are frequently mirrored in modifications to suit online education needs, which are motivated and driven by the need to train employees for the new orientations. Open standards are becoming more prevalent in e-learning.

1.4.2 General elements needed for e-learning

Some of the common elements required for e-learning are as follows.

1.4.2.1 Content

The knowledge to be transmitted is the major emphasis of learning material, and it guides the mode of transfer (for instance, the subject of mathematics is not similar to the subject of history).

1.4.2.2 Collaboration

Beyond typical instructor-led training, real-time collaboration methodology provides a variety of employment options.

1.4.2.3 Skills management

Employees and supervisors can validate on-the-job experience through management skills, which are comprised of a variety of components. This, in combination with competency and evaluation, allows businesses to track how learning activity connects to and fits with business goals.

1.4.2.4 Assessment

It requires all of the components to correctly assess an individual's proficiency in various abilities. Web-based examining as well as valuation systems with full hypermedia competences are among the assessment options available.

1.4.2.5 Learning management

The learning management system (LMS) connects all the strategy's elements. An LMS may help join the dots between session planning, delivering, and assessment. Whether it is handling courses like Computer Based Training (CBT), Instructor-Led Training (ILT), Web Based Training (WBT), document-based training, or a combination of training regimes, an LMS can really focus on providing a highly centralized location to handle all factors of coaching, which includes meeting student's needs and generating reports. An effective LMS can launch, monitor, and present data from a variety of resource providers' courses, as well as integrate with other business-critical platforms like Enterprise Resource Planning (ERP).

1.4.2.6 Integrated system

Online education or digital learning must go beyond merely substituting technologies for training rooms to turn a profit. Blended instructional media addresses the need for more just-in-time and project-grounded learning, productivity assistance, accessible and distant education, professional guidance, and a broader choice of activities and events as studying becomes more connected with work. Furthermore, to get the best possible business outcomes, e-learning platforms must be used to link training to business objectives. Educator-led coaching would prevail to perform a vital role for numerous motives: it is the optimal transfer method for some types of high-level education system, it is the preferred method of learning for some people, and it is the preferred method of training for many trainers.

1.5 CYBER SECURITY AND EDUCATION

1.5.1 Building digital trust

Higher education is a much more diverse setting than it was some years ago, and online learning technologies now provide considerable student involvement. Students are becoming more aware of IT and IS concerns, thus course providers' overall learning methods must be inextricably connected with IS/IT approaches in order to satisfy learner demands today, as well as in upcoming years. In terms of accessibility, safety, and guarding personal information, both digital immigrants and natives will have greater hopes of their online education system. This might involve the safe storage of a student's bank account information in connection with course fees and other purchases. Universities in the United Kingdom possess a considerable amount of intellectual property in the form of research and other academic resources, making them ideal targets for cyber-criminals. Scholars and scientists will anticipate that their delicate research and economically confidential material will be protected from robbery or misuse. Organizations must examine their cyber security vulnerabilities and choose advanced software, personnel, and process configurations.

1.5.2 Bring your own device and remote access

Bring Your Own Device (BYOD) creates a number of database security issues as the device is kept by the client/user rather than the data administrator. Learners are competent and confidently utilize technology for communication, extraction of information, teamwork, and as a platform for education and training. They want cordless devices and also entry to the institution's system, such as any online classroom environments, not only from the organization's static PCs in a dedicated computer laboratory, but also from their personal gadget (iPad, cell phone and so on) in different on- and off-campus locations. It is critical that all personal data processing managed by the data controller is guaranteed to comply with the DPA of 1998. The DPA is founded on eight "good information handling" principles. These grant people certain rights over their personal information and impose certain duties on the organizations in charge of processing it. Each organization's specific hazards will be addressed differently by a BYOD policy. An important problem to tackle is which private details may be managed on a personalized device and which should be retained in a more limited context. Institutions and corporations should analyze whether learners, lecturers, or employees who are using their own individual devices handle non-corporate information regarding the device's user or any other users. Users must, therefore, maintain any private information related to the user in compliance with the DPA guidelines.

1.5.3 Learning management system security

Contemporary e-learning platforms that provide digital interactive and collaborative education do not meet all of the required security criteria. The vast majority of interactive educational experiences are designed and implemented with pedagogical principles in consideration, yet safety issues are frequently underestimated. Youngsters providing false curriculum assessments, displaying a believable fake persona to others, intruding into restricted or highly confidential conversations, changing the date stamps on submitted work, as well as a mentor gaining access to students' personal details are all examples of unfortunate circumstances that adversely affect the educational workflow and also its governance. Some scholars recommend using a scheme focused on Public Key Infrastructure (PKI) modelling techniques, which help in providing critical safety characteristics as well as offering internet cooperative education, including presence, integrity, identity management, privacy, non-repudiation, access control, fault control, time stamping, and audit service. PKI presupposes the deployment of Public Key Cryptography (PKC), the most extensively used mechanism for authenticating an identity of the sender or encoding a text sent through online. For the encryption and decryption of messages, old-style conventional cryptography has generally required the production and distribution of an undisclosed key. This private key system has the critical drawback that communications may readily be decoded if the key is found or intercepted by someone else. As a result, on the internet, PKC as well as PKI are the favored methods.

1.5.4 Largest cyber security threats in higher education

Mobile devices are popular among technology enthusiasts as well as initial users, with newer gadgets appearing on sites across the country. On a daily basis, a rush of unique and better smart mobiles with superior versions of OS (including tablets, new Android smartphones, iPads, and transportable internet service access systems) are produced and created primed for infiltration and prepared to assault a communications network of universities. It is thus crucial to back these systems while keeping a comprehensive picture of their connectivity links, as well as communications with the academic system.

1.6 SECURITY THREATS, DETECTION AND PROTECTION IN DISTRIBUTED E-LEARNING SYSTEMS

1.6.1 Cyber security issues

Software assaults (worms, denial of service, macros, viruses), espionage, acts of theft (illegitimate apparatus or information), and burglary of intellectual property are all major security risks to E-Systems (piracy, copyright, infringement). E-learning systems offer several unique characteristics, such as a wide range of users, numerous uses, and data to download and upload. E-Systems are susceptible to a number of safety and security risks.

1.6.1.1 Authentication

Insecure communication due to faulty verification and also session supervision.

1.6.1.2 Accessibility

Denial of Service (DoS) attack.

1.6.1.3 Secrecy attacks

These include information leaking and poor error handling; unsafe encrypted storage; and insecure direct object reference.

1.6.1.4 Integrity attacks

Cross-site request forgery, inability to limit URL access, malevolent file execution, cross-site scripting, buffer overflows and injection issues are all examples of vulnerabilities.

A threat is a type of thing, person, or other entity that poses a threat, such as Trojan horses or phishing. Password-based authentication schemes are particularly vulnerable to phishing assaults, which are getting increasingly complex and need robust preventive measures and responses.

1.6.2 Privacy concerns

Most researchers emphasize the ethical as well as technological difficulties of using a monitoring device to observe and evaluate the variety of human-to-computer communication that takes place in online education, distance learning, and collaborative learning. They've elevated safety and confidentiality to the top of the priority list for students, educators, and academics who employ student monitoring and private student information. Participants will get a better awareness of security problems, allowing them to avoid security risks while also increasing their personal and their learning environments' security. The providers of the online educational atmosphere, as well as the educators who transmit the material, are focused on ensuring a protected classroom atmosphere and the safe storage of private student info. Students construct their own opinions on the classroom atmosphere and are worried about the safety of their private details. Information recorded on security and privacy concerns in technology-enriched learning revealed that the persons rated the below elements in order of descending significance: Raising awareness > data security > credibility of learning resources > uninterrupted accessibility > location and address privacy > single sign-on > digital rights management > legislation > anonymous or unspecified usage.

1.7 MODIFIED DEEP NEURAL NETWORK BY PROPOSED FITNESS-BASED BUTTERFLY OPTIMIZATION ALGORITHM

1.7.1 Modified deep neural network

DNN [11] contains two hidden layers that aid in the mapping of "output and input data." Due to the growing number of training iterations, it is still difficult to achieve the decision limit. "Training speed and classification accuracy" are improved by constructing two hidden layers. The total node count is computed as in Equation (1.2)when the hidden layer is taken into consideration.

$$nv = \sqrt{av + bv + cv} \qquad (1.2)$$

The input layer node count is supplied by av, the output layer node count is supplied by bv, the hidden layer node count is supplied by nv, and a constant value is supplied by cv. A non-linear fitness capacity is employed as an initiation function in the buried layer. The sigmoid is employed as an activation function, as demonstrated in Equation (1.3).

$$SV = \frac{1}{1 + e^{-xv}} \qquad (1.3)$$

As stated in Equation (1.4), xv provides the input data, and the mapping function MV_{fv} is used to activate it.

$$MV_{fv} = \text{sigm}\left(w_{iv}x + \beta_{iuv}\right) \qquad (1.4)$$

The bias is denoted by β, whereas the weight matrix is denoted by ω.

The DNN provides advantages such as being well-supported for all applications, having sophisticated capabilities, ultimate platform flexibility, and so on. However, it is URL-dependent, which entails a bulk value of data, and increases the cost to consumers, and so on. To address these flaws, the hidden neurons of a DNN are optimized, resulting in MDNN. This MDNN has advantages such as improved security, ease of usage, and dependability. The major objective of the MDNN is to optimize the hidden neurons of DNN with the consideration of insecure information ratio minimization. It is shown in Equation (1.5).

$$OB = \arg\min_{\{HN_{DNN}\}}(IIR) \tag{1.5}$$

Here, the objective function is shown by OB, hidden neurons of DNN are shown by HN_{DNN} and the insecure information ratio is provided by IIR correspondingly.

1.7.2 F-BOA

The suggested F-BOA is utilized to improve the classification performance. Finding optimum or suboptimal solutions is not straightforward in general. The main advantage of adopting a heuristic method is that it gives a rapid, easy to implement and to comprehend answer. These algorithms appear to be useful, and they may be used to provide realistic and fast short-term answers to scheduling and planning issues. The butterflies symbolize the BOA [12] search agents that are employed in the optimization process. A butterfly produces a less intense fragrance that is connected with the butterfly's wellbeing. A butterfly's fitness varies as it moves from one position to the next. The fragrance disseminates private data among the butterflies. The global search period begins when one butterfly recognizes the fragrance of some other butterfly. The butterfly will wander randomly when it does not perceive a fragrance from a neighborhood, which is referred to as the local search stage.

Each single fragrance has its own personality and smell. This sets the BOA apart from the other meta-heuristics. Three terms influence the processing and feeling of the modality: power exponent pf, stimulus intensity sj, and sensory modality sn. The size of the actual/physical stimulus is represented by this word. This word is linked to the solution's/fitness. The butterfly's exponent, in which the intensity is raised, is represented by power. Response compression pf, linear response, and regular expression are all possible with this option. When the scent rises more quickly than the response expands. When compared to, response compression sj occurs when grows slowly. When anything grows in a proportionate way fh, it's called a linear reaction. The formulation fh and variation of sj are two aspects of butterflies' natural behavior. The encoded goal function is associated with the name butterfly. Because the word *fh* is a relative one, the surviving butterflies must be aware of it. As shown in Equation (1.16), the scent is calculated as a vital role of the stimulus' physical intensity (6).

$$fh = snsj^{pf} \tag{1.6}$$

In this case, *sn* and *pf* is between [0,1].
The following are some of the features of all varieties of butterflies:

- The complete colony of butterflies tends to emit a scent that attracts other butterflies.
- Each and every butterfly flutters on an arbitrary track or follows the awesome-smelling butterfly.
- The geography of the goal function determines the stimulus intensity.

The start-up, iteration, and final stages are the three steps of BOA. During the initialization step, the algorithm specifies the goal function as well as its solution space. The values are also allocated to the parameters. The program then produces a population of butterflies initially, for the optimization phase. The data is saved by assigning a defined amount of RAM. The fitness and scent values are kept and computed while the butterfly location is generated at random. The search is carried out in the iteration phase utilizing the created fake butterflies. The butterflies adapt their movement to various locations and assess their fitness levels during this phase. The procedure begins by calculating the fitness values of the butterflies at various points in the output area. Following that, these butterflies generate the scent, as shown in Equation (1.6). During the global search phase, the butterfly follows the route of the fittest solution/butterfly gg^*, as shown in Equation (1.7).

$$z_n^{l+1} = z_n^l + \left(ran^2 \times gg^* - z_n^l\right) \times f\,h_n \tag{1.7}$$

The current iteration which is said as the present best solution is indicated by gg^*, whereas the solution vector z_n for the nth butterfly in iteration count l is denoted by z_n^l in Equation (1.7). The term *fh* represents the scent of the nth butterfly, whereas the term *ran* represents a random integer in the interval [0, 1]. The local search phase is described by Equation (1.8).

$$z_n^{l+1} = z_n^l + \left(ran^2 \times z_s^l - z_m^l\right) \times f\,h_n \tag{1.8}$$

The mth and s^{th} butterflies from the solution space are denoted by z_m^l and z_s^l. If they are members of the same swarm, the above mathematical equation becomes a local random walk and *ran* represents a random integer in the range [0,1]. The BOA has several advantages, including exciting environment-inspired implications for practical uses and global optimization challenges, elegance, rapid convergence, and excellent localized search capabilities, to name a few. It does, though, have drawbacks, such as sliding into a local optimum rather than attaining the global optimum. As a result, the fitness idea is merged into BOA to increase its worldwide searching capabilities, and it is dubbed F-BOA.

In the traditional BOA, the random number is assigned between [0,1]. But, in the developed F-BOA, the random number is assigned using the fitness concept as in Equation (1.9).

$$ran = \frac{curr(OB)}{mean(OB)} \quad\quad (1.9)$$

In the above equation, the current fitness is shown by $curr(OB)$ and the mean fitness is shown by $mean(OB)$ respectively. The pseudocode of F-BOA is given below, and its flowchart is in Figure 1.2.

Pseudocode of the proposed F-BOA

Start
Objective function $h(z), z = z_1, z_2, \dots, z_{dj}, di$ = dimension count
The initial population of nc butterflies are produced $z_n = (n = 1,2,\dots,nc)$
The term $h(z_n)$ describes the stimulus intensity sj_n at z_n
The switch probability pc, power exponent pf and sensor modality sn are defined
while the end criteria is not met do
    for each and every butterfly bc in the population do
$$fh = snsj^{pf}$$
End for
Find best bc
For every butterfly bcdo
$$ran = \frac{curr(OB)}{mean(OB)}$$
    If $ran < pc$ then
$$z_n^{l+1} = z_n^l + \left(ran^2 \times gg^* - z_n^l\right) \times f\,h_n$$
    Else
$$z_n^{l+1} = z_n^l + \left(ran^2 \times z_s^l - z_m^l\right) \times f\,h_n$$
    End if
End for
Update pf
End while
Output best solution
Stop

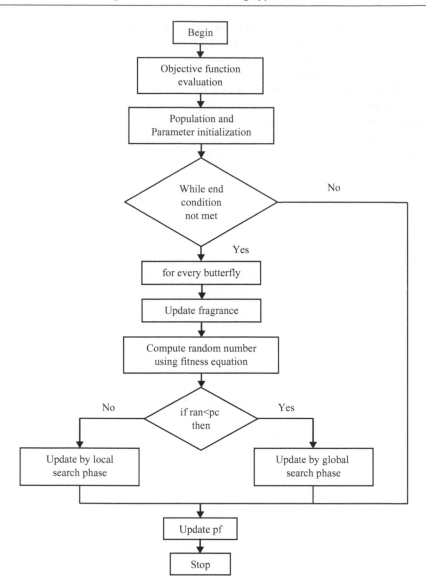

Figure 1.2 Flowchart of proposed F-BOA.

1.8 RESULTS AND DISCUSSIONS

1.8.1 Experimental setup

The information from data sets 1 and 2 [13] is safeguarded in the user support architecture by an experimental procedure of ML that detects cybercrime. The python platform is used to implement and verify the proposed

model. During the study, instructors' attention grew as they progressed from the classroom to the dashboard's informative level. After analyzing the dashboard's community stage, teachers offered interventions when they believed the community needed to take disciplinary action to enhance cohesiveness.

The following research focuses on the success of ML students, lowers susceptible cybersecurity facts, and also improves the learning scheme in user-based methods.

1.8.2 Learner's activity ratio analysis

An educator who is devoted to evaluating and choosing learning assignments, relying on the informational gateways that these actions engage, considers these actions and also the type of job that an educator may do annually, as indicated in Figure 1.3(a) and (b). Educators can be clearer and more transparent regarding their strategies in various sets if they can recognize a learning emphasis in a structured methodology. Table 1.2 shows the values obtained by the proposed and the other conventional methods in students' activity ratio analysis.

1.8.3 Performance analysis of learners

Machine learning techniques can predict student performance and identify children at risk early on, allowing appropriate actions to be taken to improve student outcomes. As is depicted in Figure 1.4(a) and (b), the research provides two data sets focusing on learners' overall performance of their usage of internet as an educational tool as well as its influence on social networks. Table 1.3 shows the values obtained in the students online learning performance analysis performed with the proposed and the other conventional methods.

1.8.4 Insecure information analysis

Technical training patterns, as shown in Figure 1.5(a) and (b), will be assessed and benefited from in order to minimize repeating attacks and adapt developing activities. This will make it easier for cybersecurity professionals to detect and respond to security vulnerabilities on a real-time basis. It will help firms invest their funds more effectively by reducing the amount of time invested on monotonous tasks. Table 1.4 shows the values obtained in the insecure data analysis by the proposed and other conventional methods.

1.8.5 Accuracy analysis

The proposed framework provides a complete backdrop along with methodology for hazardous user authentication process to the business security center. In a nutshell, methods to create labels with F-BOA-MDNN study

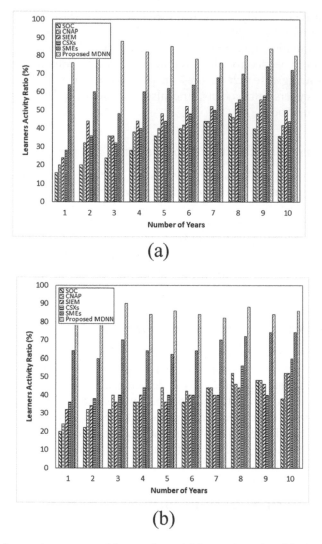

(a)

(b)

Figure 1.3 Increasing count of learner's activities ratio using (a) dataset 1, and (b) dataset 2.

notes, contrast host, user duties and IP, choose machine-learning (ML) algorithms, evaluate results, and construct appropriate equipment.

Figure 1.6(a) and (b) shows the learning system's configuration. Furthermore, even with simple ML algorithms with severely imbalanced as well as limited labels, the learning system may learn from the data sources. Table 1.5 shows the values obtained in the accuracy analysis by the proposed and other conventional methods.

Table 1.2 Analysis of growing count of the learner's activities ratio

	Growing count of the learner's activities ratio in 10 years (%)	
Methods	Data set 1	Data set 2
SOC	25	30
CNAP	35	45
SIEM	42	55
CSXs	45	60
SMEs	73	75
Proposed F-BOA-MDNN	80	90

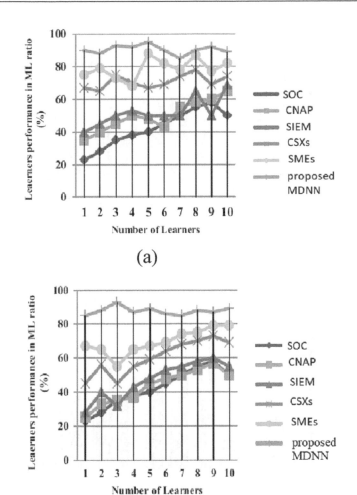

(a)

(b)

Figure 1.4 Learners' performance orientation using (a) dataset 1, and (b) dataset 2.

Table 1.3 Analysis of students' online learning performance

Methods	Students' performance analysis for 10 students (%)	
	Data set 1	Data set 2
SOC	50	50
CNAP	65	50
SIEM	70	55
CSXs	75	70
SMEs	80	80
Proposed F-BOA-MDNN	90	91

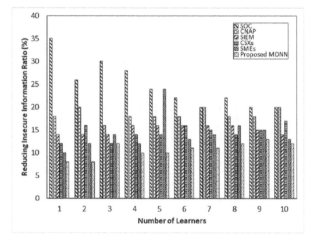

(a)

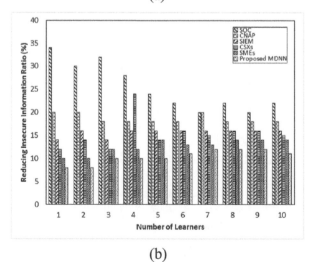

(b)

Figure 1.5 Insecure Information Minimization (IIR) using (a) dataset 1, and (b) dataset 2.

Table 1.4 Minimization of insecure data analysis

	Minimization of insecure data for 10 students (%)	
Methods	Data set 1	Data set 2
SOC	98	95
CNAP	76	75
SIEM	58	56
CSXs	40	41
SMEs	26	28
Proposed F-BOA-MDNN	11	10

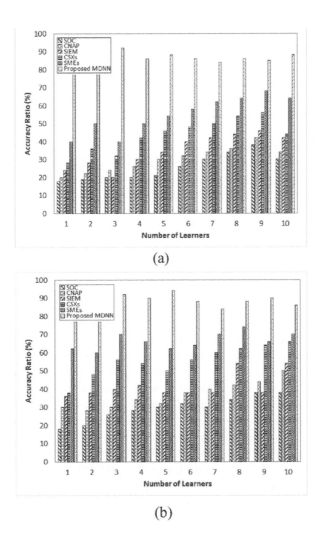

(a)

(b)

Figure 1.6 Learning system's accuracy using (a) dataset 1, and (b) dataset 2.

Table 1.5 Precision of the learning model analysis

Methods	Precision of the learning model for 10 learners (%)	
	Data set 1	Data set 2
SOC	30	30
CNAP	32	50
SIEM	42	58
CSXs	45	65
SMEs	68	70
Proposed F-BOA-MDNN	89	89

1.9 CONCLUSION

The chapter's main objective is to look at all current data theft tactics that make use of cybersecurity knowledge. The data connected with e-learning is initially obtained from conventional, publicly available database sources. User-centric approaches such as "learner assistance, teacher support, learning centers, and feedback" are described based on the acquired data sources. Furthermore, the classification is performed using the well-performing deep learning algorithm DNN, with the hidden neurons tuned using the proposed F-BOA with the goal of minimizing the insecure information ratio, resulting in MDNN. This MDNN categorizes the final output as either secure or insecure data. Finally, the suggested F-BOA is compared to current heuristic-based and classifier algorithms in terms of several analyses that describe the superiority of the presented F-BOA. Finally, in F-BOA-MDNN, the proposed method's approaches are estimated to be a growing amount of learner's practices ratio of 86.2%, achievement orientation of learners in ML ratio of 89.05%, unsafe data as well as information is significantly lowered through the cybersecurity ratio of 88.6%, learning precision of the system in user-centric frameworks ratio of 91.3%, and cumulative outcome ratio of 97.2%.

However, research into how to increase the quality of courses should continue. Online assessment approaches can help to promote a student-centered design; however, several faults must be addressed. New trends include online assessment components into flipped classrooms, circumventing the total cost of the professor position, as well as utilizing superior quality videos created by worldwide professionals. Open education provides fantastic potential for both online and traditional classes, but more research is needed to achieve consensus on best practices for online assessment production and use. These can be considered as directions for future research.

REFERENCES

1. J. L. Martín Núñez, E. Tovar Caro, and J. R. Hilera González, "From Higher Education to Open Education: Challenges in the Transformation of an Online Traditional Course", *IEEE Transactions on Education*, vol. 60, no. 2, pp. 134–142, 2017.
2. G. Naveh and D. Bykhovsky, "Online Peer Assessment in Undergraduate Electrical Engineering Course", *IEEE Transactions on Education*, vol. 64, no. 1, pp. 58–65, 2021.
3. T. G. Cleaver and L. M. Elbasyouni, "Student Online Assessment Behaviors", *IEEE Transactions on Education*, vol. 48, no. 3, pp. 400–401, 2005.
4. M. Farrow and P. J. B. King, "Experiences with Online Programming Examinations", *IEEE Transactions on Education*, vol. 51, no. 2, pp. 251–255, 2008.
5. J. S. Jeong and D. Gonzalez-Gomez, "Assessment of Sustainability Science Education Criteria in Online-Learning through Fuzzy-Operational and Multi-Decision Analysis and Professional Survey", *Heliyon*, vol. 6, no. 8, pp. 1–11, 2020.
6. H. Lawrence-Benedict, M. Pfahl, and S. J. Smith, "Community of Inquiry in Online Education: Using Student Evaluative Data for Assessment and Strategic Development", *Journal of Hospitality, Leisure, Sport and Tourism Education*, vol. 25, p. 100208, 2019.
7. M. Cukusic, Z. Garaca, and M. Jadric, "Online Self-Assessment and Students' Success in Higher Education Institutions", *Computers and Education*, vol. 72, pp. 100–109, 2014.
8. I. M. Venter, R. J. Blignaut, K. Renaud, and M. A. Venter, "Cyber Security Education is as Essential as "the Three R's"", *Heliyon*, vol. 5, no. 12, pp. 1–8, 2019.
9. D. Gürdür Broo, U. Boman, and M. Törngren, "Cyber-Physical Systems Research and Education in 2030: Scenarios and Strategies", *Journal of Industrial Information Integration*, vol. 21, p. 100192, 2021.
10. M. N. Katsantonis, I. Mavridis, and D. Gritzalis, "Design and Evaluation of COFELET-based Approaches for Cyber Security Learning and Training", *Computers and Security*, vol. 105, p. 102263, 2021.
11. S. Ramesh and D. Vydeki, "Recognition and Classification of Paddy Leaf Diseases Using Optimized Deep Neural Network with Jaya Algorithm", *Information Processing in Agriculture*, vol. 7, no. 2, pp. 249–260, 2020.
12. S. Arora and S. Singh, "Butterfly Optimization Algorithm: A Novel Approach for Global Optimization", *Soft Computing*, vol. 23, pp. 715–734, 2018.
13. E. Abu Amrieh, T. Hamtini, and I. Aljarah, "Students' Academic Performance Dataset", 2016, https://www.kaggle.com/aljarah/xAPI-Edu-Data.

Chapter 2

Survey of risks and threats in online learning applications

Dahlia Sam and K. Nithya
Dr. M.G.R. Educational and Research Institute, Chennai, India

S. Deepa Kanmani
Sri Krishna College of Engineering and Technology, Coimbatore, India

Adlin Sheeba
St. Joseph's Institute of Technology, Chennai, India

A. Shamila Ebenezer
Karunya Institute of Technology and Sciences, Coimbatore, India

B. Uma Maheswari
St. Joseph's College of Engineering, Chennai, India

Jennifer Daffodils Amesh
The American College, Madurai, India

CONTENTS

DOI: 10.1201/9781003264538-2

In recent years, especially since the COVID-19 pandemic, education systems have experienced a sudden transition toward online learning. Online learning, also referred to as e-learning or digital learning, has become the new norm after universities and schools around the globe had to shut down suddenly without prior planning. In the corporate world, several online courses that train toward finding jobs are offered online to enable professionals to upgrade their skills and increase their competency. Online learning can be described as the method of teaching learning wherein all the stakeholders including the tutors, students, and the teaching resources are connected via the internet. This method of education makes use of content storage and uses internet-based technologies through which students communicate with teachers as well as with fellow students. This method of learning is fully dependent on the web or internet for its full execution. However, despite all the services provided by the internet for uninterrupted learning, it is also inevitably the platform of all security threats. Owing to the emergency transition to e-learning, educational institutions, teachers, and students were not equipped to handle the situation. Not all students or teachers had proper laptops or stable internet connections. Even educational institutions were not prepared with proper cybersecurity measures. As a result, online classrooms were at increased risks of cyberattacks. Popular platforms of online learning and video conferencing including Moodle, Google Classroom, Blackboard, Coursera, Google Meet, and Zoom , all had various threats, too. The different security threats could directly or indirectly affect online learning systems include virus threats, hacking, SQL injection, phishing attacks, brute force attack, denial of service, spyware threats, and social network threats , most from external intruders. Security risks also include MITM attack, cross-site request forgery (CSRF), masquerade, cross site scripting (XSS), IP spoofing, rootkits, ARP cache poisoning, session hijacking, stack-smashing attacks, or session prediction. This survey of various possible threats or risks involved in online learning may be an eye-opener for e-learning providers in implementing security strategies. As digital learning will continue to be a necessity from now on, even end users like students and teachers will have better awareness about the potential threats within the platform they are using for digital learning and take precautionary measures. Educational institutions can consider steps to improve security like improving authentication, authorization, and confidentiality, or training security professionals. This chapter will also aid researchers who are trying to develop better online learning systems for the next generation; systems that are not only more user friendly but also more secure and safer personal learning environments that assures the security of online classroom sessions or assessments.

2.1 INTRODUCTION

One of the main effects of the COVID-19 Pandemic was the sudden shift to digital learning. Schools shut down across the globe and billions of children were left without meeting their teachers. As days went by, out of necessity, education systems changed drastically. Teaching was done remotely using online learning platforms. Even people who had never tried out online courses had to begin using them. Many others took online courses to learn about technical advancements. Not only academic courses, but even extra-curricular classes started going online. The usage of internet services increased from 40% to 100%. Video-conferencing platforms like Zoom, Google, and Meet, among others, saw an increased usage of about ten times.

With the ubiquitous use of digital platform for education, use of content repositories to store content and to help students interact with teachers and with fellow students is also required. The growth of online learning has brought many benefits but, at the same time, has also allowed many security threats. Since online learning is completely dependent on the internet, both teachers and students are contiguously exposed to all kinds of security issues associated with the internet. Educational institutions, students, and teachers had to adopt this methodology of teaching-learning without prior planning or proper security measures.

This pandemic has totally changed the future perspective of education industry. Hybrid learning is sure to continue even after the pandemic settles down. Massive open online courses (MOOCs) have already become part of most educational institutions in the past decade. Along with this, other digital platforms and learning management systems (LMSs) will continue to find their place in institutions. It is a known fact that virtual school is more than just teaching via video conferencing tools. It is a total paradigm shift in pedagogy involving knowledge of the blended learning environment by educators, parents, and students. Maintaining a balance between online and offline is a crucial aspect to be considered while designing the timetable, lesson plans, examination schedule, and so on. Blended learning goes beyond the four walls of classrooms. It facilitates students to learn at their own time and pace, as well as creating better opportunities for combined studies and more.

Before analyzing the threats and risks involved in online education, it is worth considering the advantages it provides. Online learning enables students to pursue personalized learning courses. Many online resources help students to explore the various options available before choosing one. Digital learning has made each student an independent learner. Online learning also makes it possible for students to learn almost anywhere and anytime and gives students the flexibility to choose their schedule. An online learning environment also gives shy students freedom from the irrational behavior of fellow students.

In spite of all these benefits provided by online learning environment, it is also a known fact that this transition to online learning has been really challenging for all the stakeholders. Parents have to plan for new purchases or for setting up a virtual learning space for their children. Educators need to be trained, institutions need to subscribe to necessary video conferencing tools and even students will have to get accustomed to the new mode of education. This also makes it important to secure students and educators from unauthorized threats, risks, and attacks.

2.2 BACKGROUND AND RELATED WORK

There has been considerable work carried out in the area of online learning in the recent past. Having a secured online learning environment means being protected from malicious users and misuse of digital resources. Thus, it can be said that security in online learning has three main aspects: the CIA Triad – confidentiality, integrity, and availability. "Confidentiality" is the protection of sensitive data from being misused by unauthorized persons, and the prevention of unauthorized disclosure of data or information. Since large numbers of users, including students' tutors, students, and administrators access any online learning platform, a login system is essential. Along with this a strict delimitation of registered users and appropriate user groups is required. For protecting personal information, authentication and encoding are implemented. The second important element in maintaining security is "integrity", which means the protection of data from unauthorized changes made intentionally or accidentally. It can also be seen as the way to avoid improper system alterations. Maintaining integrity ensures that any data or information is not modified, damaged, or removed either maliciously or accidentally. It ensures that the data is in its correct and complete original form. Access control is the main method used for maintaining integrity in the digital learning platforms. Availability refers to readiness for providing correct service. It means that data and other resources are easily accessible for all authorized persons in a timely manner. Availability is usually damaged by denial-of-service attacks.

Information and communication technology and digital learning applications, according to Graf (2002), can cause many security risks, including loss of integrity, confidentiality, and availability. They may also cause exposure of sensitive data, and piracy of public data. Generally, e-learning related security issues are linked to users' poor experience of measures taken to protect digital security, malicious behaviors, and lack of knowledge about security mechanisms that need to be adopted in e-learning. One example is that in most institutions, the system administrators install firewalls and anti-virus software to ensure proper protection of learning resources. Alwi & Fan (2010) continued to enhance the technology used for security in their online learning systems. Recently, most people have acquired basic knowledge about security and even skills have improved. However, security issues including data manipulation by outsiders or insiders, like students, and loss of confidentiality could still happen once in a while. Security is important in order to retain the educators' and students' trust in using the online learning environment because any kind of risk would dramatically affect users' perceptions of the reliability of the online learning system. Thus, it is essential to identify the factors that are responsible for security issues in digital learning environments and also to identify the shortcomings of existing security protection measures available. Only then can countermeasures be planned and developed for mitigating the risks.

Security or any privacy issues in online learning were also examined by El-Khatib et al. (2003). With relation to the "Privacy Principles," the privacy needs for e-learning systems were examined. The capacity of some of the existing security handling technologies were analyzed, including network security methods, policy-based security, trust-based systems, and privacy management. Ma et al. (2009) developed a model for detecting malicious or insecure websites. They used lexical or host-based factors of the URLs that were being visited. The gathered URL features were combined with labelled URLs from a web email provider and the URLs were classified as either malicious or non-malicious.

Information security threats in a digital learning environment were investigated by Alwi et al. (2010). Each application in the managed learning environment (MLE) system that was used in e-learning was subjected to a threat analysis. The threat analysis was carried out using a Microsoft-adapted methodology. This research yielded a list of information related security threats for e-learning applications, as well as a matrix of threat risk for e-learning. This study only looked at application system vulnerabilities, not host or network vulnerabilities in e-learning and, as a result, discovered information security concerns specific to e-learning applications.

May and George (2011) presented a study on online learning security and privacy issues. The core part of their study was to track students' activities on computer-mediated tools. The security and privacy aspect of the online learning was also covered. The objective of the proposed work is to improve awareness of the security issues around online learning. Important elements of security in online learning is described by Luminita (2011) They identified authentication, access control, data integrity, and content protection as major issues. The cryptography and secured network protocols are the basic methods that provide information security. The key issues of Moodle are examined in these works.

Application of a security metric to cyber learning systems was discussed by Arfa et al. (2012). They identified six components of e-learning system as follows: the browser, application server, web server, database server, mail server, and firewall server. They also classified the security requirements into authentication, availability, confidentiality, integrity, non-repudiation, and privacy.

Online learning is a platform where the internet is the backbone. As the internet is more vulnerable to security attacks, online learning has to be protected from these attacks. E-learning security threats are as follows: spyware attacks, virus threats, hackers, adware, phishing threats, trojan attacks, viral website threats, and threats to online social networks.

The students, the teachers, and the controlling authority are the three main entities of the online learning system. On every level, integrity and security have to be maintained. The different loopholes available on the internet and in the learning system are the weak points through which the hackers can enter the system. Sharma and Karforma (2012) discussed different risks faced by online learning systems and remedies to those risks in order to build trustworthy and secured systems. Awareness of potential risks associated with online learning by providers was examined by Chen et al. (2013). The authors considered the protection measures that need to be followed to reduce those risks. They adopted two methods for this survey. First, an extensive search was conducted in the Web of Knowledge and other similar academic databases like the ACM Digital Library. Second, a blog-mining method was used to dig deeper into security threats and risks in e-learning.

An attempt was made by Bandara (2014) to reveal the popularity of internal cyberattacks and lack of proper policies and procedures. An online learning system needs a standardized architecture and also specific requirements for security. They listed the security threats and the methods to detect and protect against these threats. A security management model was also proposed with proper understanding of security requirements, planning, implementing, maintaining, and evaluating. Zafar et al. (2014) considered online learning systems by a combination of multi agents and system security standards. They listed efforts that have been taken to make systems secure. The PMA3 (multi-agent platform) is combined with three critical security issues namely: trust, authorization, and authentication to model the security requirements.

Shyamala and Visalakshi (2015) discussed the two ways by which IP spoofing is done. The first one uses online IP masking tools to mask the IP. The second one uses offline tools like TOR. The IP spoofing may lead to different types of attacks and consequences. Many online learning institutions are racing to implement ICT without first adequately analyzing and evaluating any security risks that may arise. As a result, Singh (2015) focused on security challenges in e-learning as well as security solutions to protect enterprises that access and manage information over multiple networks via the internet. This research work also discussed the impact of e-learning systems that lack suitable IT policies and processes.

As e-learning grows in popularity and reach, so will the need to comprehend security issues, especially when employing open and dispersed environments like e-learning platforms. The objective of this chapter is to highlight some critical security concerns that must be addressed when creating and using an e-learning platform. To fulfil the above objective, Asmaa et al. (2016), covered fundamental ideas of computing security, as well as key features of e-learning platforms that bring new vulnerabilities and attack vectors.

The influence of security vulnerabilities and implementation challenges that obstruct successful e-learning implementation was examined by Saidu et al. (2016). Their review focused on the impact of online learning security concerns and the viability of e-learning implementation. This study discovered that for the e-learning platform, a feasible and comprehensive approach model that incorporates both biometric fingerprint and cryptography authentication techniques is required. For e-learning to be sustainable, it is advised that appropriate and uninterruptible bandwidth and electricity be provided. Many organizations are turning to e-learning for some of its advantages, such as lower costs, faster delivery of resources, effective learning methods, and reduced environmental impact; however, security is often overlooked. One of the most important considerations in ensuring good content delivery on the web is the security of the digital learning system. Adetoba et al. (2016) provided an overview of e-learning, security difficulties, and challenges, as well as current and recent research in the field of e-learning security.

Various cyberattacks were discussed by Marius et al. (2017) and a novel algorithm was proposed to generate strong passwords to protect the personal data. A random password method is used to generate stronger passwords. Classical passwords are vulnerable to dictionary attacks, but random passwords are much more resistant to dictionary attacks. Kanimozhi et al. (2018) proposed a cloud-based online learning method with proper access control. This mechanism ensures that only authorized users can access the cloud resources. The access control is combined with key management to protect the e-learning environment. Anderson (2019) discussed the impact of social media in online learning; the challenges, and disadvantages. The important issue is loss of data control. Various solutions to the above issues were discussed as follows. The first solution discussed was institutionally-owned social media where all the data and communication are owned by the institution. The second one was decentralized social media applications.

The internet is the backbone of all online learning systems, and as such, it is inherently insecure. Because of the large number of people communicating via the internet, information security and privacy are extremely important. Data are vulnerable to a variety of security threats and vulnerabilities as a result of data exchange through the internet. Ekereke and Akpojaro (2019) provided a comprehensive examination of the security challenges that arise when using digital learning platforms for educational delivery in Nigeria. The study concludes with several key recommendations for ensuring a secure e-learning environment in Nigeria. They also discussed digital watermarking, access control using firewall, SMS authentication, dual or triple authentication methods, cryptography, and biometrics authentication security techniques. Barbu and Perețeanu (2020) discussed the BYOD (bring your own device) concept in which the students and employees can bring their own computers/devices to access the private networks of the universities/companies. This can lead to major security issues as personal data are vulnerable to attacks.

The major shift to the e-learning paradigm provided a feasible and convenient way of learning during the COVID-19 period. Even though we benefited from several advantages of online learning, this system paved many paths for our personal data risks. The risks associated with online learning have been categorized into two dimensions. The first one is general risks that include non-availability, theft, illegitimate use, integrity violation, unintentional threats, privacy violation, deliberate attacks, or natural threats. The second one is specific stakeholders' risks like content developers' risks, instructors' risks, and institutions' risks. Even though the LMS uses traditional authentication techniques, some hackers may be willing to exploit such a system's flaws in order to cheat. User authentication and end-user surveillance are more difficult in this circumstance. Multifactor adaptive authentication methods are used to create a system that allows for simultaneous authentication. Jagadamba et al. (2020) proposed an efficient human intervention and low-cost adaptive authentication system for e-learning environments.

Cloud technology provides many benefits to users, including quick and simple deployment methods, lower costs, constant resource availability, scalability and elasticity, and the ability to easily adapt to the needs of organizations. The use of cloud computing technology in the e-learning domain is a continuous process by which teaching and learning methods adapt to the current technology-based society. The features provided by this type of architecture can benefit both students and teachers by leveraging the electronic environment in a dynamic and interactive process of learning, teaching, and evaluation. If no specific security measures are installed, more frequent cyberattacks might cause severe material damage. The majority of cyberattacks take advantage of security flaws created by technical flaws and faulty network devices. Brumă (2020) compared the key weaknesses of cloud technology with current security measures, which might lead to serious security issues including data breaches.

Globally, educational institutions have been compelled to shut down completely or partially, moving from physical class to online academics. Cloud computing and e-learning has resulted in a new type of system known as cloud-based e-learning systems. These systems blend cloud computing advantages and benefits with e-learning platforms. This combination provides various options for improving the efficiency and ease of use of e-learning systems, as well as contributing to the optimal conditions for using distant learning systems. Cloud-based e-learning systems, on the other hand, pose certain issues in two key areas: security and storage. A new architecture to address these two issues. is built on a new security layer that is in charge of managing and storing all transactions in order to establish a security key, and provide the opportunity to utilize data generated in the future to recommend systems.

Shams et. al. (2019) briefly explored the usefulness of cloud-based e-learning, as well as its concerns, challenges, and benefits, in their study. The findings imply that a cloud computing platform for e-learning is both viable and effective, providing a clearer picture of the cloud computing landscape.

On the basis of scalability, types of services, shareable content object reference model (SCORM), pricing, usability, and other factors, a review of many cloud-based e-learning solutions was conducted. Despite the benefits, the fundamental difficulty with cloud-based e-education is the privacy and security of outsourced data. Existing systems keep all documents in the same storage space, use the same authentication process for all users, and utilize the same encryption strategy for all documents. Devi Priya, and Sumalatha (2021) proposed a secure framework for e-education in the cloud environment, which uses multiple-factor authentication to effectively authenticate cloud users based on their roles and activity. The VGG (Visual Geometry Group) 2F convolutional neural network is used to extract accurate aspects of the biometric face modality. The VGG2F model improves the accuracy of biometric face authentication, and a hybrid combination of encryption techniques with varied key sizes applied to the documents resists various attacks.

Amor et al. (2020) proposed a new fog computing e-learning scheme. The learning contents are stored in the edge server. The user's device need not be used to encrypt the content. Instead, this is done at the fog server, thus improving efficiency. The course and examination contents were encrypted by IBBE (identity-based broadcast encryption) and CP-ABE (ciphertext-policy attribute-based encryption) techniques, thus improving the security. A secured profile-matching mechanism was also presented in this study and was designed to find colleagues within the vicinity in an efficient and secure way.

2.3 RISKS AND THREATS IN ONLINE LEARNING

Based on the literature review and online sources, it can be seen that online learning is exposed to various security risks and threats. These are discussed in detail in the following sections.

2.3.1 ARP cache poisoning

Address resolution protocol (ARP) is the protocol that is used for proper communication within the network and helps any device to reach another specific device on the network. It translates the internet protocol (IP) address to a media access control (MAC) address and vice versa. Most commonly, devices use ARP to contact the router or gateway that enables them to connect to the internet. An ARP cache is maintained by the hosts along with a mapping table for IP addresses and MAC addresses. This is used to connect with destinations on the network.

The ARP protocol was not designed to be secure. This means that if an HTTP request is sent to an unauthorized party, it can be accepted even if the host has never received it. Moreover, ARP spoofing, also referred to as ARP poisoning, is a category of man-in-the-middle (MitM) attack that could allow attackers to intercept communication between network devices. These types of attacks are possible in online learning environments.

In this type of attack, when the attacker has access to the network, they scan to determine any two devices' IP addresses, maybe a workstation and a router. The attacker then uses a spoofing tool, like Arpspoof or Driftnet, and sends out ARP responses that are forged. These forged responses show as if the correct MAC address of both the router and workstation IP addresses is the MAC address that is, in fact, the attacker's. This way both the router and workstation are under a false impression and connect with the attacker's machine, instead of with each other. The two devices also update their ARP cache entries and as a result start communicating with the attacker instead of communicating directly with one another. The attacker becomes the secret middleman spying on all communications. This is illustrated in Figure 2.1 below.

2.3.2 Rootkits

Another possible threat in online learning environments is from rootkits, which is a collection of software programs or a single program that gives remote access to any actor to gain control over any computer. Not always, but most of the time rootkits open a door for malicious software like viruses, ransomware and others, to enter the victim's system. Rootkits also attempt to prevent the malicious software from being detected by deactivating any endpoint antivirus software that may be installed.

Rootkits can be installed during phishing attacks and trick users into permitting the rootkits to be installed on their systems. Often this also gives administrator access to remote cybercriminals so they can access the system. Once the rootkit is installed, it gives the remote actor complete access to control almost every aspect of the operating system (OS). Few antivirus programs struggle to detect these rootkits and most antimalware programs can detect and remove such rootkits too.

Rootkits depend on clandestine methods to get control over computers since they are non-effective by themselves. Rootkits are installed like any

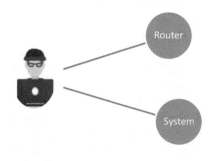

Figure 2.1 ARP cache poisoning.

malicious software, sometimes by email phishing campaigns, executable malicious PDF files, crafted malicious Word documents, or by downloading software infected with the rootkit from risky websites and so forth. Unsuspecting users give permission for rootkit installer programs to be installed on their computers, and later these rootkits are installed and concealed, until some hackers activate them. Rootkits include malicious tools like password-stealing tools, banking credential stealers, antivirus disablers, and bots for denial-of-service attacks among others.

A rootkit attack can result in malware infection, removal of essential files, interception of personal information such as emails to steal personal data like credit card numbers, sensitive data being stolen, modification of system configurations, and so forth.

2.3.3 SQL injection

Another possible attack in online learning is by SQL(Structured Query Language) injection wherein a code penetration might cause loss of database. This is one of the most common online hacking techniques through webpage input where malicious code is placed in SQL statements. Malicious users use this SQL injection to manipulate the application's web server. SQL injection usually occurs when any user is requested to input their username and password. Instead of the username, an SQL statement is given that will run undetected on the database.

There are other types of SQL injection attacks as well as passing the login algorithms. A few other attacks include: updating, deleting, or inserting some data, getting user login details, downloading and installing trojans or other malicious programs, and exporting valuable data such as passwords or credit card details to the hacker's remote server.

The impact of SQL injection can be severe. The intruder retrieves all the important user details present in the database such as credit card information or social security numbers. Intruders can also gain access to the administrator portal or delete some user data from the database. With so many online applications and bank transactions being used these days, the role of back-end database servers becomes very important to prevent the intruder from exploiting SQL injection and compromising the entire server.

2.3.4 Session hijacking

In a protected network, TCP (Transmission Control Protocol) session hijacking is another security attack that is seen. IP spoofing is the most commonly seen method of session hijacking, where an attacker uses source-routed IP packets and inserts commands with an active communication that is going on between two nodes on a network. The attacker disguises themself as an authenticated user. This type of attack is caused due to the common practice that authentication is usually done at the beginning of any TCP session.

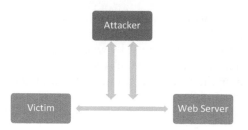

Figure 2.2 Session hijacking.

Man-in-the-middle attack is another type of session hijacking, wherein the attacker uses a "sniffer," observes the communication between devices, and gathers the data being transmitted. Another way of doing session hijacking is by using packet sniffers and is shown in Figure 2.2. It can be seen that attacker uses packet sniffers to get the victim's session ID and gain access to the server.

2.3.5 Credential prediction

Credential prediction, also referred to as session prediction is a technique of hijacking or impersonating any website user. The attacker guesses the unique value that identifies a particular session. As a result, the attacker gains control to issue website requests with the compromised user's privileges. Most of the websites authenticate the user when communication is initially established. Users typically prove their identity by providing unique username and password combinations, which are referred to as credentials. Instead of giving these confidential credentials again and again with each transaction, websites generate a unique session ID. Subsequent communications between the user and the web site are authenticated with this as proof. If an attacker is able to predict this session ID, malicious or fraudulent activity becomes possible.

2.3.6 Stack-smashing attacks

Stack is a memory structure that is used in many well-known programming languages to store values. After memory is allocated for the variables on the stack, it has to be carefully managed so that data values that are stored in them do not exceed the allocated stack space. If they exceed, the additional data can overwrite other data stored on the stack. This could cause problems for these other variables and the program control flow.

If any malicious security cracker can intentionally exceed the stack space allocated for any variable, the malformed data can be used to indirectly affect program control flow. This category of security compromise is referred to as a stack-smashing attack. This might eventually lead to a root attack of the OS too. This can be extremely dangerous. Most vulnerabilities can only affect specific parts of the system, but stack-smashing attacks can often cross the limits and affect other parts of the system.

2.3.7 Phishing attacks

Phishing attacks are a typical feature in online learning and interactions. Phishing response is a major business, influencing security software markets, affecting e-commerce adoption and involvement, and defending corporate brand and image. Phishing is a type of malicious code attack that is often used to obtain sensitive information from users, such as login credentials and credit card details. It happens when a hacker poses as a trustworthy entity and convinces a victim to open an email, instant message, or text message. The user is ultimately fooled into malicious websites, which can result in spyware installation, system freeze as part of a ransomware attack, or the disclosure of confidential information. An attack can be devastating. Illegal purchases, financial theft, and identity theft are examples of adverse outcomes for individuals.

Phishing, in its simplest form, combines social field and complicated attack vectors to create the impression or misdirection in the view of the email reader that the validity of what is being offered or asked is not only true, but convincing enough to compel the receiver to take some action (Lacey et al., 2015).

An example of phishing could be via a mass email, claiming to be from a particular website, which is sent to as many members as possible. The user's password is set to expire, according to the email. To renew their password within 24 hours, they must visit that website for renewal. Influence strategies used in phishing emails are given in Table 2.1. below.

Table 2.1 Influence strategies used in phishing emails

Approach	Definition
Professional	Claims made by a person or organization claiming to be an authority figure.
Immediate	The receiver is given a minimum amount of time to answer.
Agreement	Aims to effectively help the recipient in some way.
Social claims	Convinces by saying that others have replied to the email.
Benefit	If the recipient responds, the sender claims to provide a significant benefit.
Penalty	If the receiver does not answer, the sender claims that they will suffer somesort of loss.
Limited	This indicates that a deal or chance is restricted in some way e.g., for the firstfive responses.

Researchers have spent the last decade attempting to uncover the major elements that may influence an individual's sensitivity to phishing emails. As a result, a variety of theoretical frameworks have been developed and applied. According to the IPPM (IP Performance Measurement) (Vishwanath et al., 2011), the content of a phishing email, such as the influence techniques it contains, the use and validity of email signatures, and the sender address, all impact the likelihood that an individual will respond. The model claims that the existence of specific influencing strategies, such as urgency, act to control people's limited selective attention (e.g., a crucial time limit).

For example, when comparing participant responses to authentic, phishing, and spear-phishing emails it is done with confidence, scarcity, or social testimonials influence approaches (Butavicius et al., 2016).

According to the scam, the extent to which heuristic processing strategies are used when evaluating emails varies depending on the recipient's characteristics.

A variety of technological and other support methods may be in place inside an organization to assist users with information security issues. For example, automated system alerts, particular phishing warnings sent through email, and IT phishing-reporting tools and methods, can all help to minimize perceived threats and increase self-efficacy in the office. Unfortunately, there is very little study of how individuals think about these mechanisms, how they affect perceptions of vulnerability and identity, and if employees think they are helpful when dealing with spear phishing (Williams et al., 2018).

2.4 DISCUSSION

Security threats in online learning can be analyzed from two aspects – the user side and the management side. When considering the user side, emerging ICT applications and injudicious user activities could be the main causes of security issues in e-learning platforms. Along with the usual security risks inherent in the online environment, the growth of social media like Instagram and Facebook among others, has allowed a range of new security breaches with even higher security impact. The types of cyberattacks and the malicious content on the different web applications are rapidly increasing, both in the frequency of occurrence and in their sophistication. These days, educators are using social media sites as an aid to support blended learning. This in itself could pose various security risks to gullible instructors and students. For example, personal data that is shared on social media sites can be misused in many ways. Recent research has shown that social media sites are increasingly being used for delivering malware more than the previously popular method of email delivery.

Security issues in online learning can also be analyzed from the standpoint of the user. Security mechanisms often used in online learning programs miss out on usability. Also, security discipline is not centered on the users and therefore they tend to overlook even the most serious security risks.

From the management perspective, online learning service providers have made quite a few mistakes. Threats often not only come from outsiders, but also from insiders. Online learning providers can also be the cause of security risks as they are responsible for the present underdeveloped security measures and policies.

To make things worse it is evident from this pandemic that many online learning providers have rushed into adopting information and communication technology out of necessity, without fully understanding possible security concerns. Even the online course and platform designers take into consideration only the quality of the course content and the technology used but ignore security aspects. Even though almost all universities and educational institutions install firewalls and antivirus software to protect their resources, they do fail to perform information system security management.

2.5 CONCLUSION

Based on the extensive study done, it is obvious that security aspects have not been the prime focus of online learning software. Since the pandemic, online learning has become somewhat mandatory. It is therefore, crucial that these online learning environments are made more secure. As many researchers have rightly pointed out, security aspects are often not represented as high priority in any educational environment. The main reason why security risks inherent in online learning have not been considered seriously is because security issues may not have caused damage in the realm of digital learning as alarming as they have done in the world of business. Even though no serious security issue has yet happened in the world of e-learning, it is a good idea to be vigilant. The security of e-learning environments is much needed and should be a top priority, especially in this era when much education has shifted online.

BIBLIOGRAPHY

Adetoba, B. T., Awodele, O. and Kuyoro, S. O. (2016). E-learning security issues and challenges: A review. *Journal of Scientific Research and Studies*, 3(5), 96–100.

Ahmad, A. and Elhossiny, M.A. (2012). E-learning and security threats. *IJCSNS International Journal of Computer Science and Network Security*, 1215–19.

Aissaoui, K., Amane, M., Berrada, M. and Madani, M. A. (2022). A new framework to secure cloud-based e-learning systems. In: Bennani, S., Lakhrissi, Y., Khaissidi, G., Mansouri, A., and Khamlichi, Y. (Eds.) *WITS 2020. Lecture Notes in Electrical Engineering*, vol 745. Springer, Singapore.

Alwi, N.H. M., Fan, I.-S., Lytras, M.D. et al. (Eds.) (2010). Information security threats analysis for e-learning. In *Technology Enhanced Learning, Quality of Teaching and Educational Reform, Proceedings of the 1st International Conference TECH-EDUCATION, CCIS*, vol. 73, Athens, Greece, pp. 285–291.

Amane, M., Aissaoui, K., and Berrada, M. (2021). A Multi-agent and Content-Based Course Recommender System for University E-learning Platforms. In: Motahhir, S., and Bossoufi, B. (Eds.) *Digital Technologies and Applications. ICDTA 2021. Lecture Notes in Networks and Systems*, vol 211. Springer, Cham. doi: 10. 1007/978-3-030-73882-2_60

Amor, A. B., Abid, M. and Meddeb, A. (2020).Secure fog-based E-learning scheme. *IEEE Access*, 8, 31920–31933.

Anderson, T. (2019). Challenges and opportunities for use of social media in higher education. *Journal of Learning for Development*, 6(1), 6–19.

Arfa Rabai, L.B., Rjaibi, N. and Aissa, A.B. (2012). Quantifying security threats for e-learning systems. In *International Conference on Education and e-Learning Innovations*, pp. 1–6.

Asmaa, K. and Najib, E. K.; STIC Laboratory, Chouaib Doukkali University. (2016). E-learning systems risks and their security, *International Journal of Computer Science and Information Security (IJCSIS)*, 14(7), 193–200.

Bandara, I., Ioras, F. and Maher, K. (2014). Cyber security concerns in e-learning education. pp. 0728–0734.

Barbu, M. and Perețeanu, G.-C. (2020). Cyber security approaches in e-learning. 4820–4825. doi: 10.21125/inted.2020.1323.

Brumă, L.M. (2020). Security vulnerabilities in cloud based E-learning. In *The International Scientific Conference eLearning and Software for Education*, Bucharest, vol. 1.

Butavicius, M., Parsons, K., Pattinson, M. and McCormac, A. (2016). Breaching the human firewall: social engineering in phishing and spear-phishing emails. arXiv: 1606.00887.

Chen, Y. and He, W. (2013). Security risks and protection in online learning: asurvey. *International Review of Research in Open and Distance Learning*, 14, 108–127.

Devi Priya, K. and Sumalatha, L. (2021). Secure framework for cloud-based e-education using deep neural networks. In *2021 2nd International Conference on Intelligent Engineering and Management (ICIEM)*, pp. 406–411.

Ekereke, and Akpojaro, J. (2019). Security challenges in accessing e-learning systems: a case-study of Sagbama. *Bayelsa State*, 4, 1049–1054.

El-Khatib, K., Korba, L., Xu, Y. and Yee, G. (2003). Privacy and security in e-learning. *International Journal of Distance Education Technologies (IJDET)*, 1(4), 19.

Fouzia, Shersad and Sabeena, Salam. (2020). Managing Risks of E-learning During COVID-19. *International Journal of Innovation and Research in Educational Sciences*, 7(4), 348–358.

Gabor, A. M., Popescu, M. C. and Naaji, A. (2017). Security issues related to e-learning education. *IJCSNS International Journal of Computer Science and Network Security*, 17(1), 60–66.

Graf, F. (2002). Providing security for eLearning. *Computers & Graphics*, 26(2), 355–365. doi: 10.1016/S0097-8493(02)00062-6

Jagadamba, G., Sheeba, R., Brinda, K. N., Rohini, K. and Pratik, S. K. (2020). Adaptive E-learning authentication and monitoring. In *2020 2nd International Conference on Innovative Mechanisms for Industry Applications (ICIMIA)*, pp. 277–283.

Kanimozhi, S., Arputharaj, K., Devi, K. and Selvamani, K. (2018). Secure cloud-based e-learning system with access control and group key mechanism. *Concurrency and Computation: Practice and Experience*, 31, e4841. doi: 10.1002/cpe.4841.

Lacey, D., Salmon, P. and Glancy, P. (2015). Taking the bait: a systems analysis of phishing attacks. *Procedia Manufacturing*, 3, 1109–1116.

Luminita, D. (2011). Information security in e-learning platforms. *Procedia – Social and Behavioral Sciences*, 15, 2689–2693. doi: 10.1016/j.sbspro.2011.04.171.

Ma, J., Saul, L.K., Savage, S. and Voelker, G.M. (2009). Identifying suspicious URLs: an application of large-scale online learning. In *Proceedings of the 26th Annual International Conference on Machine Learning (ICML '09). Association for Computing Machinery*, New York, NY, USA, pp. 681–688.

May, M. and George, S. (2011). Privacy concerns in e-learning: is using tracking system a threat? *International Journal of Information and Education Technology*, 1(1), 1–8.

Mumtaz, Nazia, Saqulain, Ghulam Saqulain and Mumtaz, Nadir. (2021). Online academics in Pakistan: COVID-19 and beyond. *Pakistan Journal of Medical Sciences*, 37(1), 283–287.

Saidu, A., Clarkson, M. A. and Mohammed, M. (2016). E-learning security challenges, implementation and improvement in developing countries: a review, *International Journal of Computer Science and Mathematical Theory*, 2(2), 20–25.

Sharma, D. and Karforma, S. (2012). Risks and remedies in e-learning system. *International Journal of Network Security & Its Applications*, 4. doi: 10.5121/ijnsa.2012.4105.

Sharma, P., Agarwal, K., and Chaudhary, P. (2021). E-learning platform security issues and their prevention techniques: a review. *International Journal of Advance Scientific Research and Engineering Trends*, 6(8), 51–59.

Shersad, F. and Salam, S. (2020). Managing risks of e-learning during COVID-19. doi: 10.13140/RG.2.2.12722.63689.

Shyamala, K. and Visalakshi, U.S. (2015). Mitigating IP spoofing to enhance security in multi-agent based e-learning environment. *Indian Journal of Science and Technology*, 8. doi: 10.17485/ijst/2015/v8i17/63910.

Siddiqui, S., Alam, S., Khan, Z. and Gupta, A. (2019). Cloud-based e-learning: using cloud computing platform for an effective e-learning. doi: 10.1007/978-981-13-2414-7_31.

Singh, N. (2015). E-learning security concerns and measures, *Journal of Scientific and Technical Advancements*, 1(3), 139–141.

Vishwanath, A., Herath, T., Chen, R., Wang, J. and Rao, H. R. (2011). Why do people get phished? Testing individual differences in phishing vulnerability within an integrated, information processing model. *Decision Support Systems*, 51(3), 576–586.

Williams, E. J., Hinds, J., and Joinson, A. N. (2018). Exploring susceptibility to phishing in the workplace. *International Journal of Human-Computer Studies*, 120, 1–13.

Zafar, A., Alghazzawi, D., and Hamid, S. (2014). E-learning systems and their security. *MAGNT Research Report*, 2, 83–92.

Chapter 3

Approaches to overcome security risks and threats in online learning applications

Adri Jovin John Joseph
Department of Information Technology, Sri Ramakrishna Institute of
Technology, Coimbatore, India

Marikkannan Mariappan
Department of Computer Science and Engineering, Government
College of Engineering, Erode, India

CONTENTS

DOI: 10.1201/9781003264538-3

The COVID-19 pandemic affected educators and students on a very large scale globally. School education and higher education were affected drastically as educational institutions and universities were forced to close due to the global pandemic. It was because of online learning applications that education got back on track. Online learning happens through different modes, whether through massive open online courses, through virtual meeting platforms or open online learning platforms. The utilization of web and mobile learning applications has increased exponentially in recent years following the COVID pandemic. With the growth in the usage of online learning applications, the threat posed toward the end users of online learning applications has also increased in recent years. Most online learning applications are web applications. Therefore, online learning applications are susceptible to all types of security attacks as described by the Open Web Application Security Project (OWASP). Some commonly identified attacks on online learning platforms are: buffer overflow, eavesdropping of the network, guessing of user passwords, a replay of cookies, credential stealing, privilege promotion, unauthorized access, trapdoor mechanisms, spamming, tunnelling, a replay of sessions by outsiders, man-in-the-middle attack, HTTP manipulation, manipulation of cookies, SQL injection, cross-site scripting, and information disclosure among others. These are carried out viathe online learning platform and have a direct impact on the educator and learner. Service providers face a lot of threats. It is reported that most online learning service providers have faced distributed denial of service attacks in recent years. This has raised a major concern in the usage of online learning platforms specifically when the assessments are time-bound. Apart from these, phishing attacks have also increased in recent years, especially the imitation of online learning platforms of universities and major online learning platform providers. Many end users have been affected due to these attacks. This chapter presents a detailed review of the threats faced in the usage of online learning applications, the risk classification, and the impact on the end users. It also presents various possible approaches that can be followed to prevent and mitigate the risks of using online learning applications.

3.1 INTRODUCTION

It might be an astonishing fact to learn that online education had prevailed even before the internet came into being in the 1960s. Early online education started with the broadcasting of course content through radio, after which it made its evolution through television in the mid-1950s. Many of us may be surprised to know that the University of Wisconsin started a telephone-based distance learning program for physicians in 1965. It was in 1976, that the Coastline Community College started the concept of a virtual college with no campus. In the 1980s various online courses were started with the advent of the internet. By the start of the 2000s, most universities all over the world started offering courses and course modules in online mode. A huge revolution in education started with the introduction of massive open online courses (MOOCs) in the latter part of the 2000s, when Edutech started booming as a new industry (Dai et al. 2016). During the COVID-19 pandemic, this reached a peak due to factors like easy accessibility to online content, free offerings by leading MOOC platforms, and non-availability of physical classrooms, among others.

In 2020, when the COVID-19 pandemic curtailed the movement of people, most sectors were affected. Owing to the very long lockdown, one of the worst-hit sectors was the education sector. Most people believed that the curfew would only last for a few days, but the prolonged curfew paved the way to new horizons in the education sector. Governments and regulatory authorities started exploring new ways of providing continuing education for students. Nearly 0.32 billion students were affected in India, according to the United Nations Educational, Scientific and Cultural Organization (UNESCO) (Alvi and Gupta 2020). Online education was the solution that was offered. The next questions raised were concerned with affordability, accessibility, and flexibility (Dhawan 2020). We must be thankful to the online learning platform providers who gave online education as a free offering. Larger corporations provided their costly software for free so that even educators and aspirants could afford the platforms. E-learning platforms have developed to find out various user preferences and display learning contents which are interesting to the end users (Deborah et al. 2014). Some educators offered face-to-face lectures through platforms such as Zoom, Google Meet, and others, whereas some started posting content on platforms like Moodle or Blackboard. It was even possible for people to conduct assessments through these online platforms in a secure manner (Deborah et al. 2019). Blended learning became a common practice during this period of the pandemic (Aguti et al. 2014). The world could appreciate the strength of Edutech companies. Thus, education was served in an "anywhere, anytime" mode. Online learning became no more just an option, but a necessity.

3.2 SECURITY RISKS AND THREATS

Online learning happens through web applications that are developed and deployed in a web server, in most cases, over the cloud (Malik et al. 2016). When it comes to online learning, the data being in the public domain is prone to several threats (Shersad and Salam 2020). Today, most online applications are made of elements defined in Web 2.0. Hence, they have high exposure to a lot of vulnerabilities, since most of the site owners focus most on the functionality rather than on the security of the system (Lawton 2007; Chen and He 2013). Online users need to be aware of these risks while using online learning platforms. As Edutech grew, so, too, did issues related to security (Baby and Kannamma 2014).

The Open Web Application Security Project (OWASP) has listed the top ten vulnerabilities (OWASP Top 10: 2021) right from the early 2000s. The most recent list has a few updates compared with the list published in 2017, as is illustrated in Figure 3.1. The vulnerabilities faced by online learning platforms will be viewed from the OWASP perspective. Apart from these, there are some other threats faced by online learning platforms such as phishing, malware attacks, and so forth.

The various vulnerabilities are discussed in detail below.

3.2.1 Broken access control

Access control ensures that the resources in a platform are not utilized by a user or an outsider without appropriate permission. If a broken access control occurs, it may lead to modification/destruction of data or may disclose the data to unknown recipients. Some of the common vulnerabilities that fall under this category are:

- Some servers may not have been configured to provide the least privilege or deny-by-default policy. This may lead to a scenario where an unauthorized user may gain access to the contents of the server or access to all the data will be available to everyone by default.
- In some systems, the access control may be delegated through the arguments in the URL or the access string of an Application Programming Interface (API) or by a sophisticated tool that is designed to analyze the source and pass inputs to a webpage.
- Access to other users' accounts by using some unique identifier. In some learning management systems, the data about a student can be

Rank	2017	2021
1	Injection	Broken Access Control
2	Broken Authentication	Cryptographic Failures
3	Sensitive Data Exposure	Injection
4	XML External Entities	Insecure Design
5	Broken Access Control	Security Misconfiguration
6	Security Misconfiguration	Vulnerable and outdated components
7	Cross-site Scripting	Identification and Authentication Failure:
8	Insecure Deserialization	Software and Data Integrity Failures
9	Using components with known vulnerabilities	Security logging and monitoring failures
10	Insufficient Logging and Monitoring	Server-side Request Forgery

Figure 3.1 OWASP top 10 vulnerabilities: 2017–2021. (Source: OWASP).

accessed using their roll number or a faculty may be accessed using their faculty identity.

- In some systems, the access controls may be passed to pages using POST. In case the access control argument is missed due to certain factors, the user may be provided with over-privileges. This may also lead to the elevation of privileges.
- Manipulation of the metadata through tampering with the JavaScript Object Notation (JSON) web token, cookie manipulation may lead to elevation of privileges.

3.2.2 Cryptographic failures

This was previously known as sensitive data exposure. As per the privacy laws prevailing in most countries the personal information, health records, business secrets, and financial data should be protected, and any service provider should ensure that these data are not breached at any cost. It is required to guarantee that the following measures are undertaken:

- Check whether any data in the learning system is transmitted as plain text. Perform an audit to ensure that no external traffic enters the learning system without appropriate permission. In the case of any plain text transmission, there is a possibility that sensitive information may get leaked.
- In most of the old servers, older cryptographic algorithms may be used. This may be prone to attacks. The cryptographic algorithms used in the systems are required to be updated regularly, failing which an attacker may find the vulnerability and attack the server. Some of the hash functions like MD5 and SHA1 are deprecated due to the presence of vulnerabilities.
- The crypto keys used in a system need to be regularly updated. If a common crypto key is used, then they may be prone to chosen plain text or chosen ciphertext attack. Hence a proper key management tool needs to be deployed in a system.
- Encryption should be forced by the webserver. A failure of encryption in the HTTP header may lead to exposure of data.
- The server certificate should be appropriately validated by a certifying authority. Failure to do so may result in compromise of data.
- Most servers deploy a block cipher mode of operation. Some of these require an initialization vector to initiate the encryption process. A failure to secure the initialization vector or improper management of the same may result in compromise of data. Using an inappropriate block cipher mode of operation may also result in security breaches. Zoom was an online learning platform that was affected by such a security breach.

- Passwords need to be protected by cryptographic keys. Failure to do so may result in the release of passwords. Previously certain hashing algorithms like MD5 were used to store the passwords in an encrypted form, but later on, the technology proved that MD5 hashes can be decrypted using rainbow tables.

The randomness of the cryptographic keys should follow cryptographic requirements and should meet the requirements of confusion and diffusion, failing which the cryptographic technique may not be effective.

3.2.3 Injection

This was the most popular vulnerability that topped the OWASP list for years. It has recently slid to third position. Some of the major causes for this vulnerability are given below.

- It is required to validate the input given by a user. The user may accidentally or purposely append special characters which may be escape sequences or appending statements for Structured Query Language (SQL). Failure of filtering and sanitization of input may result in injection.
- Queries that are sensitive to the database engines may be provided as input from the user which may display extra data or sensitive data from the database.
- Queries sensitive to the database engine may be concatenated which may contain stored procedures or commands. This extracts/updates/ delete the data in the database.

3.2.4 Insecure design

This is a confusing term when viewed from a software engineering perspective. The term insecure design does not mean that the design is inefficient, rather it indicates that the design of the software lacks control over the functionalities. It does not mean that a secure implementation results in a secure design. An insecure design means that the controls required to defend against attacks may not be present in the software. This is caused since an application is designed to meet business needs but does not have appropriate requirement specifications concerning its security profile.

3.2.5 Security misconfigurations

Misconfiguring a system may result in several security issues. This is a platform-based problem. The reasons behind security misconfigurations are as follows:

- Most applications are hosted today over the cloud (Hashemi and Hashemi 2013). Every cloud provider has its own custom security configurations. The documentation related to security configurations is usually vast and hence misconfiguration of minute options may be ignored. Moreover, there are possibilities that the default access privileges may be configured, which may lead to the public accessibility of resources.
- Sometimes some ports, services, or accounts that are not in use may be active and administrators of the learning system may be unaware of these open ports, services, or types of accounts, which the attacker may use to intrude into a system.
- Systems may have default usernames and passwords. It may be username: root and password: password. These may not be used by the users, but they may have added new users. These default users in a system may have privileges to access the root folder. This, when unchanged, could be used by an attacker.
- Whenever an error is encountered in a system, a detailed log of the error is usually created. This log, when it provides detailed information about the error, may provide certain information to an attacker.
- Most systems are upgraded at regular intervals. Sometimes, administrators or users fail to notice the new security upgrades and may not configure them accordingly.
- Systems may not have been upgraded properly even after multiple information from the vendors. One well-known attack that happened due to lack of upgrade was the WannaCry Ransomware attack worldwide in May 2017 on Windows XP.

3.2.6 Vulnerable and outdated components

There are different types of updates provided by a company or a service provider. Some of them may be feature updates, whereas others may be security updates. It is required to keep security services up to date to overcome security vulnerabilities. This may be caused due to various reasons which are listed below:

- There may be some updates on the server side, and some updates on the client side. Some updates need to be synchronized. A certain version of server-side updates requires complimentary client-side updates, failing which they may not function. This is due to issues related to backward compatibility.
- A software or web application depends on various factors like the operating system, web server, database management system, library files which all require an avalanche of updates. Any asynchronous update may cost the performance of the others.

- Regular scans for vulnerabilities in a system need to be done, failing which it may not be possible to get up-to-date information about recently identified vulnerabilities.

3.2.7 Identification and authentication failures

In an online learning system, it is essential to confirm the identity of the students or the facilitator to ensure authenticity. There are several authentication-related attacks reported which are caused by various reasons listed below:

- An attacker may gain access to a list of usernames and passwords. For example, for freshmen in an institution, the username may be their roll number and a default password may be given. This may be used by the attacker. This is called credential stuffing. There are popular websites that disclose EZproxy login credentials reported every year.
- There are many automated tools available to initiate a brute-force attack for a known username or a username-password combination. They may be used to log in to an online service.
- Most users avoid changing the default password offered to them because of which they may get disclosed to an attacker. Another case is that the user may have passwords like 'password' or dictionary-based words, which can be easily identified by the attacker.
- Many online services use credential recovery mechanisms by using the 'Forgot password?' link. Users recover lost passwords by using security questions. An ineffective and commonly used response may provide access to an attacker. Credential recovery mechanisms need to be foolproof.
- Most online services today offer multi-factor authentication. One of the best guidelines for multi-factor authentication is that one factor needs to be in the hands of a user, whereas the other factor should be automated. If both are in the hands of a user or if both factors are automated, it may become ineffective.
- For each session, a session identifier is created by the online service. If the identifier is visible, the identifier may be used to initiate another session by the attacker.
- In recent days, single sign-on (SSO) has become a popular mode of authentication. It requires only one credential to log in to multiple websites. The session IDs generated by the source may not be properly invalidated even after logging out, or may not be invalidated even after long inactive periods.

3.2.8 Software and data integrity failures

In a real-world application scenario, a system relies on several factors like plugins, content delivery networks, and library files, among others, from trustworthy and unverified sources. Failure of any one of these may compromise software and data integrity.

Consider a learning platform like Moodle, which provides support to many plugins to enhance the functionalities. These plugins are integrated into the learning management system and may operate using a third-party source/platform. These are required to be updated regularly. Any malicious injection in these plugins will result in the compromise of the entire learning system. While updating these plugins, users should be careful that they update them from a reliable source. Hackers could provide a re-engineered version of the update and may try to install the same in the learning system which may lead to further problems related to integrity.

3.2.9 Security logging and monitoring failures

An online system that is deployed in the cloud is accessed by users from different locations and different backgrounds. It is not possible to restrict access or verify the access for every user every time they log in. The system must possess a continuous logging and monitoring system which logs the breaches or violations that happen. However, following are some circumstances where the logging fails:

- In most systems, the logging and monitoring start only after the user logs in to the system. Login attempts made by a user, or high-value transactions made by the user may not be logged in many cases.
- Error messages or warning messages may be unclear. This may result in a poorly formed log message which may not help the administrator to identify the exact problem. Providing a clear log message to the user may end up in a problem. Similarly providing an unclear log message to the administrator will also end up in a problem.
- Most applications use APIs and plugins received from third parties to enhance their functionalities. Errors or transactions happening using these APIs or plugins in the systems may not be logged appropriately.
- In most systems, the logs are recorded properly. But the problems start with monitoring. They may not have an alerting threshold mechanism. Most service providers do not have a well-defined response escalation process since they are more conscious of business functionality rather than the security issues.
- Most systems cannot trigger an alert when they are scanned by a dynamic application security testing tool, or when penetration testing is done. This provides information about the security lags in the system facilitating the hacker gaining access to the system without the knowledge of the administrator.
- In general, attacks are done in real time and do not provide sufficient time to recover. An active real-time security alert system may not be available in most cases to alert the security professionals in an organization.

3.2.10 Server-side request forgery

Most web applications are designed to work with a request from the user based on the URL supplied to them. URL validation is not done in most cases, which may lead attackers to destinations which they request. This is termed server-side request forgery (SSRF). This may not be controlled by the firewall or the network access control list since the crafted URL input may seem to be legitimate and will not violate any access policies. Since most web applications are designed to provide convenience for the end user, they ignore the concept of URL validation and hence SSRF has become a prominent attack type in recent days, especially in online learning applications.

As per the Microsoft Security Intelligence report released in June 2020, nearly 61% of 7.7 million malware attacks countered by the organization were from the education industry (Kaspersky 2020). Students and teachers who are less used to online learning became targets of most malicious attacks since most of them were not aware of cybersecurity measures. Kaspersky, in their report, stated that there was an exponentially high number of distributed denial-of-service attacks in 2020, compared to the previous year. The report also stated that the most troubled software was Zoom and Moodle. It was also observed that the attacks were mostly encountered in Russia and Germany.

Figure 3.2 gives an outline of the number of malware attacks reported during the period January–June 2019 and January–June 2020, when the pandemic reached its peak. One of the most affected online learning platforms was Zoom, where the number of attacks reported during the period January–June 2020 was 167,657 against the 120 attacks reported during the period January–June 2019. This is a 139614% increase in the malware attacks that were exclusively focusing on Zoom. It should be observed that 99.5% of attacks that happened during the period January–June 2020 were over the Zoom platform. This brings Zoom into the spotlight for further timeline analysis of the incidents that happened during the period January–June 2020.

Figure 3.3 offers a baseline on the critical timeline faced by Zoom which forced it to perform a SWOT Analysis from a cybersecurity perspective.

Online learning is prone to several security issues. Early research on security issues related to online learning (Furnell and Karweni 2001) suggested that it is open to threats due to malicious software, denial of service, masquerading, and data theft among others. The most common security attacks on online learning platform users include phishing, malware attacks and Distributed Denial-of-Service (DDoS) attacks.

Despite the non-profit nature of academic institutions, it might be observed that several attacks have been targeted toward academic resources. The 1998 Audit Commission IT Fraud & Abuse survey states that 59% of respondents who are related to academics have registered an IT abuse. It was in 2000 when it was found that attrition.org maintains an archive of hacked websites belonging to 26 universities.

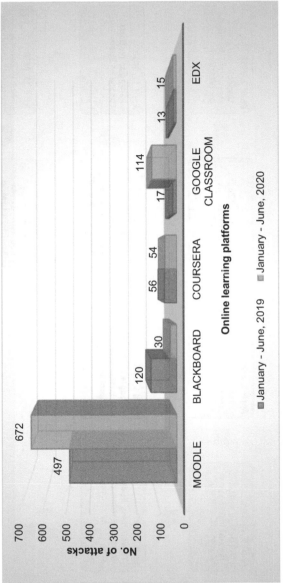

Figure 3.2 Number of malware attacks (January–June 2019 vs January–June 2020).

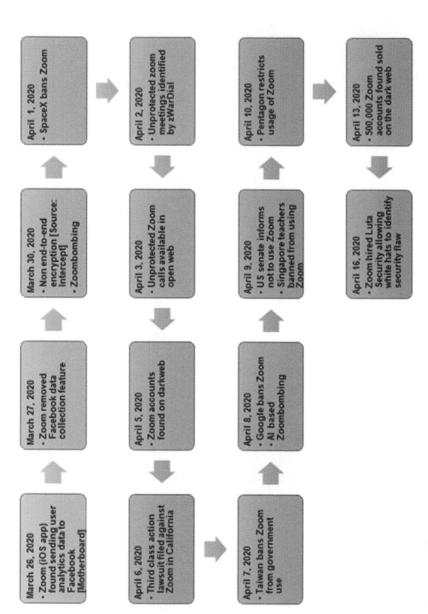

Figure 3.3 Timeline of events – security flaws in Zoom.

When providing an e-learning platform, it is required to address these issues related to security (Zamzuri et al. 2013):

For students:

- Privacy and confidentiality of personally identifiable data
- Authentication
- Accountability
- End-to-end encryption for all communication
- Confidentiality of works submitted
- Integrity
- Confidentiality of student grades
- Reliability of service provider
- Availability of service provider
- Confidentiality of exams

For learning service providers:

- Privacy and confidentiality of personally identifiable data
- Authentication
- Accountability
- Access Control
- Intrusion detection
- End-to-end encryption for all communication
- Confidentiality of works submitted
- Integrity
- Prevention of unauthorized access
- License control
- Confidentiality of exams
- Availability

To overcome these issues, proper protection software such as antivirus software needs to be put in place. Not only does an antivirus program protect the system, but the implementation of an appropriate information technology policy, periodic scanning and monitoring of files and data, and prevention of installation of unauthorized software are also required to protect the system from any security risk.

3.3 REMEDIES

Considerable research into encountering risks and threats in online learning started in the late 1990s when researchers found that the learning community was sliding toward online learning. A security framework for online distance learning (Furnell et al. 1998) suggests that online learning should focus on authentication, accountability, access control, non-repudiation, and protection of network communication. SDLearn is a framework that was introduced in 1998 to protect authentication and communication between students. It also provides different levels of access rights for the learning resource provider (LRP).

The vulnerabilities described by OWASP can be overcome by certain practices in programming or in configuring.

3.3.1 Broken access control

Some of the practices that can prevent a broken access control are as follows:

- Classify the various resources. Earmark the resources that must be provided with public access. Deny access to all other resources. Provide appropriate access to resources for legitimate users of the learning system.
- Create an access control mechanism once. Reuse it throughout the application. Redundant creation of an access control mechanism may lead to misconfiguration.
- Disable directory listing for webroot folders like htdocs and www among others.
- In case of failure of access, it should be logged appropriately and the administrator should be informed whenever required.
- Use stateless session identifiers than stateful identifiers since an attacker may gain access to the data from stateful identifiers.

3.3.2 Cryptographic failures

Some of the practices that would reduce the possibilities of cryptographic failures are as follows:

- Classify the data processed, stored, and transmitted by the online learning platform. Earmark those data which fall under privacy laws such as healthcare data which is governed by the Health Insurance Portability and Accountability Act (HIPAA), financial data which is governed by the Payment Card Industry Data Security Standard (PCI-DSS), personally identifiable data which is governed by the General Data Protection Regulation (GDPR) in the European Union, and the California Consumer Privacy Act (CCPA).
- Store sensitive data on the server if, and only if, it is required to be stored. If such data could be sought from the user whenever and wherever required, those data will not be stored. Data related to credit card/ bank account should not be stored unless essential.
- Data that is stored in databases or files should essentially be encrypted. Users should also ensure whether their data is end-to-end encrypted.

- Service providers should ensure that they are using the strongest and latest encryption algorithms and keys. They should also ensure that they are using secure protocols. Continuous upgrade of systems is a key requirement for online service providers, but the cost involved in the upgrade is much less compared to the loss occurring in business due to failure of upgrades.
- Use a strict implementation of HTTPS. Enforce HTTPS and prevent usage of HTTP to ensure that there is no plain text transaction. This should be ensured by the end user also. A detailed description of the same is provided below under phishing, which focuses on the end-user perspective.
- Care should be taken with data that is cached in the system. Cached information containing sensitive data may contribute to an information breach. This should be implemented at the system level.
- Take care that the system does not use any classical protocols like FTP or SMTP. In case of unavoidable circumstances where it is required to transmit data using these legacy protocols, take care that the data transmitted is not sensitive.
- It is advisable to use authenticated encryption since it ensures the confidentiality and authenticity of the data. This may not be available in simple encryption since it ensures confidentiality and does not look into the authenticity of the data.
- It is always better to avoid deprecated cryptographic functions. Hence, staying up to date with information security standards is mandatory for most systems.

3.3.3 Injection

Below are some practices that could help to control vulnerabilities that cause injection.

- In general, it is not possible to avoid the use of special characters in input values provided by the user. Passwords may have special characters to enhance security and to increase the search space in case of attacks. However, the inputs can be validated from the server-side which may greatly control the occurrence of injection.
- It would be better to use controlling keywords in SQL like LIMIT to prevent complete disclosure of the contents of a table.
- Use customized functions to process the inputs rather than passing the inputs directly to the queries in the database.

3.3.4 Insecure design

Steps to overcome insecure design is not an easy task. A secure design ensures that the application is secure against most of the known attacks.

One should continuously update one's knowledge against threats to ensure secure design. Threat modelling is one approach using which secure design can be achieved. Learning from mistakes is another approach to achieving a secure design. It is an abstract process that does not require a well-defined method or tool to achieve.

3.3.5 Security misconfigurations

The problems caused due to security misconfigurations can be avoided by the following practices.

- It is advisable to run a security check and disable the ports, protocols and services which are not in use. It is also recommended to uninstall the programs and applications that are not in use.
- It is required to review all the permissions available in the cloud and review whether the applications are using the appropriate permissions since the cloud is a third-party platform.
- Update the applications and tools whenever required and prompted. Usually, the systems are designed to prompt updates when available.
- Change the default passwords once the initial configuration is complete.

3.3.6 Vulnerable and outdated components

To avoid problems due to vulnerable and outdated components, it is required to follow the below procedures.

- Some of the unnecessary files, components and libraries may be available in the system even after an update, and need to be deleted or uninstalled appropriately.
- There may be multiple websites that claim to provide an update of the outdated components. It is always recommended to download the updates from the official website.
- Security patches may be provided by service providers whenever required. Proper updates of the security patches need to be done at regular intervals.

3.3.7 Identification and authentication failures

Identification and authentication failures are quite common in most online environments since the end users of the systems are located in different geographic locations. Some of the practices that could reduce the occurrence of identification and authentication failures are discussed below.

- Most systems use a username and password to authenticate a user. It is recommended to implement multi-factor authentication wherever possible. This may reduce the possibility of the reuse of stolen credentials. Though multi-factor authentication may give certain pain points to the user, it is recommended to use it, depending on the application and the risk of attack.
- One usual practice among end users is the use of default user credentials. It is always recommended to change the credentials whenever required, especially those which are associated with an administrator.
- Whenever a password is being set by a user, perform a weak password check. This helps the user not to make use of dictionary words and also forces the user to create a password with multiple combinations. Guidelines for setting passwords should be issued to the users.
- The National Institute of Standards and Technology (NIST) has provided guidelines for the complexity, length, and other security features that can be included at the time of setting the password. This can be implemented since the guidelines are found to be promising in most cases.
- A brute-force attack can be initiated over an account if any part of the credential is known. Hence, if there is a failure in login attempts, limit the number of attempts. This is usually followed in banking websites, where three failed attempts result in locking the account for a day or until an appropriate explanation is sought. It is always best practice to log the details related to login scenarios.
- In some web applications, the session identifier is placed in the URL. This is a great threat since the session identifier may be reused if recorded by a hacker. It is best practice to hide the session identifier from the user visibility.

3.3.8 Software and data integrity failures

Software and data integrity failures may lead to malicious activities that are initiated by a hacker. Some mechanisms that can be used to reduce this risk are as follows.

- The source code or a module in the software may be altered or appended during the time of transmission. It is good practice to provide a hash of the file that can be verified by the end user or the file can be protected by a digital signature through which the end user can verify the integrity of the software.
- It is always good practice to have all the dependencies and library files inside the local repository which is used to provide the service. For example, the Bootstrap framework which is used as a User Interface (UI) library can be stored in the local repository along with the library

files or may be derived from the actual source through a Content Delivery Network (CDN). It is always recommended to receive it from the local repository than deliver it through CDN which increases the possibility of a crafted request or response that initiated an attack.

- There may be known vulnerabilities in an application right from the deployment of an application. This may be identified using a software supply chain security tool. Though this might not make the application immune, it may at least reduce the occurrence of known vulnerabilities in the application.
- Care should be taken such that the data which is unencrypted or unsigned should not be shared with any clients.

3.3.9 Security logging and monitoring failures

Logging and monitoring are important tasks that need to be performed while working in an online cloud environment for hosting the learning services. Some of the best practices are listed below.

- Most systems do not log the failed attempts made by an end-user. It may be an invalid login attempt, input validation failures, specific resource access attempts using URLs, or others. A system should be designed in such a way that it logs all activities about active users of the system once they start accessing the service even before the login itself.
- Though logging may be implemented throughout the website, it should be ensured that a proper log management mechanism is available in the system.
- Log data may be subjected to injection attacks which may divert the administrator from accessing useful log data. Care should be taken to ensure that the logging is not prone to any attacks.
- Whenever a transaction of high priority or value is done, care should be taken in such a way that it leaves an audit trail. The logs should be stored in an append-only mode so that deletion or manipulation of the data will not be possible.
- Use of commercial logging software is recommended in cases where developers may not be aware of the logging process.

3.3.10 Server-side request forgery

Server-side request forgery is a challenging task since it involves in-depth knowledge about the network activities and application-level functionalities to execute the same. A few recommendations are given below.

- Use a deny-by-default rule in the firewall, so that illegitimate users may not gain access to the system.

- It is required to validate the input received from the client may it be an URL or a user credential.
- Care should be taken such that data is communicated with the client only in encrypted form and not in raw form.
- Keep a constant check on the ports and services available in the system.

3.3.10.1 Phishing attacks

Some effective practices against phishing attacks are described below.

- Websites that provide reliable services are usually secured by Secure Socket Layer/ Transport Layer Security (SSL/TLS). One common observations on websites that possess an SSL certificate is that the URL starts with https://. If the user encounters such websites displaying an URL just starting with http://, it is advisable not to access such websites.

Figure 3.4 shows the difference between a legitimate website and an illegitimate website. A difference could be noted concerning the padlock symbol near the URL. The URL starting with HTTPS will have a padlock icon near it whereas the URL starting with HTTP will have the padlock icon with a red cross.

- Ensure that you are visiting a legitimate website. Check the format and spelling of the URL multiple times before starting any transaction with a website. It is advisable to read reviews about the website. Also, check the domain registration data if possible. "Who is lookup" is one popular way to verify the domain registration data.
- Verify the email address when you receive an email from an unknown sender. If you receive an email offering free services or an email containing unidentifiable characters, be cautious. Read reviews of the free service or the URL specified in the email. Do not click the contents in the email without making an appropriate review.
- It is also good practice to read the content before clicking any content in an email. Reputed organizations do not send poorly formatted content or content with grammatical errors.
- Do not open attachments if the sender insists upon them. It is a good practice to visit the official website and browse or download the content from the official website.
- Users can install a cloud-based anti-phishing solution if they can afford it.

Figure 3.4 Differences between legitimate and fake URL.

3.3.11 Malware attacks

The most common advisories for users to encounter malware attacks are as follows.

- In general, users must download the standalone version of the online learning platform or addons from their official website only. In case of download of mobile applications, it is always recommended to download them from verified platforms like Google Play, or Microsoft Store. Most users are prone to malware attacks when they download applications from unofficial sources or when they install a pirated version of the application.
- It is always recommended to have a strong password. Most platforms have password requirements. It is good practice to change the password in regular intervals so that one can reduce the risk of the password being compromised. It is not good practice to use phone numbers, names, or any personally identifiable data as passwords since they are prone to social engineering attacks. Websites like https://haveibeenpwned.com/ help users to find whether their online credentials are under security breach. These websites also list the possible sites where the breach had occurred, thereby helping users to change the password wherever required.

3.3.12 DDoS attacks

DDoS is one of the most vigilant attacks against a service provider which should be addressed mostly at the end of the service provider. The DDoS attack can be encountered by the following methods.

- DDoS attacks are those which do not allow legitimate users to access a particular resource. In the case of most DDoS attacks, it is the responsibility of the service provider to ensure uninterrupted service to the user. This is possible by deploying cybersecurity specialists who could respond to DDoS attacks in an appropriate manner. They must be prepared to encounter the problems even on holidays or weekends, since a DDoS attack may be initiated at any time by the attacker.
- Further, it is advisable to deploy an appropriate DDoS solution from professional vendors who encounter DDoS attacks. Users should be careful that they do not become a victim or a contributor to the DDoS attack.

3.4 CONCLUSION

This chapter provides an overview of the threats and attacks prone to online learning platforms. It also provides a wide range of mechanisms and practices to encounter these security issues at the time of deployment by the service provider and at the time of utilization by the end user.

REFERENCES

Aguti, Beatrice, Robert J. Walters, and Gary B. Wills. 2014. "Effective Use of E-Learning Technologies to Promote Student Centered Learning Paradigms within Higher Education Institutions." *International Journal for E-Learning Security* 4 (2): 391–98. doi:10.20533/ijels.2046.4568.2014.0051.

Alvi, Muzna, and Manavi Gupta. 2020. "Learning in Times of Lockdown: How Covid-19 Is Affecting Education and Food Security in India." *Food Security* 12 (4): 793–96. doi:10.1007/s12571-020-01065-4.

Baby, Ann, and A. Kannamma. 2014. "Information Security Modelling In an E-Learning Environment." *International Journal of Computer Science Issues (IJCSI)* 11 (1): 195–200.

Chen, Yong, and Wu He. 2013. "Security Risks and Protection in Online Learning: A Survey." *International Review of Research in Open and Distance Learning* 14 (5): 108–27. doi:10.19173/irrodl.v14i5.1632.

Dai, Huu Phuoc Nguyen, András Kerti, and Zoltán Rajnai. 2016. "E-Learning Security Risks and Its Countermeasures." *Journal of Emerging Research and Solutions in ICT* 1 (1): 17–25. doi:10.20544/ersict.01.16.p02.

Deborah, Lazarus Jegatha, R. Karthika, P. Vijayakumar, Bharat S. Rawal, and Yong Wang. 2019. "Secure Online Examination System for E-Learning." *2019 IEEE Canadian Conference of Electrical and Computer Engineering, CCECE 2019* 2019-January (October 2019). doi:10.1109/CCECE43985.2019.9052408.

Deborah, Lazarus Jegatha, Ramachandran Baskaran, and Arputharaj Kannan. 2014. "Learning Styles Assessment and Theoretical Origin in an E-Learning Scenario: A Survey." *Artificial Intelligence Review* 8 (4): 801–19. doi:10.1007/s10462-012-9344-0.

Dhawan, Shivangi. 2020. "Online Learning: A Panacea in the Time of COVID-19 Crisis." *Journal of Educational Technology Systems* 49 (1): 5–22. doi:10.1177/0047239520934018.

Furnell, S. M., and T. Karweni. 2001. "Security Issues in Online Distance Learning." *Vine* 31 (2): 28–35. doi:10.1108/03055720010803998.

Furnell, S. M., P. D. Onions, U. Bleimann, U. Gojny, M. Knahl, H. F. Röder, and P. W. Sanders. 1998. "A Security Framework for Online Distance Learning and Training." *Internet Research* 8 (3): 236–42. doi:10.1108/10662249810217821.

Hashemi, Sajjad, and Seyyed Yasser Hashemi. 2013. "Cloud Computing for E-Learning with More Emphasis on Security Issues." *International of Computer, Electrical, Automation, Control and Information Engineering* 7 (9): 1023–28.

Kaspersky. 2020. "Digital Education: The Cyber Risks of the Online Classroom." *Securelist.* https://securelist.com/digital-education-the-cyberrisks-of-the-online-classroom/98380/.

Lawton, George. 2007. "Web 2.0 Creates Security Challenges." *Computer* 40 (10): 13–16. doi:10.1109/MC.2007.367.

Malik, Abdul Rahman, Shahzad Sarfraz, Umar Shoaib, Ghulam Abbas, and Muhammad Atif Sattar. 2016. "Cloud Based E-Learning, Security Threats and Security Measures." *Indian Journal of Science and Technology* 9 (48). doi:10.17485/ijst/2016/v9i48/96166.

OWASP Top 10: 2021. 2021. https://owasp.org/Top10/.

Shersad, Fouzia, and Sabeena Salam. 2020. "Managing Risks of E-Learning During COVID-19." *International Journal of Innovation and Research in Educational Sciences* 7 (4): 2349–5219.

Zamzuri, Zainal Fikri, Mazani Manaf, Yuzaimi Yunus, and Adnan Ahmad. 2013. "Student Perception on Security Requirement of E-Learning Services." *Procedia – Social and Behavioral Sciences* 90 (InCULT 2012). Elsevier B.V.: 923–30. doi:10.1016/j.sbspro.2013.07.169.

Chapter 4

Secure data aggregation and sharing for online learning applications

Chen Wang, Jian Shen, and Tianqi Zhou
School of Information Science and Technology, Zhejiang Sci-Tech University, Hangzhou China

Huijie Yang
School of Computer and Software, Nanjing University of Information Science & Technology, Nanjing, China

CONTENTS

The COVID-19 pandemic has led to the widespread use of online learning applications. Theoretical research of online learning has been widely carried out. However, the security and reliability of related data in online learning applications is still an issue that needs to be resolved. This chapter proposes a secure data aggregation and sharing framework for online learning applications. The framework is designed to ensure the trustworthiness evaluation based identity authentication of online learning users, privacy-preserving data storage of online course data, and the sharing of various important online learning data. First, authentication considers not only the

DOI: 10.1201/9781003264538-4

identification but also the trustworthiness of the users. Assisted by cloud computing, the trustworthiness evaluation of a user is calculated according to the different attributes of the user. Second, oblivious random access memory (ORAM) is utilized to realize user privacy-preserving and access-traceless storage. Additionally, the utilization of key agreement and group signatures achieves traceable group data sharing, supporting anonymous multi-users in online learning. The main purpose of the framework is to protect users from information leakage and data tampering caused by various possible attacks during the online learning process.

4.1 INTRODUCTION

Due to the COVID-19 pandemic, online learning has become one of the fastest-growing fields in the past year. Education is the top priority for the future development of regions, countries, and the entire world. Nowadays, online learning has become an important part of global education. One of the main advantages of online learning is that the age, location, or time of the learning participants are not obstacles. In the future, with the deepening of globalization, cross-regional communication and learning will be one of the most likely development trends. In terms of online learning, collective intelligence (CI) has great potential in improving collaboration, social learning, and problem solving. Tenorio et al. (2021) surveyed the most representative CI solutions in online learning applications. This shows that a large amount of online learning data has a wide range of application values. The collection, aggregation, and analysis of courseware, videos, student responses, and other data involved in online learning can contribute to the development of the education field. The aggregation and sharing of online learning data will be driven by technologies such as artificial intelligence and the Internet of Things to further improve the entire education process (Wang et al., 2021a, 2021b).

The structure of an online learning system is illustrated by Figure 4.1. Using personal terminals such as computers, tablets, and mobile phones, through network connections, teachers and students can attend classes, conferences, and exams online. Students, teachers, and other staff first authenticate themselves to the system. The authenticated users carry out normal teaching activities in the system. The data generated during the teaching process is transmitted to the cloud server for storage. Users of the same or different identities may form diverse groups to achieve various teaching contents (Zhou et al. 2021).

However, because online learning connects the teaching content of lecturers and their assistants with students through internet technology, this requires the security and reliability of network transmission. Reliable online learning applications require that their functions will not be affected by various network attacks such as Distributed Denial of Service (DDoS). Secure

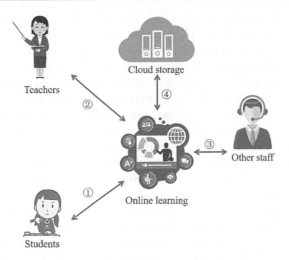

Figure 4.1 The simplified structure of an online learning system.

online learning applications require that the identities of functional users (including lecturers, teaching assistants, and audiences) are trustworthy, and can guarantee user information security. At the same time, the content of online learning needs to have a secure and efficient storage solution to ensure the copyright and privacy of the teaching content.

The motivation for this chapter: Current online learning solutions either only focus on user access control, or only consider using data for teaching effect analysis. The latest user identity authentication methods do not consider all aspects of the user's attributes, or evaluate the user's trustworthiness based on these attributes. Besides, with the continuous iteration of cloud storage technology and data transmission technology, course recordings and student feedback are often outsourced and stored on servers in the form of videos. The improper use of these data may seriously affect the privacy of users. In addition, the collection and analysis of the educational data of online learning under the premise that the privacy of users is effectively protected is one of the issues that need to be resolved urgently.

Our contribution: In this chapter, a novel secure data aggregation and sharing framework is presented for online learning applications. The contributions of this chapter are listed as follows:

- **Trustworthiness evaluation based identity authentication is proposed for online learning**. In the process of online learning, personnel are complicated. Since education is of great importance, it is necessary to ensure the trustworthiness of personnel identities. In this phase, the constant and instant attributes of a user are selected to value its trustworthiness. The trustworthiness evaluation result is utilized as a part of its signature for authentication.

- Privacy-preserving data storage is designed based on oblivious random access memory (ORAM) to avoid the leaking of private educational data. A large number of courses and participant-related data are stored in the cloud server to meet the needs of online learning applications. This leads to possible data leakage and data tampering problems. In this phase, the trustworthiness value is treated as an access proof for the access of cloud data in the system. Improved ORAM structure is utilized in this phase to achieve the protection of personal privacy, especially the access pattern of users.
- **Anonymous and traceable data sharing is presented for online group competitions.** According to differing actual needs, participants may be divided into multiple groups to start work or study. In addition, in some specific scenarios, members may need to remain anonymous. Block design based group key agreement is utilized in this phase for online group cooperation. Anonymity is implemented to meet the use of common online learning scenarios such as competitions and exams. The feature of traceability is implemented to satisfy the tracing of malicious users in anonymous scenarios. This feature is also required when the results of anonymous competitions are announced.

4.2 RELATED WORK

Online learning is considered a unique educational context comparing with other teaching and learning formations, as is discussed by Anderson (2004). Raitman et al. (2005) investigated the security of collaborative online learning. The results denied the validity of administrative identification and proved the importance of pre-identity authentication in online learning examinations. At the same time, higher requirements were put forward for anonymity and traceability technology for online learning. Yong (2007) designed the meta-format of digital identities of online learning to protectthe privacy of users' digital identity. Weippl and Ebner (2008) further presented security and privacy challenges in online learning.

Alwi and Fan (2010) believed that access control alone in online learning applications is not enough to prevent internal attacks. Lai et al. (2019) tried to intervene in the educational process of online learning through automatic detection of students' personality traits. They believed that collecting additional features such as text and images related to students is needed to obtain a larger data set to better predict personality traits. There is no doubt that such behavior may lead to the disclosure of user privacy. Therefore, how to use the large amount of data generated by online learning applications to achieve better teaching is an important issue worth exploring.

Atherton et al. (2017) proposed to evaluate student engagement and academic outcomes through analysis of online learning data. Preuveneers and Joosen (2019) designed an edge-based browser method for analyzing different behavior patterns aggregated from online learning user by using secure multiparty computing. This method lacks monitoring of the client's behavior, which may lead to the occurrence of cheating.

Wang and Yu (2021) proposed an evaluation strategy that uses deep learning and collaborative filtering technology to analyze the optimization of online learning evaluation from online course evaluation data and student comments. The proposed personalized exercise recommendation method based on deep knowledge tracing is considered to have the ability of improving the quality of online learning. However, this evaluation strategy does not consider the privacy protection of the original data.

4.3 PRELIMINARIES

Here are listed the main technologies involved in this chapter, including trustworthiness evaluation, improved ORAM, and block design.

4.3.1 Trustworthiness evaluation

Trustworthiness evaluation is the concept that by collecting various attributes of a user and using methods such as model construction and weighting ratio, the trustworthiness of the user can be calculated. The result can be used as an evaluation criterion for identity authentication, or as a condition for access control. The following Equation (4.1) is utilized to calculate the trustworthiness of a user by Wang et al. (2020).

$$\mathfrak{C}(t) = \left(1 - \frac{\delta}{\theta \cdot (1 + \Delta t)}\right) \cdot \frac{\sum\limits_{i=1}^{m} \mathfrak{W}_i \mathfrak{a}_i}{m}(t) + \frac{\delta}{\theta \cdot (1 + \Delta t)} \cdot \mathfrak{C}(t^-) \qquad (4.1)$$

where $\mathfrak{W}_i$ is the weight of the i-th attribute of the user. δ denotes that the previous evaluation result $\mathfrak{C}(t^-)$ should be accounted for. Δt is the time interval between time t and time t^-. θ is used to control the annealing speed of the previous result.

4.3.2 Oblivious Random Access Memory (ORAM) and improved ORAM

To protect the access pattern of stored data, researchers have focused on an idea called oblivious random access memory (ORAM). ORAM is designed to protect the traces left by users accessing data in storage devices, thereby protecting personal privacy.

An improved ORAM structure is proposed by Shen et al. (2021). A one-way circular linked table in a binary tree is utilized to promote the

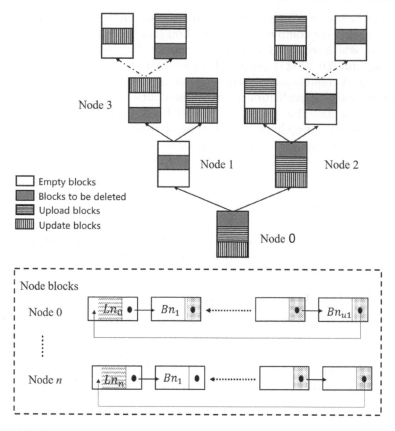

Figure 4.2 The structure of the improved ORAM.

performance of ORAM schemes. Figure 4.2 shows the improved ORAM structure. The structure is a complete binary tree with n depth and $2^n - 1$ nodes. Each node is considered as a one-way circular linked table.

4.3.3 Block design and $(v, k + 1, 1)$-design

Block design is one of the important concepts in combinatorial mathematics. A balanced incomplete block design (BIBD) is defined by Definition 3.1:

Definition 3.1

Let $V = \{0, 1, 2, ..., v - 1\}$ be a set of v elements and $B = \{B_0, B_1, B_2, ..., B_{b-1}\}$ be a set of b blocks. Note that, B_i is a subset of V and $|B_i| = k$. For a finite incidence structure $\sigma = (V, B)$, if σ satisfies the following conditions, then it is a BIBD, which is called a (b, v, r, k, λ)-design.

As is mentioned above, the number of elements of the set V is denoted as v and that of blocks is denoted as b. Note here that, k is the number of elements in each block and r and λ are two parameters. Let $k = r$ and $b = v$, a symmetric balanced incomplete block design (SBIBD) is constructed, which is called $(v, k + 1, 1)$-Design. A detailed explanation can be found in Shen et al. (2017).

4.4 MAIN IDEA

In this section, the novel secure data aggregation and sharing framework for online learning is introduced in detail. The scheme consists of three different parts: trustworthiness evaluation based identity authentication, privacy-preserving data storage, and anonymous and traceable data sharing.

4.4.1 Overview of the proposal

The proposal of this chapter is a framework for secure data aggregation and sharing for online learning applications. This framework is designed on the basis of trustworthiness evaluation, improved ORAM and $(v, k + 1, 1)$ block design. As shown in Figure 4.3, the framework consists of three phases:

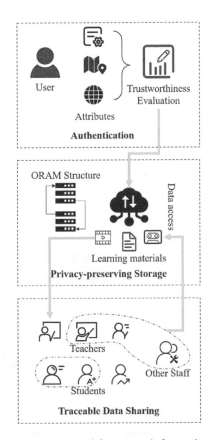

Figure 4.3 The overview of the novel framework for online learning.

authentication, privacy-preserving storage, and traceable data sharing. In the first phase, the system authenticates the identification of registered users. Trustworthiness evaluation is implemented by the system according to the different attributes of the users. A user with a high trustworthiness level may have the chance to access the data stored in the cloud. In the second phase, learning materials such as course videos, audio recordings, courseware, and documents, are stored in the cloud. To protect the privacy of the users and the course copyright, an improved ORAM structure is utilized to achieve secure data access. In the third phase, due to the actual needs of applications, it may be necessary to form various groups among different users. Block design is utilized to ensure secure group data sharing. In some special scenarios, group users can be guaranteed to be anonymous, and at the same time, authorized administrators can trace the identity information of any user if needed.

4.4.2 Trustworthiness evaluation based identity authentication

The first part of this framework is trustworthiness evaluation based identity authentication, as is shown in Figure 4.4.

First, the system needs to securely collect various constant attributes of users. For student users, these data may be the student's school status, valid certificates, and biological information. For the teacher user, these data may be the teacher's qualification, valid certificate, biological information, and

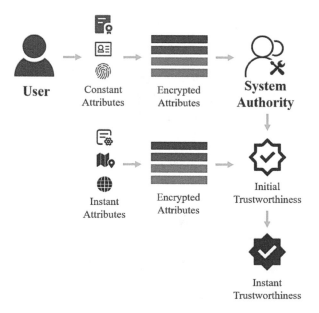

Figure 4.4 The process of the update of trustworthiness evaluation.

so on. The system authority calculates an initial trustworthiness of the user. This value will be sent to the user as a part of its signature.

The user chooses two random numbers $x_u, r \xleftarrow{R} \mathbb{Z}_p$ and computes $Y_u = g^{wu}$ and $R = h^r$. ID_u, Y_u, R, and the attributes of the user $Attr$ are sent to authority by a homomorphic encryption algorithm. The authority calculates its trustworthiness. If the user is a trustworthy one, the authority generates two random numbers $c_u, r' \xleftarrow{R} \mathbb{Z}_p$ and computes $R' = w^{r'}$. The signature for the user is shown in Equation (4.2):

$$\sigma_u = \left(g_0 g_1^{H(V\,P_u)} Y_u R^{r'} \prod_{i=1}^{N_i} \eta_i^{H(I_{ij})} \right)^{\frac{1}{x+c_u}} \tag{4.2}$$

where $V\,P_u$ is the valid time of this signature, N_1 is the number of attributes, and I_{ij} is items of the attributes according to $Attr$. After receiving a message including c_u, R', σ_u, $V\,P_u$ from the authority, the user verifies the signature as Equation (4.3).

$$e\left(\sigma_u, \tilde{g}g^{C_u}\right) \overset{?}{=} e(g_0, g) \cdot e(g_1, g)^{H(V\,P_u)}.$$
$$e(Y_u, g) \cdot e(R', g)^r \cdot \prod_{i=1}^{N_1} e(\eta_i, g)^H (I_{ij}) \tag{4.3}$$

Second, during the process of online learning, according to the instant attributes such as behavior log, location, network connection, etc., the system authority updates the trustworthiness into a instant one. This trustworthiness value will also be sent to the user as a part of its signature. The user will prove themselves to the system by zero knowledge proof.

4.4.3 Privacy-preserving data storage

The authenticated users are allowed to request some data on the cloud. Algorithm 1 shows the process of accessing data. As is illustrated in Figure 4.5, take users 1 and 2 for example. User 2 wants to download the data M of user 1. User 2 sends its real request Q together with other fake requests Q_1, Q_2, ... The identity ID of the user, its trustworthiness T, the number of the requested data block and the operation it wants to deal with the data are listed in Q. User 1 finds the number of the data block and searches for the answer to the request $A = (a, H)$, where a is a random number generated when the data is stored, and H is the corresponding head pointer.

Also, fake answers are made for the fake requests. The real one is sent to user 2 by user 1 using oblivious transfer technology. The answers are sent to the cloud server and the server gives the corresponding encrypted data. User 2 then uses the answer from user 1 to decrypt the requested data.

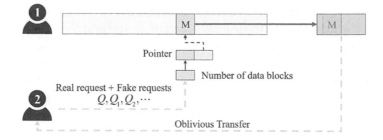

Figure 4.5 The process of privacy-preserving data access.

4.4.4 Anonymous and traceable data sharing

This phase mainly solves the problem that some users wish to form a group for work scheduling, learning sharing or group cooperation. To meet the needs of a wider range of teaching activities, this stage also allows the anonymity of users. In addition, when a user violates regulations, the system can track the user, or, after the anonymous validity period ends, the system can disclose the identity information of the members. The process is shown in Figure 4.6. There are two steps for the members of a group to generate the group session key.

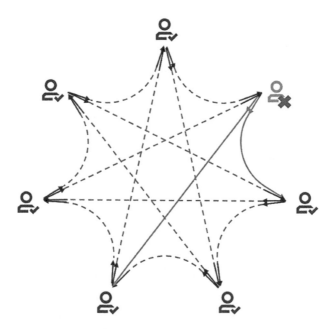

Figure 4.6 The process of privacy-preserving data access.

Algorithm 1 AccessOperation()

Require:
    user ID_i, data $D = d_i$, trustworthiness T_i, average of users' download times Uc_{av};

Ensure:
    Message M or unreadable;
```
 1: for d_i ∈ (1, m) do
 2:    while ID==auth(ID_i, T_i)   do
 3:       if Uc_i ≤ Uc_av then
 4:          λ_1 ← DB(Hn_0, Ln_1)
 5:          (λ_1, λ_2, ..., λ_n) ←
             SB(Bn_1, Bn_2, ..., Bn_u)
 6:             Cn_i = Cn_i + 1;
 7:          if Cn_i > T_A then
 8:                run Confusion();
 9:          end if
10:       else
11:          if a'_i, == a_i then
12:                continue AccessOperation();
13:          end if
14:          Return Message M
15:       end if
16:    end while
17: end for
```

Step 1: In the first step, $\mathcal{F}_i = \hat{e}(\mathbb{G}, e_i r_i \mathcal{L}_i)$ is calculated by each user, where r_i is a random number. Let $Y_i = H_2(ID_i, \mathcal{T}_i)$, where ID_i is the identity of user i and $\mathcal{T}_i$ is their trustworthiness. Then, calculate $\mathcal{T}_i = X_i \cdot \hat{e}(\mathbb{G}, w_i r_i \mathcal{L}_i)$ and a time stamp t_i, where $X_i = Y_i^{d_i}$, $w_i = H_2(\mathcal{F}_i, t_i)$.

User i receives message $D_j = \left\{ Y_j, (\mathcal{F}_j)^{e_i}, T_j, t_j \right\}$ from user j if j is in the corresponding block according to the design of block design.

Each user receives k messages, Equation (4.4) is calculated by user i to decrypt the messages.

$$\mathcal{F}_j = \left[\left(\mathcal{F}_j \right)^{e_i} \right]^{d_i}, j \in Block_i - \{i\} \tag{4.4}$$

where d_i is the secret key of himself. Equation (4.5) shows the calculation for the user to derive $U_{i,j}$.

$$U_{i,j} = \prod_{x \in Block_i - \{j\}} \mathcal{F}_x \tag{4.5}$$

Step 2: User i receives message $\varepsilon_{j,i} = \left\{ Y_j, \left(U_{j,i} \right)^{e_i}, \left(M_j \right)^{e_i}, T_j, t_j \right\}$ from *participant$_j$* according to the rule of block design. And finally, the session key for user i is calculated as Equation (4.6).

$$
\begin{aligned}
SK &= \mathcal{F}_i \left(\prod_{j,i \in Block_j} U_{j,i} \right) \\
&= \hat{e} \left(\mathbb{G}, e_i r_i \mathcal{L}_i \right) \cdot \left(\prod_{j,i \in Block_j} U_{j,i} \right) \\
&= \hat{e} \left(\mathbb{G}, \sum_{i=0}^{\nu-1} e_i r_i \mathcal{L}_i \right)
\end{aligned}
\tag{4.6}
$$

4.5 PERFORMANCE

In this section, the performance of this framework is presented. However, different similar schemes can be combined with this framework to achieve the same purpose. Therefore, the simulation in this section is only to provide a reference for showing the performance of the framework. The simulation is implemented on the GNU multiple precision arithmetic (GMP) library and pairing-based cryptography (PBC) library[1]. C language is used to implement the simulation on a Linux system with Ubuntu 16.04 TLS, 2.60 GHz Intel(R) Xeon(R) CPU E5-2650 v2, and 8 GB of RAM.

Figure 4.7 shows the time cost of the authentication phase, which is the first phase of our novel framework. As the number of authenticated users increases, so does the time cost. However, for one user, the authentication time cost will not be affected.

Figure 4.8 illustrates the result of the computation cost of data access and session key generation. Data access is the most important part of the second phase in our framework and session key generation is the third phase. The results show us that the computation cost of the two operations increases linearly as the number of users increases. It is worth noting that within a certain range of the number of users, such an increase is acceptable.

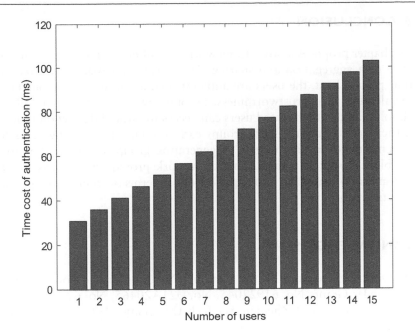

Figure 4.7 The time cost of authentication phase.

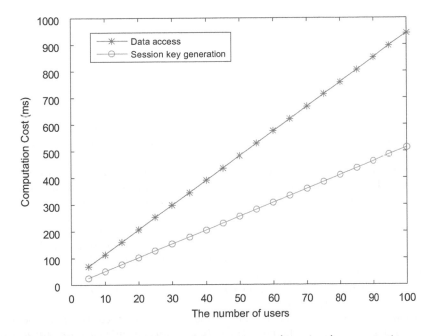

Figure 4.8 The computation cost of data access and session key generation.

4.6 CONCLUSION

This chapter proposes a novel framework for online learning which ensures secure data aggregation and sharing. The novel framework has three different phases. First, the users are authenticated according to the outcomes of evaluating their trustworthiness. Second, by using improved ORAM technology, the authenticated users can access the stored data without leaking their access pattern. Last, groups can be established among users for different online learning targets by generating group session keys assisted with block design structures. This framework provides new ideas for the development of online learning applications in terms of security and privacy protection.

ACKNOWLEDGEMENTS

This work is supported by the National Natural Science Foundation of China under Grants No. 61922045, No. U21A20465, No. 62172292, and Science Foundation of Zhejiang Sci-Tech University (ZSTU) under Grants No. 22222266-Y.

NOTE

1 https://crypto.stanford.edu/pbc/.

REFERENCES

Alwi, N. H. M., and Fan, I.-S. (2010). E-learning and information security management. *International Journal of Digital Society (IJDS)*, 1 (2), 148–156.

Anderson, T. (2004). Teaching in an online learning context. *Theory and Practice of Online Learning*, 273–294.

Atherton, M., Shah, M., Vazquez, J., Griffiths, Z., Jackson, B., and Burgess, C. (2017). Using learning analytics to assess student engagement and academic outcomes in open access enabling programmes. *Open Learning: The Journal of Open, Distance and e-Learning*, 32 (2), 119–136.

Preuveneers, D., and Joosen, W. (2019). Edge-based and privacy-preserving multimodal monitoring of student engagement in online learning environments. In *2019 IEEE International Conference on Edge Computing (Edge)*. Paris (pp. 18–20).

Lai, S., Sun, B., Wu, F., and Xiao, R. (2019). Automatic personality identification using students' online learning behavior. *IEEE Transactions on Learning Technologies*, 13 (1), 26–37.

Raitman, R., Ngo, L., Augar, N., and Zhou, W. (2005). Security in the online e-learning environment. In *Fifth IEEE International Conference on Advanced Learning Technologies (ICALT'05)*. Kaohsiung, Taiwan, (pp. 702–706).

Shen, J., Yang, H., Vijayakumar, P., and Kumar, N. (2021). A privacy-preserving and untraceable group data sharing scheme in cloud computing. *IEEE Transactions on Dependable and Secure Computing*, 19 (4), 2198–2210.

Shen, J., Zhou, T., Chen, X., Li, J., and Susilo, W. (2017). Anonymous and traceable group data sharing in cloud computing. *IEEE Transactions on Information Forensics and Security*, 13 (4), 912–925.

Tenorio, T., Isotani, S., Bittencourt, I. I., and Lu, Y. (2021). The state-of-the-art on collective intelligence in online educational technologies. *IEEE Transactions on Learning Technologies*, 14 (2), 257–271.

Wang, C., Huang, R., Shen, J., Liu, J., Vijayakumar, P., and Kumar, N. (2021a). A novel lightweight authentication protocol for emergency vehicle avoidance in vanets. *IEEE Internet of Things Journal*, 8 (18): 14248–14257.

Wang, C., Shen, J., Lai, J.-F., and Liu, J. (2020). B-TSCA: Blockchain assisted trustworthiness scalable computation for v2i authentication in vanets. *IEEE Transactions on Emerging Topics in Computing*, 9 (3), 1386–1396.

Wang, W., Qiu, C., Yin, Z., Srivastava, G., Gadekallu, T. R., Alsolami, F., and Su, C. (2021b). Blockchain and puf-based lightweight authentication protocol for wireless medical sensor networks. *IEEE Internet of Things Journal*, 9 (11), 8883–8891.

Wang, Z., and Yu, N. (2021). Education data-driven online course optimization mechanism for college student. *Mobile Information Systems*, 2021: 1–8.

Weippl, E. R., and Ebner, M. (2008). Security privacy challenges in e-learning 2.0. In *E-learn: World Conference on E-Learning in Corporate, Government, Healthcare, and Higher Education* (pp. 4001–4007).

Yong, J. (2007). Digital identity design and privacy preservation for e-learning. In *2007 11th International Conference on Computer Supported Cooperative Work in Design* (pp. 858–863).

Zhou, T., Shen, J., Ren, Y., and Ji, S. (2021). Threshold key management scheme for blockchain-based intelligent transportation systems. *Security and Communication Networks*, 2021: 1864514.

Chapter 5

A secure data-centric approach to blended learning for programming languages

C. Beulah and Christalin Latha
Karunya Institute of Technology and Sciences, Coimbatore, India

Sujni Paul
Faculty Higher Colleges of Technology, Dubai, UAE

Rajan John
College of Computer Science and Information Technology, Jazan University, KSA

CONTENTS

DOI: 10.1201/9781003264538-5

Blended learning refers to a new approach in teaching and learning in which digital learning tools are used with traditional classroom teaching for more efficient learning. This approach combines computer assisted tools for making learning a pleasurable as well as a productive process. The pandemic has made classroom learning a near to impossible activity and all teachers and students have experienced a paradigm shift towards online education. Though online learning cannot be a substitute for classroom teaching, these digital learning tools help teachers to achieve a personal touch with students and make the sessions interactive. The traditional blended learning approach needs the teacher and the learner to be in a physical classroom where digital tools are used for interaction. In an online mode of education, the same effectiveness is achieved using flipped classrooms which use digital learning tools through cloud-based learning platforms. In a flipped classroom approach, the learner may choose to learn from the digital learning resources at any convenient time.

5.1 INTRODUCTION

Blended learning and flipped classroom are novel educational approaches that have been used by instructors worldwide to impart learning to diverse types of learners. Both blended learning and flipped classroom approaches facilitate interactive learning to a great extent. Moreover, blended learning helps to customize the learning process as per the learning styles and skills of individual students using data analytics. Unlike classroom teaching, it is easier to handle a larger number of students simultaneously using blended learning approaches. This chapter details a research study that was conducted with undergraduate science students to analyze the effectiveness of learning programming languages using a blended learning approach. Digital learning tools make the data collection process during learning an easier task. The data thus collected is analyzed to provide a customized learner-centered learning environment. Data analytics can help teachers to identify weak learners precisely. It also enables them to design customized learning materials and assessment materials. The availability of digital learning platforms helps students to complete their customized assignments.

Group activities were also facilitated through these platforms. Platforms such as Slido, Kahoot, Nearpod, and Plickers helped to make learning more interactive and enjoyable. Data mining techniques were used for identifying students' study patterns and analyzing their performance on assessments. The results of data mining algorithms were used to customize the learning materials as well the assessment materials to enhance the students' learning. The feedback obtained from the students was found to be satisfactory. The following conclusions were drawn from the results. Tools such as Zoom, Google Meet, Google Classrooms, Kahoot, Plickers, and Slidos were widely used for online teaching. Blended learning tools help in developing communication, skills, and knowledge, meeting individual learning needs, and offer better understanding through recorded lectures, and doubt clearing. But these tools were found to be less effective in providing a convenient and interactive learning environment for hands-on practical sessions. The teachers faced many challenges in digitizing the entire course during the pandemic. Project-based learning, problem-based teaching, and flipped classroom technologies could be effectively used for teaching programming language concepts.

Storytelling and programming are an ideal combination when introducing programming concepts to beginners. A story structure always has a beginning, middle, and end. This gives a foundation to organize scripts into manageable chunks. Students are usually reluctant to learn programming languages; some find it difficult to understand the logic of the programs. To motivate students to learn, program storyboards help a lot. Students can understand the steps in a program in the form of a story and write scripts to code them. This makes them first solve the problem on a piece of paper, understand it by themselves and interpret this into scripts. This chapter provides a detailed analysis of teaching programming languages made simple in a blended learning environment.

5.1.1 Blended learning

Computers have become an inevitable part of everyday life. People use computers for various purposes. Since computers are used in various fields, the younger generation is expected to be techno-savvy, especially in using computers. This is applicable not only to software professionals and computer programmers but also to people working in other areas. For example, nowadays computer programming is used in the medical field for medical imaging, data analysis in medicine, and for diagnosis of various diseases, while doctors now perform computer-assisted or robotic- assisted surgeries and so on. Similarly, we find that computers are used in basic science streams like physics, chemistry, botany, and zoology and also in various technological streams such as mechanical engineering, thermal engineering, biotechnology, aeronautics, civil engineering, biomedical engineering, and so on. Computer programming is also used in smart farming and precision farming, and various other fields in agriculture. Therefore, computer programming has become a part of the curriculum for almost all the programs at college level as well as at school level. Despite the fact that programming is not a piece of cake for many, students have programming courses as a mandatory requirement in the curriculum of most of the programs offered at college level. The majority of technological advancements are based on computer programming. So, irrespective of the field of work, today's employees are expected to be techno-savvy and familiar with computer programming.

Classically, programming is taught in classrooms. In the earlier days, the "talk and chalk" approach was used to teach programming. Teachers would explain problem-solving using algorithms. Then they would teach how algorithms could be represented using a flowchart and proceed with how to transform the algorithms into a program in a programming a language. They would use a blackboard for teaching this way. After the introduction of smart classrooms, this approach was simplified. Teachers used to demonstrate programs in real time programming environments and students also found it interesting to learn. Blended learning is a new approach to teaching and learning in which digital learning tools are used with traditional classroom teaching for more efficient learning. This approach combines computer-assisted tools for making learning a pleasurable as well as a productive process. Blended learning offers the convenience of providing hands-on sessions to students in a computer lab. Another similar approach, namely flipped learning, uses digital learning tools through cloud-based learning platforms. In a flipped classroom approach, the learner may choose to learn from the digital learning resources at any convenient time. Nowadays, teachers have the facilities for using augmented reality also in online teaching. This makes the learning experience interesting as well as interactive.

5.1.1.1 Blended learning models

Blended learning can be implemented through different models. These models describe the methods that can be used for hybrid teaching. There are twelve models in blended learning. Figure 5.1 shows the blended learning models [1].

  i. Station rotation blended learning
     In this model, students are divided into batches, and they are rotated through different stations on a fixed schedule, where at least one of the stations is an online or computer-assisted learning station. This model is widely used in elementary schools.
 ii. Lab rotation blended learning
     In the lab rotation model, student batches are scheduled to work in a dedicated computer lab on a rotation basis.
iii. Remote blended learning
     This model is also referred to as enriched virtual learning. In this model, the students will have to complete online coursework while

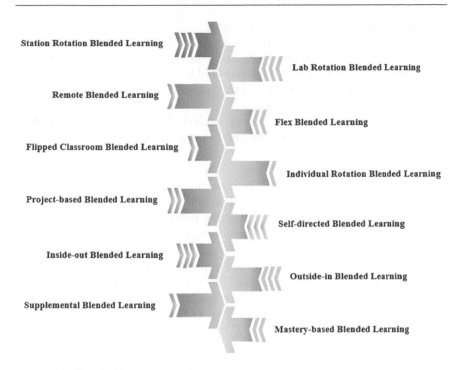

Figure 5.1 Blended learning models.

meeting the teacher only intermittently or only when needed. In this model, students study online, or in a physical classroom, and learn at home. Unlike the flipped classroom model, the remote blended learning model does not require the teacher to be with the student during the learning phase.

iv. Flex blended learning

In flex blended learning, online learning or physical classroom learning is considered to be the main course of learning and the student is directed to offline activities at times. Activities are allotted using flexible schedules. The teacher is available for the students during the learning process, except for homework assignments, and provides face-to-face support on a flexible and adaptive basis, as and when required, through activities such as group discussions, group projects, and individual tutoring.

v. Flipped classroom blended learning

In flipped classrooms, students are provided with offline content through cloud-based learning platforms. Students can refer to the materials at their own convenient time and then complete assignments in online mode, either guided by a teacher or by working with peers. This model flips the traditional roles of teacher and student and hence the name.

vi. Individual rotation blended learning

This model allows the students to rotate through online and offline stations on an individual basis based on a schedule. Unlike other rotation models, the student is not required to rotate through every station; they can rotate only to the required stations based on their activities.

vii. Project-based blended learning

Project-based learning is a model in which the student uses both online learning and face-to-face instruction and collaboration to complete project-based assignments.

viii. Self-directed blended learning

In the self-directed blended learning model, students achieve their personal goals using a blend of online and physical classroom learning. This model may be used for meeting mentors, having some personal inquiry with teachers, and achieving self-directed learning goals.

ix. Inside-out blended learning

In the inside-out blended learning model, a student is required to learn beyond the classroom premises but still requires the advantages of physical and digital spaces. Expert guidance and support are required on a daily basis in this model. Project-based blended learning is an example of this model.

x. Outside-in blended learning

In the outside-in blended learning model, students plan and begin their activities in a physical or digital environment outside the classroom. The activity is then completed inside the classroom. This helps students to implement innovative ideas and try implementing the theoretical concepts they learned in the classrooms. Guidance and support from the instructor are needed on a daily basis for this model as well.

xi. Supplemental blended learning

In this model, students supplement physical classroom learning with online work and vice versa. They implement the concepts learned in a classroom environment using some online or simulation tools, or they learn the concepts in an online environment and complete some related activity in a classroom. So, critical learning objectives are met entirely in one space and the supplementary experiences this space cannot provide may be met in the opposite space. For example, the students may learn about a robot in a physical classroom environment, and they can try simulating one in simulation software like Webots.

xii. Mastery-based blended learning

In this model of blended learning, students rotate between online and classroom learning based on the completion of mastery-based learning objectives. The teacher should be careful in designing the assessment since the use of manual or digital assessment tools is either powerful or complicated depending on the mindset of the designer.

5.1.1.2 Advantages and Disadvantages

Blended learning has many advantages and disadvantages. Teachers can experience a personalized and customized training experience in blended learning environments and can assess the students at a convenient time. It is easier to track employee performance and skill development. Training costs can be reduced to a larger extent. There is more possibility of collaboration between teachers and students and peer learners. Blended learning can have some adverse effects as well. Students are assumed to have basic technical knowledge and a willingness to learn. Higher technology setups may include investment in hardware and software and may extend to maintenance costs as well. Offered resources may not be fully utilized by the students. There is a greater dependency on technology.

5.2 CHALLENGES IN TEACHING PROGRAMMING LANGUAGES

Diversity in Background Knowledge: Teachers face a lot of challenges when it comes to teaching programming languages because of the wide diversity in students' background knowledge, fear of programming, and problems in learning syntax [2]. The study discussed in this chapter focuses on novice learners who are learning a programming language for the first time at college level. When it comes to teaching a programming language to a class, the teacher has the task of addressing heterogeneous learners from different backgrounds. A majority of them could be novice learners, some with a passion for programming, some with a disinclination towards programming, and some who have already learned some programming languages. Focusing on each student's individual needs is a difficult task when it comes to classroom teaching. Blended learning approaches are more effective in such cases. They help provide customized materials and attention to different types of students. When programming is taught online, teachers can check the code, and guide the learners through the virtualized platforms. Collaborative coding can also be developed through online platforms.

High Failure Rate: Being a technical subject, teaching programming languages, is time-consuming. Most of the students find the subject difficult to grasp. On an average, only around 70% of the students from non-computer streams pass in programming languages when the instruction is offered in traditional classroom mode. The high failure rate is attributed to the difficulty level and complexity of the subject, interest in learning a new technology, and the time taken to acquire the required expertise. Students from non-mathematical backgrounds find computer programming as one of their toughest subjects. But blended learning practices help in improving the effectiveness of learning. The percentage of students passing in programming language courses increased to 88% when a blended learning approach was followed.

Lack of Individual Attention: Another challenge that is faced by teachers in a traditional classroom approach is the provision of individual attention to the students. In modern-day classrooms, the number of students is usually above 50. In a class of one-hour duration, teaching a programming concept requires providing at least three to four examples. The more the number of examples, the more the learner grasps the concepts. But when examples and exercises are given in the classroom, the teacher has to monitor and assist all the students in the class. Paying attention to individual students is a cumbersome task in a traditional classroom. The blended and flipped classroom approaches help teachers to solve this problem to a greater extent. Online classrooms also enable teachers to provide customized assignments and evaluate and guide students in an appropriate way [3].

Failing to cope up with Logic and Syntax Together: Learning the logic of problem-solving and coding the solution using new syntax simultaneously is a challenge faced by many novice coders. Most of the concepts in programming are abstract and, therefore, difficult for the students to conceptualize. As per statistics, there is a high drop-out rate witnessed in programming courses [4]. Many novice learners view programming like any other subject and try a rote learning approach rather than grasping meaningful concepts. This makes it difficult for them to understand the concepts and apply them appropriately for solving problems. Syntax-free, problem-solving courses help in this aspect. Such courses focus on teaching logic alone which helps the students learn the concepts properly. Tools such as Raptor, can help students to grasp programming concepts faster. After getting trained in such tools, students may be given the task of learning a programming language along with syntax. Another alternate approach is to teach a programming language with light syntax such as Python initially and introduce other languages such as C, C++, and Java later. Some of the literature even suggests introducing an object-oriented approach initially [4].

Disinclination towards Programming: Teachers also face the challenge of imparting programming knowledge to students who are disinclined toward programming. Some students have a natural disinterest in programming for various reasons. Software concepts are more abstract, and the output of applications is not concrete all the time. Most of the applications produce only an intangible, abstract output. This makes many students lose interest in programming. Some students try learning programming in a rote way, and this makes understanding logic a tough task for them. Some students have a general tendency to feel that programming is not their cup of tea, and they have a perception that they cannot understand programming. This makes them unable to concentrate on programming concepts and learn them. Teaching such students is a big challenge for teachers.

Teachers who teach coding have to overcome all the above said challenges to make their teaching effective. Therefore, it is essential for them to adapt to novel strategies for making the students learn effectively, and blended learning makes these approaches feasible and easier. Some of these strategies will be discussed later in this chapter.

5.3 STUDENT-CENTERED LEARNING

Traditional classroom teaching is more of a teacher-centered approach than a student-centered approach. Teacher-centered approaches tend not to empower students in their own learning since there is little or no room for student engagement activities [5]. Teachers try molding each learner through providing individual attention, but classes with large numbers of students, students with different learning styles, different learning abilities and different learning needs makes a student-centered approach more challenging for a teacher [6]. Time-constrained learning is also another drawback of traditional classroom teaching in catering to the needs of individual learners. Blended learning platforms help teachers to offer student-centered learning that can focus on individual learners, making the learning process convenient for everyone. The ubiquitous nature of blended learning platforms also helps in this aspect. Student-centered learning requires customization of the materials provided to the students as well as of the methods through which they are trained. A student-centered approach makes the learning process more meaningful and interesting for the students. In addition to that, rigorous and personalized assessments can help learners to get the maximum out of the process.

Student-centered learning approaches support remote learning in which the students can learn individually using the study materials and assignments or in groups. They also experience the freedom of learning at their own pace. This helps even weak learners to learn effectively [7]. The teacher also is relieved of the stress of focusing on the needs of the students learning at different speeds. During the COVID-19 pandemic, these approaches helped both students and teachers to make the learning process easier and more effective. At this juncture, it is also necessary to mention that blended learning approaches do not sideline or undermine the role of a teacher in the education process but in fact, require the expertise of the teacher to make the learning process effective as well as easier [8, 9].

Student-centered education empowers students and equips them with conversational skills, problem-solving skills, and critical thinking skills. Student-centered learning strategies involve students in all phases of learning such as planning, implementation, and assessment. Most of the blended learning approaches are student-centered by nature. They provide flexibility in time, place, and pace of learning and therefore, meet the needs of all the students. Students have the flexibility of learning wherever they can, whenever they need, whatever they need, and in whichever method they like. This keeps them engaged and motivated and makes the learning process simple.

A student-centered approach offers many advantages. Rotation models, remote models, and project-based models help students to take up challenges and move forward in finding solutions. It also provides them the flexibility to collaborate and work together, thus developing team spirit. Students are also familiarized with technology and use technology for problem-solving. In addition, students get hands-on experience by practicing what they have learned in the classroom using simulation tools and development environments.

Though the blended learning paradigm is effective for both teachers and students, the transformation process may also be challenging for both teachers and the students especially when this paradigm needs to be adapted by teachers who are less techno-savvy and find the approach more challenging. Some students also find it difficult to adapt to the new norm.

5.4 LEARNING STYLES

Learning styles describe how learners acquire, select, interpret, organize, and retain information. Different approaches are required for motivating and instructing learners with different learning styles. Learning-style-based approaches are used in teaching programming as well. State-of-the-art research reveals that such approaches focus on increasing student performance [10, 11]. Learning styles can also be taken into account while teaching programming languages. Using different strategies on different learners based on their learning styles can improve their learning process. Based on the literature, the learning patterns of learners can be categorized into five learning styles.

5.4.1 Verbal/Linguistic learners

These types of learners prefer to learn by reading, speaking, and writing. Programming languages can be taught to such types of learners by providing coding snippets and providing them with an environment to apply them. Concepts and syntax can be taught, and programming assignments and the concepts learnt can be practiced through blended learning platforms such as Codeboard, Google Colab, etc. for them to practice. This model helps the learners not only to understand the concepts but also to apply them in problem solving.

5.4.2 Visual/Spatial learners

Visual learners prefer colorful learning environments, graphic organizers, images, and use of visual media. Such learners find learning impressive if concepts are taught with pictures, charts, and different colors. When using chalk and talk for teaching, different colored chalks can be used for writing syntax on the board. Keywords can be written with one color, user-defined terms with another color, optional components with another color, and so on. Such students also love to copy the writing to their notebooks using different colored pens. While programming, such students prefer to use text editors

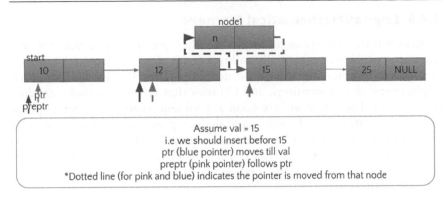

Figure 5.2 Teaching linked list insertion operation to visual learners.

with different colors. While teaching subjects like data structures, pictures are impressive for such learners.

Figure 5.2 shows a sample of teaching data structures to visual learners. Visual representations such as flowcharts, data-flow diagrams, and entity-relationship diagrams are also appealing for such learners. While doing project assignments, their assignments may be designed in such a way that the assignments are image-based. For example, assignments such as demonstrating a sorting algorithm using an animation would be more interesting for them and motivate them to solve the problem easily as well as understand it effectively.

5.4.3 Auditory/Musical learners

Auditory learners are learners who love sounds, rhythms, and music. Audio lectures, audio books, podcasts, and videos are appealing learning materials for them. Many blended learning platforms help teachers to upload audio lectures and videos which can be highly attractive to these types of learners. They also love to listen to lectures and speeches with varied tone and intonations. There are learners who have the practice of completing assignments with their headphones on. Assignments to these types of learners can be in the form of videos, short films, vlogs, and podcasts.

5.4.4 Physical/Kinesthetic Learners

Kinesthetic learners prefer to learn using activities that need a physical touch such as movement, hands-on activities etc. Such types of learners enjoy fixing broken code, debugging, and developing full-fledged code from a partial design. These types of learners can be taught by giving some introduction on a concept, partially designing a related application, and then allowing them to develop it into a product or an application. They like assignments which involve demonstration, coding, and hands-on activities.

5.4.5 Logical/Mathematical learners

Logical learners are systematic learners. They prefer systematically working out a problem, sequentially following the steps, understanding cause and effect, and running simulation activities. They like logical workflow applications, documentations, and libraries that rely on an understanding of hierarchy. These learners are good at problem solving by defining problems using mathematical models and deducing solutions. They have good critical thinking ability and problem-solving skills. They are also interested in solving puzzles, challenges, and games. Application-oriented teaching of programming languages is the most appropriate type of approach in teaching such students.

5.4.6 Interpersonal and Intrapersonal learners

Apart from the twelve above-mentioned learning styles, learners may also be categorized as interpersonal or intrapersonal. Interpersonal learners like to learn in a social environment getting them involved in social activities. They prefer learning in groups, participating in activities like hackathons and group discussions. On the other hand, intrapersonal learners prefer learning alone and focus on self-reflection.

5.5 STRATEGIES USED FOR TEACHING PROGRAMMING LANGUAGES

Various approaches have been used for teaching programming languages. The type of approach that is followed depends upon the type of students in the classroom. This section discusses the different strategies that are used for teaching programming languages.

5.5.1 Talk and chalk approach

The traditional style with chalk and board is a very good approach to teach programming. This will be an active approach which involves both the teacher and the students. The teacher solves a sample on one side and can give another sample for a student to come and solve. Concepts and programs are easily conveyed as there is "talk and chalk" from both the teacher and the students too. Students become more connected with other students in learning the programs as they are doing it along with the teacher. Teacher has to clearly organize the content as a roadmap so that the board can be divided, and every section can be used accordingly. As technology has advanced, smart boards and pens can also be used in solving the problems using programs. These handwritten notes in the classroom could be saved and sent to the students after the class. Many different surveys have shown that the "talk and chalk" method outperforms other PowerPoint-based teaching methods [12].

5.5.2 Hands-on programming approach

A hands-on approach is a successful approach in teaching programming. This is a learning-by-doing approach wherein students are not just listening to the teacher but engage themselves with the subject matter by creating their own programs or practicing the teacher's program. This is the best way of active learning where students are engaged in working on the problem. They are actively creating knowledge rather than just passively consuming it. Hands-on is the best method for giving students more practice. Teachers can understand the grasping level of their students whether all were able to complete the program or if they need some more examples to fully understand. Hands-on learning for programming is an easy way for the teachers to show the students the exact purpose of learning programming that can be used in the real world.

McLeod describes a learning style theory, namely, Kolb's experiential learning style theory which is shown in Figure 5.3. Kolb's experiential learning style states that effective learning is seen when a person progresses through a cycle of four different stages: (1) having a concrete experience , followed by (2) observation, report and reflection on that experience, which leads to (3) the formation of abstract concepts (analysis) and generalizations (conclusions), which are then (4) used to test the hypothesis in future situations, resulting in new experiences [13].

5.5.3 Programming tool-based approach

Programming refers to the art or writing instructions to inform the computer what it needs to do. Scratch is a tool that can be used to teach programming. It is a good visual programming language with color coded blocks of code

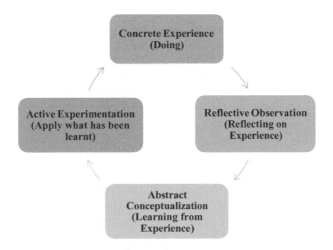

Figure 5.3 Kolb's experiential learning style theory.

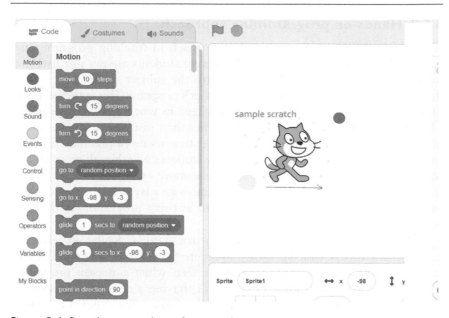

Figure 5.4 Sample screenshot of a scratch project.

clipped together. This is a great tool for developing programming skills in learners and training them to be professional coders. Coding is fun, but it depends on the way programming is taught to students.

If tools like Scratch are used to teach coding with fun it creates a great enthusiasm in students for doing their own code and analyze the results. Figure 5.4 shows a sample Scratch project. This Scratch programming encourages the development of logical thinking when students search for solutions to the problems.

Students can program in a more structured and organized way by grouping the color box, dragging it and releasing it to obtain immediate results and test them. Tools like Scratch allow students to simply create movement, add sounds, change scenarios, or create games, contributing to developing and enhancing their creativity. Such tools help beginners to learn programming skills easily and make programming more interesting for even those who have a strong disinclination towards it.

5.5.4 Storytelling approach

To motivate the students in learning programming, storyboards help a lot. Students learn the steps in programming in the form of a story and then use scripts to program them. This makes them first solve the problem by themselves on a piece of paper and then interpret it into a script so that the computer understands it and produces the necessary output. One form of digital storytelling that has recently emerged uses programming as a media text production tool. Just like new media studies, programming-as-writing relies upon words, images, and sounds to create multimodal digital stories.

5.5.4.1 How to create stories

First, always take the correct data. Second, synthesize, which means use a combination of data sets, contemporary ideas, and other parameters to reach to some conclusion. A data story that is more abstract relies heavily on hypotheticals which may not resonate with many people. For example, let's consider the open data on transportation issues. Instead of developing a story about a famous city, keep the data story connected to the city saying that the data belongs to this specific city. Also illustrate the consequence of that data on an individual family in that particular community.

5.5.4.2 Pen–paper approach

Initially you need to script your ideas before you start structuring your story, as this is essential for the final product. The most important thing to dramatically improve your analytics is to have a story to tell. A flow that you can generate can have a lot of friction in your end result.

Aristotle's classic five-point plan helps deliver strong impacts:

1. Deliver a story or statement that arouses the audience's interest.
2. Pose a problem or question that has to be solved or answered.
3. Offer a solution to the problem raised.
4. Describe specific benefits for adopting the course of action set forth in the solution.
5. State a call to action.

Well, you're sketching the actual content you've described in your story outline and your abbreviated story. You're figuring out the details – things like which chart you should use, what type of text is on the page with the visualization, what type of labeling will be needed to draw attention to the key ideas, maybe even things like color, or at least how you'll use it color. So, you need to keep sketching and playing around with different visuals until it's perfect.

Often this will lead you to flaws in your story structure and/or new ideas for a different approach that's worth experimenting. Sometimes you'll capture ideas for things like the copy you'll write at the same time. Take notes; capture those ideas. Hence, you need to work in analogy, use your hands, organize your story structure, experiment a lot, fail a lot, test your ideas every step of the way, embrace that chaos and trust that the chaos will fade as you keep approaching.

5.5.4.3 Dig deeper to identify the sole purpose of your story

Identify closely what the idea of your story is. Ask yourself, "What am I really giving with this story?" It's never the story alone, but what the story can do to make decision making better. What you're displaying is the idea of better decision making or analytics. Develop a personal "passion statement" so that you can explain your intentions and the genuine reason for working toward them.

5.5.4.4 Use a powerful heading

Create a catchy and powerful heading, a one-sentence statement for your story, visual, or analysis. The most effective headlines are concise, specific, and offer a personal benefit. The heading is a statement that offers your audience a vision of a better understanding and a clear picture about the story outline. It's not about you: it's about them.

5.5.4.5 Design a road map

An infographics road map is one of the best methods to design and make a memorable and a visual road map. The main steps involved here will be

    a. Portray a journey to success.
    b. Explain the steps in detail.
    c. Visualize step by step instructions.

Figure 5.5 shows a sample infographic roadmap template.

5.5.4.6 Conclude with brevity

Always conclude with a very short summary highlighting the facts as trends or comparisons, ranking them in order, exploring required relationships, and revealing the surprise hidden in the data.

Padlet is a tool that can be used for summarizing concepts. Summaries help students to understand a clear picture of the problem and the solution to it. Padlet is a community-centered application that allows students to express their thoughts on the story and how the problem is identified and can be solved. Every student can put down their ideas, and they can add anything like text, documents, images, and links. These can be then summarized by the teacher to support their ideas and views on the work they have created in the Padlet as shown in Figure 5.6.

Figure 5.5 Sample infographic roadmap template.

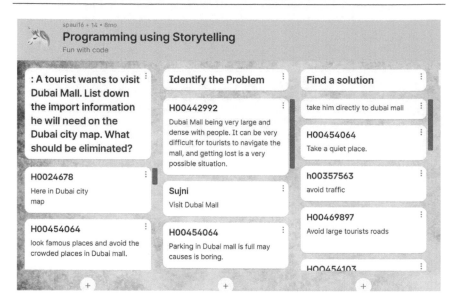

Figure 5.6 Sample Padlet.

5.6 BLENDED LEARNING PLATFORMS

Various platforms have been used by teachers around the globe for blended learning. Many open-source platforms are also available on the internet which makes usage of such platforms popular and powerful. Blended learning platforms can be classified into four categories: live streaming platforms, learning management systems, video/audio recording platforms, and assessment and interaction platforms. Let us discuss these platforms in this section.

5.6.1 Live streaming platforms

Live streaming platforms are useful in making remote and ubiquitous learning possible. They make learning easier for people who cannot learn in a classroom. Remote learning or online learning has become popular nowadays, thanks to blended learning platforms. Such platforms help working people, women at home, or people who cannot go to schools or colleges to learn and improve their career. Even students who follow regular programs in colleges and schools learn additional courses using such platforms. During the COVID-19 pandemic, many universities, colleges, and schools adapted to online learning, which allowed students to continue their studies without any hindrance.

Online learning platforms have been very active for over two decades. The popularity of online education is because of its flexibility in the mode of offering the courses and also because these courses are cheaper and affordable. Digital learning platforms also make ubiquitous and pervasive learning possible, and this makes students retain what they have learnt. Online learning enhances learners' retention rates up to 60%. It takes 40%– 60% less time than conventional learning. Videos attract learners of all age groups. As per statistics, six million students in the United States are enrolled in online programs. Online learning provides flexibility, independence, time management, and self-motivation.

Some of the tools commonly used for live streaming are Zoom, Google Meet, Microsoft Teams, and Cisco WebEx. Each of these tools have unique features and are compatible across multiple devices. Zoom is a cloud-based proprietary video teleconferencing software developed by Zoom Video Communications. Zoom allows free meetings with up to 100 participants, lasting up to 40 minutes. Users can upgrade by subscription. Zoom allows audio and video. It also allows recording of meetings and screen sharing.

Another popular software used for live streaming is Google Meet. It is a video conferencing application developed by Google. Google allows up to 100 participants to be connected for a maximum of 60 minutes. However, subscriptions allow unlimited duration. Google Meet provides a lot of features.

i. *Live captioning*: Google Meet provides fully automated live captions which helps in following up the meetings easily.
ii. *Device agnostic*: Google Meet is compatible with a variety of devices such as desktops, laptops, tablets, and mobile phones. It will work with both Android and iPhone. Google Meet also allows you to join using Google Nest Hub Max, the Google Assistant Smart Display. It also provides Google Meet hardware for a conference room setup.
iii. *Screen sharing*: Google Meet allows flexible screen sharing such as sharing an entire screen, a single chrome tab or a single application window with meeting participants. This makes sharing and collaboration easier.
iv. *Messaging during the meeting*: Chat messages can be shared with the participants during the meeting. This makes it possible to share links, files and more with other participants.
v. *Preview screen*: The preview screen adjustments enable users to adjust camera and mic. They also help the users to view all who are present in the meeting.
vi. *Adjust layouts and screen settings*: Google Meet provides different layouts and screen settings for viewing the participants.
vii. *Host controls*: Google Meet allows the meeting host to mute, remove or pin participants. However, due to privacy concerns only a participant can unmute themselves.
viii. *Full integration*: Google Meet also integrates with Microsoft 365 apps such as Outlook, which allows users to access meetings directly from a calendar, even if not a Google calendar.

Other tools such as Cisco WebEx and Microsoft Teams also provide similar features and help in live streaming. During the COVID-19 pandemic these tools helped teachers to conduct online classes and have live interactions with their students.

5.6.2 Learning management systems

A learning management system (LMS) is a type or software, usually cloud-based, that assists both teachers and students in the education process. Learning management systems are helpful for content delivery. In addition to that a LMS can also be used for creating content, monitoring student participation, and assessment of student performance. Learning management systems are not only used by educational institutions but also by other organizations for training employees. Popular learning management systems used in educational institutions are Moodle, Blackboard Learn, Schoology, and Docebo LMS. The learning management system serves as a repository for learning resources. It is also a secure environment and the contents can be accessed using secure login credentials. The teachers can control who can view the uploaded content. Most modern learning management systems are device agnostic: users can access the contents from any device. They also provide user-friendly interfaces. In addition to that, learning management systems help teachers to track the activities. They also provide content interoperability and course integration. Some learning management systems even support collaborative learning and peer learning using social media tools. In future, learning management systems could incorporate virtual reality, augmented reality, and artificial intelligence concepts which could make learning a more interactive experience [14].

5.6.3 Recording tools

One of the methods used in blended learning is facilitating learning through recorded materials. Screen-capture and screen-casting tools help to capture the screen and record an audio narration. Screencasts are considered to be one type of educational videos. Audio over the PowerPoint feature of Microsoft PowerPoint is one of the simplest of such tools. Most screen-capturing tools capture a screen with an inset video of the teacher which can give the learner a live learning experience. In addition to this, drawing tools like Annotate Meet can be used for annotating presentations. Some of the commonly used screen-casting tools are Camtasia, Collaborate, DemoCreator, CamStudio, Nimbus, PowerPoint, QuickTime, and Active Presenter. Some of them have video-editing tools also. For others, video-editing tools such as OneShot or iMovie may be used.

5.6.4 Assessment and interaction tools

Blended learning allows students to learn in a remote environment without the physical presence of a teacher or an instructor. Therefore, it is essential to monitor the progress and performance of the students on such platforms. Assessment and interaction tools aid the teachers in evaluating the performance of students in blended learning. Various formative assessment tools such as Plickers, Kahoot, Slido, NearPod, and Google Forms are used in blended learning environments for evaluating the students. Plickers is a tool that is commonly used by teachers since it is free and does not require the students to be techno-savvy. Therefore, this tool is used by teachers from all streams. Kahoot and Slido are other commonly used tools for online interaction and formative assessment. Google Forms is also used by teachers for assessment. Most of these tools are web based and students can use them in a browser itself. They do not require any installation by the student. Socrative is an assessment tool which can be used to track the progress of students in the tests like Google forms. EdPuzzle is another tool that can be used for assessment of video lectures.

5.7 SECURITY IN BLENDED LEARNING

Educational institutions around the world were pushed to remote and blended learning due to the global COVID-19 pandemic. This is still a very big part of education and is definitely foreseen to continue in future. Due to this situation, a review of data privacy with the events from the previous year's data has definitely to be considered. A global pandemic has no compromise on data privacy measures.

A cause-and-effect diagram, called the fishbone diagram, is a visual way to help in the identification of potential causes of issues under consideration in safe blended-learning data, and then organizing ideas into various categories. This analysis is extremely helpful as it helps the data-security team in finding potential causes of problems which may not be otherwise considered. Figure 5.7 analyzes the struggles that could be faced by teachers and students while adopting to a new online environment.

To enhance a sustainable data quality program, first, the IT operations team has to identify the issues of bad data. If this is not rectified properly, the wheels keep spinning and resources are constantly used only for correcting issues but without addressing their root cause. Data quality root cause analysis techniques need to be used.

The IT operations team must guarantee that the e-learning content formed is kept secure from unauthorized users. There are certain hybridized encryption techniques that protect shared data better than others in e-learning. This employs a two-tier approach that comprises compression techniques and encryption algorithms that will compress and encrypt the specified data to build it in a more protected way. Initially the given data will be compressed by means of a novel lossless compression algorithm called a binary code indexing and encoding (BCIE) algorithm, which is preceded by the procedure of hybridized encryption that utilizes both RSA (Rivest-Shamir-Adleman) and AES (Advanced Encryption Standard) encryption algorithms along with a novel algorithm called a SCELL (self-loop code enfilade linked list) algorithm. Ultimately the decryption process for the specified data proceeds for the user prospect in which the compressed decrypted data is

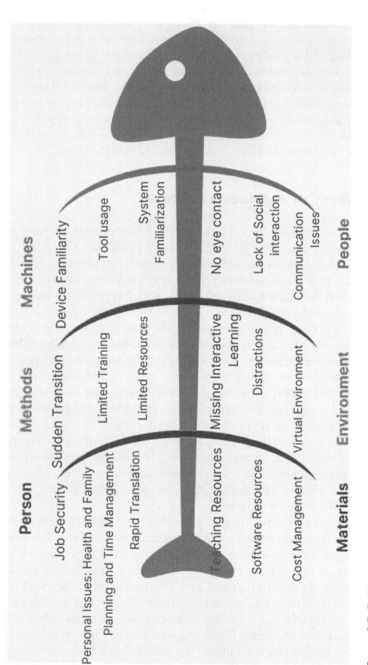

Figure 5.7 Fishbone analysis for challenges faced in blended learning.

decompressed. By managing this kind of high security, the unauthorized user is not capable of accessing the equivalent original data. Only the concerned owner of the data can carry out any actions on the original data and only authorized users can utilize the content. In this way many different techniques are used to maintain data privacy [15].

Blockchain has a greater potential for implementation in blended learning systems because of its massive openness, and online secure database that e-learning platforms require. This can be implemented on various platforms as per the information security policy of the institutions. A mutual-healing group key distribution scheme based on the blockchain could be adopted for a highly secure environment [16].

5.8 SUMMARY

This chapter discusses the importance of blended learning to provide an effective learning environment for learning programming languages. Blended learning environments help both teachers and students, making the learning process easy as well as effective. A variety of blended learning models are available from which teachers can choose to provide an efficient mode of education based on the subjects they teach. Though there may be some challenges to be overcome while using blended learning approaches, it is not at all a big issue in today's world of technology. Blended learning approaches can also be easily used to target different types of learners. Apart from this, these approaches help instructors to follow a variety of strategies to teach courses like programming languages. Hands-on experiences are made effective, thanks to the diversity of computer-aided teaching and assessment tools. Moreover, today's technology also enables in providing a secure, student-centered learning environment. However, there are a few drawbacks that must be addressed while implementing these approaches. These technologies expect both students and teachers to be well-versed in using computer hardware and software. Higher technology setups may include investment in hardware and software and may extend to maintenance costs as well. Effective utilization of resources requires cooperation from students. Despite these shortcomings this technology may well overtake many other traditional methods of education in the near future.

REFERENCES

1. *12 of the Most Common Types of Blended Learning.* (n.d.). Teach Thought. Retrieved October 8, 2021, from https://www.teachthought.com/learning/12-types-of-blended-learning/.
2. Danijel, R., Tihomir, O., and Alen, L. (2009). New Approaches and Tools in Teaching Programming. *Conference Paper*, pp. 49–57. https://www.academia.edu/25099209/New_Approaches_and_Tools_in_Teaching_Programming.

3. Mishra, I. (2018). *Teaching Programming Online – Challenges and How to Address Them.* Teaching Programming Online. Retrieved October 10, 2021, from https://blog.wiziq.com/teaching-programming-languages-online/.

4. Lahtinen, E., Ala-Mukta, K., and Jarvinen, H.-M. (2005). A Study of the Difficulties of Novice Programmers. *ACM SIGCSE Bulletin, 37*(3), 14–18. https://doi.org/10.1145/1151954.1067453.

5. McMillan, A. C.. (2020). *Student-Centered Learning Strategies.* Teach Hub. Retrieved October 7, 2021, from https://www.teachhub.com/teaching-strategies/2020/07/student-centered-learning-strategies/.

6. Beulah, C., Kirubakaran, E., and Ranjit Jeba Thangaiah, P. (2018). An Evolutionary Approach for Personalization of Content Delivery in E-learning Systems Based on Learner Behavior Forcing Compatibility of Learning Materials. *Telematics and Informatics, 35*(3), 520–533. https://doi.org/10.1016/j.tele.2017.02.004.

7. Christudas, B. C. L., Paul, S., Ezra, K., and Venkatraman, S. (2010). Personalization of e-Learning Using Data Mining. *The International Journal of Learning: Annual Review, 17*(4), 585–594. https://doi.org/10.18848/1447-9494/cgp/v17i04/46972.

8. Singh, J., Steele, K., and Singh, L.. (2021). Combining the Best of Online and Face-to-Face Learning: Hybrid and Blended Learning Approach for COVID-19, Post Vaccine, & Post-Pandemic World. *Journal of Educational Technology Systems, 50*(2), 140–170. https://doi.org/10.1177/00472395211047865.

9. Sudderth, A. (2022). *What Is Student Centered Learning and Why Is It Important?* XP Superschool. Retrieved January 6, 2022, from https://xqsuperschool.org/rethinktogether/what-is-student-centered-learning/.

10. Carelli Oliveira Maia, M., Serey, D., and Figueiredo, J. (2017). Learning Styles in Programming Education: A Systematic Mapping Study. *IEEE Frontiers in Education Conference*, pp. 1–7. https://doi.org/10.1109/FIE.2017.8190465.

11. *Understanding Your Individual Learning Styles in Relation to Learning to Code.* (2017). Medium.Com. Retrieved October 10, 2021, from https://medium.com/career-change-coder/understanding-your-individual-learning-styles-in-relation-to-learning-to-code-3ad24ebec551.

12. Sharma, A., and Kumar, N. (2018). Importance of Talk and Chalk Method of Teaching: Dental Students' view in Preclinical Years. *International Journal of Healthcare Education & Medical Informatics, 5*(3), 11–15. https://doi.org/10.24321/2455.9199.201812.

13. McLeod, S. (2013). *Kolb's Learning Styles and Experiential Learning Cycle.* Simplypsychology.Org. Retrieved October 10, 2021, from http://www.simplypsychology.org/learning-kolb.html.

14. Brush, K. (2019). *Learning Management System.* Techtarget.Com. Retrieved October 8, 2021, from https://searchcio.techtarget.com/definition/learning-management-system.

15. Qwaider, W. (2012). Information Security and Blended Learning System Environment. *International Journal of E-Learning Security, 2*, 147–151. https://doi.org/10.20533/ijels.2046.4568.2012.0019.

16. Chien, H., Wang, Y., Vijayakumar, P., He, D., Kumar, N., and Ma, J. (2021). Self-Healing Group Key Distribution Facilitating Source Authentication Using Block Codes. *Security and Communication Networks, 2021*, 1–11. https://doi.org/10.1155/2021/2942568

Chapter 6

Centralized key distribution protocol using identity-based encryption techniques in cloud computing environments

S. Ambika and A.S. Anakath
E.G.S. Pillay Engineering College, Nagapattinam, India

S. Rajakumar
University College of Engineering Ariyalur, Ariyalur, India

R. Kannadasan
VIT University, Vellore, India

S. Senthilkumar
University College of Engineering Pattukkottai, Rajamadam, India

CONTENTS

DOI: 10.1201/9781003264538-6

Currently, a group gathering is performed as an online meet conducted in online meeting platforms such as Zoom, Google Meet, Go To Meeting, Webex Meet, or Microsoft Teams among others. In none of the cases, do all members join the gathering at the same time. Group communication becomes inevitable nowadays and group size is also increasing. This leads to issues pertaining to the scalability characteristics of distributed systems. As the group size grows gradually, the size of the key domain also expands proportionately. It is a difficult and challenging task to filter unauthorized persons and those hacking the data in the distributed network. The storage size for maintaining this large quantum of keys becomes a disputed issue in a group conversation environment. This issue also occurs in new user registration to enter the group, as well as in group members leaving the group, because during these two events, key updation must be performed by regeneration of the group key. Applications based on multi-cast as well as multi-media key distribution is the very big ongoing issue, and the certificate authority (CA) is responsible for transmitting the key in a secure way to the end entity. However, of primary concern is the security of such data being transferred through the distributed clouds characterized in a centralized configuration. In a group communication environment, security threats arise when new users join the system as well as when existing users remove themselves from the gathering. At this stage utmost care must be taken while a new user's entry occurs, or users depart from the system. In order to resolve the previous issues based on the computational and storage complexity in the certificate authority as well as the end user, it becomes imperative to initiate a method. A group key plays an essential and important role in proving its robustness, and its use for encrypting the data needs to be secured. At the event of a user entering the group conversation, this group key identifies the quorum of members present in the group as well as identifies the state of the group, even if a member exits the chat for any reason. It is possible that at any instant of time, changes may occur in group size and the group key updates the group information inevitably. Safeguarding and securely distributing the group key is an important issue to be considered in achieving the security of group communication. In this chapter, we present a centralized key distribution protocol using attribute-based encryption to provide security for the shared data pertaining to a group. This proposed protocol provides superior security and improved efficiency in generating and distributing group keys in a distributed environment.

6.1 INTRODUCTION

Distributed processors are connected through communication networks to form distributed systems. The user of the system feels that he/she alone is using the entire system and hence this provides a logical view of it as a unique system. But in reality multiple processors are located in distant places and appropriately communicate with each other to fulfil the tasks of the whole system. The distributed environment has two possible communications: peer level communication, and centralized communication. Applications such as peer-to-peer communication, Skype, Facebook, WhatsApp, PAY-TV, video conferencing, email, Twitter, and online network games all run in a distributed environment. Such applications are exposed to security attacks and threats. In this scenario, distributed group communication is the most optimistic approach to provide secure group communication in many emerging network applications.

6.1.1 Distributed group communication

In a distributed network, each user can act as a client who accesses the services, or as a server who provides services to other users of the same network to utilize the resources in a shared manner without using a key server. Group communication falls into two categories: centralized group communication, and distributed group communication. In a centralized group communication, only one user acts as a sponsor user or key server, who maintains the information about the participating users and also manages the entire system, while the remaining users act as participating users. In this scheme, a key server alone is responsible to generate, distribute, and update the keys of the group users participating in the communication. The major challenges of a centralized group key management scheme include scalability overhead, which means that the entire group communication depends on the single key server, and also the operation of key updation becomes an overhead when the group size varies dynamically. The other challenge is storage overhead, which influences the efficiency of the system because of the burden of maintaining a large number of keys in a single server. Moreover, if the key server fails, the entire group will be lost or affected. In addition, maintaining forward and backward secrecy is a very difficult task at the moment a user enters or leaves the group. Figure 6.1 shows the system model for secure communication in a centralized group communication environment.

In contrast to the centralized secure group communication, distributed group key management scheme does not use a fixed key server, instead any user from the group may be granted the privilege to act as a key server. Therefore, peer users are able to send data to the remaining users of the group. In this scenario, all the other peer users act as participating users in the group with respect to the sending peer. In this scheme, any user belonging to the group may be assigned responsibility for generating, distributing, and updating the keys for the other users in the group. All individual users are able to compute the common group code from the secure code transmitted by other users pertaining to the same group. Figure 6.2 shows the system model for secure communication in a distributed group communication environment.

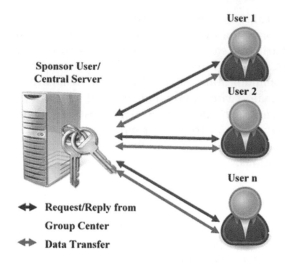

Figure 6.1 System model for centralized secure group communications.

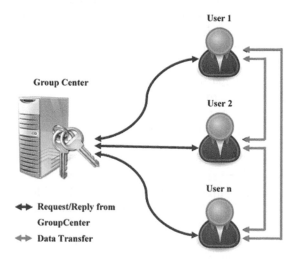

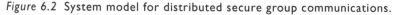

Figure 6.2 System model for distributed secure group communications.

6.1.2 Cloud security workload model

A unique work assignment put on a specific cloud that is to be performed with specialized capacity is referred to as a cloud workload. The case may be a web server on the internet, a database supporting big data, a Hadoop system using MapReduce, or a container, amidst of a variety of things available in a cloud network. Cloud security workloads are ways to safeguard these cloud workloads. The cloud service provider has great concern for the security of the workload in the majority of cases. But in certain scenarios,

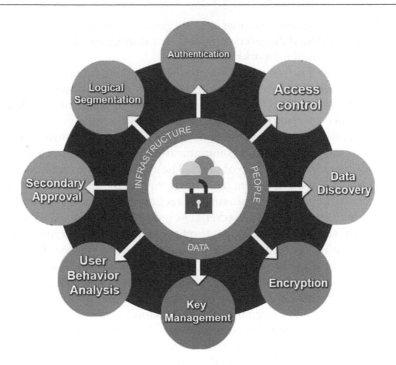

Figure 6.3 A typical cloud security workload model.

like infrastructure-as-a-service (IaaS), the user must take additional care to assess the security concerns of the cloud service. In such instances, the user has to apply policies, mechanisms, and access control related to security, to protect the workload of the cloud object. Figure 6.3 shows a typical cloud security workload model that can be observed in a distributed cloud network.

- **Authentication.** A security breach can happen for data and services in cases where private data is shared for access, or these data are allowed to be accessed by users without proper authorization. Authentication mechanisms protect from such unwanted entry to access data in a cloud environment.
- **Access control.** When the data is available among a group of users or in the public domain, it must be viewed and used only by the intended users, although other users may also be authorized to use the data. In such cases, various access control mechanisms may be implemented based on need and use. For example, role-based access control can be implemented in distributed transactions in a financial information system.
- **Data discovery.** The need for ascertaining the data, followed by finding it in the cloud, leads to the requirement for proper regulation of

data in a protected manner and its removal when its usage expires. Cloud workload discovery supports monitoring and detecting security threats in cloud networks.

- **Encryption.** Enciphering is the process of making intelligible data into an unintelligible format. So, unauthorized users without the proper deciphering method in hand are not able to view the intelligible data, and hence encryption protects the data in the cloud.

- **Key management.** Cloud systems are a utility of the distributed computing environment, and communication occurs for sharing data and resources among a group of users. The exchange of secret keys allows secure access to the data and resources in the cloud. Therefore, it becomes imperative to provide protection in generating, distributing, and managing the secure secret keys used to access the cloud data.

- **Logical segmentation.** This method fragments the wide range of cloud workstations into chunks of cloud network. Nevertheless, logical segmentation does not involve any additional hardware due to the fact that the cloud infrastructure is already well administered, and it must not compromise the security of data in the cloud network. Measures must be taken to safeguard data in the cloud segments.

- **Secondary approval.** This is implemented as a two-person rule for specific management activities which could cause considerable impact on the cloud service. This secondary approval controls and averts sensitive distractions both of an unexpected nature, or purposefully done by a privileged user of the cloud network.

- **User behavior analysis.** Also referred to as User and Entity Behavior Analytics (UEBA), this gathers information, and coalesces and examines user data in measurable values and unmeasurable values, such as characters of the user. This includes user interaction with websites or webservers, and accessing the objective of their access in the cloud environment. By learning user behaviors, malfunctioning users can be identified, and data can be protected from them: hence cybersecurity can be achieved in the cloud systems.

6.1.3 Mise-en-scène work

With rapid technology development, cloud computing plays a vital role in many applications such as industry, healthcare technology, and so on. In cloud computing, clients provide the data to the cloud for storage and other business purposes, with the cloud service provider acting as the trusted commercial enterprise. Information represents a critical resource for any association, and thus, cloud clients are divided into cloud suppliers and their potential rivals, in order to secure the data [1]. Cloud-based services include Platform as a Service (PaaS) and Software-as-a-Service (SaaS). Other cloud industry provider services are IBM's Blue Cloud and

Amazon's Elastic Compute Cloud (EC2). These cloud service providers allow users to access several applications based upon cloud services on demand [2].

This chapter on group communication confidentiality is necessary for the purposes of software distribution, web caching, stock quote streaming, and multimedia conferencing. Encryption of group data and distribution of group keys for continuing members can be enforced by access control and making it confidential. A departing member present in the group communication cannot decrypt any future group communication after the group member leaves. This process is known as forward secrecy. Also, decryption of completed group communication cannot be made if a new member joins in the group. This process is known as backward secrecy. To keep the group key fresh, it ensures the group key distribution schemes update whenever a member joins or leaves the group. A group center (GC) can only give permission for all keys, rekeys, and client keys by using traditional schemes. It cannot handle such an arbitrary subset of group members, such as those who want to make a privileged subgroup. This kind of privileged subgroup is known as dynamic conference [3]. Sometimes, it takes a large amount of time to perform and deal with these events with no greater efficiency obtained for the GC. So, it enforces more members to join or leave the dynamic group [4]. The possibility of conferences in the group can be 2^n-n-1, where n is the number of members in the group.

In this chapter, we optimize a KeyGen algorithm by the way of enhancing the stateful key distribution protocol. Using this optimized KeyGen algorithm prioritizes the preferences to update and to distribute the members in the group [5]. To maintain the associated members in the group, the proposed algorithm can be archived using a binary tree (key tree) to articulate the keys. These keys can be coordinated in a sequence pattern by using a key called a Key Encryption Key (KEK) to pair with the leaf of the public/private key [6]. Public key roots are encrypted by using a Group Key (GK). Sub trees can be used to create a group without conferences by only covering the necessary members who need to create it. A conference key can be easily encrypted in the group for those members who want to set up the group by distributing the sub trees of the public key roots. Special operations can be used to perform more information in using public keys [7].

The main contributions of this chapter include:

1. Proposing this identity-based encryption combined with the KeyGen algorithm for cloud computing – this results in the most secured key management approach.
2. Representing this identity-based signature (IBS) for cloud computing used for authentication purposes.

Determining and comparing computational complexity in terms of communication cost and authentication time.

6.2 LITERATURE SURVEY

A literature survey related to the work adopted in this investigation is presented in this section as follows. Multigroup-based services can be co-existed on a single network for proliferating owing to the convergence of upcoming mobile technology and wireless technologies, which is an emerging communication key on mobile-multicast keys management [8]. Group Key Management (GKM) keys are inefficient as they incur overhead for rekeying to enhance GKM keys in multiple multicast group environments. Secure group communication can be made single group service for existing GKM [9]. Overhead occurs on low rekey transmission on servicing in a multiple group network across a homogeneous or heterogeneous network, if a wireless network participates on a group network that supports single and multiple members leaving the group. This chapter proposes a multicast group, namely a slot basis multiple GKM scheme, for a multiple multicast group [10]. Various kinds of problems with key management for multicast communication sessions are discussed in research works [11]. Investment pressure and single point of failure rekeying at a network causes signal loading if it mitigates one affect n-phenomenon. Symmetric Polynomial Based Dynamic Conference Scheme (SPDCS) is a special application for approximation of SGC application and it is a well-known technique [12]. Formation of privileged subgroups to allow arbitrary subsets of users to make conference schemes is the result of the extension of SPDCS. A significant problem arising is to achieve dynamic and secure multicast communication to maintain a lower computation and storage complexity. The solution is to construct a centralized group concurrent to the distribution of the protocol. It helps to improve the efficiency of the centralized group by minimizing the computation key cost for the Key Server (KS) on updated keys. It can dynamically perform busy operations effectively when a user joins or leaves in a group [13].

Public Key Infrastructure is involved in most grid-based implementations as it is evenly supported and can be easily combined with various applications on different platforms [14]. Identity-Based Encryption acts as a public key encryption process here, and a public key acts as an arbitrary string, such as a telephone number or email address. Usually, the private key generated by a Private Key Generator acts as the powerful master secret key [15]. In this way, it is inferred that everyone can verify signatures and encrypt messages beyond the dissemination of public features and the public key "strings" without prior key distribution. Based on several literature surveys, there are only a few researchers attempting to apply identity-based encryption in cloud computing. The main challenge of identity-based cryptographic system is based on key management and complexity, when implemented to avoid the attacks of certificate-based security infrastructures. Those research works did not find out the solution in identity-based encryption and signature, and did not make performance comparison analysis, or simulation.

Based on the evidence of reports in the literature, performance measures still need to be improved. Hence this proposed research work effectively points out this problem by proposing a novel approach for effective secured key distribution algorithm using identity-based encryption in the cloud. Overall, the risk belonging to the secured key distribution algorithm using identity-based encryption in the cloud and its challenges are taken into consideration to find out the best solution, which has a direct effect on many application areas.

6.3 PROTOCOL FOR IDENTITY-BASED ENCRYPTION

The stateful nature of any group key dispersion protocol exhibits the following characteristics.

- A user exits the group at any time t, then all other existing members of the group at time $t + 1$ are given permission to have shared access to the group. All the users who left the group at time t should not be permitted to access the group information.
- A user registers for participation in the group at time t, then all other users in the group are granted permission to share the secret information at time $t - 1$. The users entering the group at time t should not be given rights to share the previous secret information in the group.
- A new user enters the system at time t, then all the new members of the group are only able to share and access the secret information available on the path from the leaf node to the root node of the cluster tree.
- A user exits the group at time t, then all the group information learned by the user from the leaf node to root node of the cluster tree must be deleted from that user at time t for the user exiting the group itself.
- A user is not a member of the communication gathering neither at time t nor at time $t - 1$, then the user is not granted to recover the secret information pertaining to any leaf node to root node.

This protocol first initializes a security value n, and computes a public key value and a shared secret code. Then it discloses the public key value to the group and keeps the secret value n and the secured shared secret code as private to the group convener. The key generation algorithm computes a private key using a created public key value and the public key value is disclosed to all users present in the group interaction. The encryption algorithm encrypts the message using the public key value disclosed by the group convener. Cipher information is available after execution of this encryption algorithm procedure. The decryption algorithm deciphers the data using a customized public key, a private key, and using a public key value. The original information is retrieved as the outcome of the execution of this algorithm. The proposed protocol functions in three phases viz., group convener initialization, person joining, and person leaving the group conversation. The group convener initializes certain variables and computes the size of the group. The size of the group may increase or decrease based on a variable declared in the procedure. Cryptography based identifiers are encrypted by the protocol so as to satisfy the specified rules in order to make a public key so that whenever a user joins or leaves the group it can be easily encrypted in the cipher text based on the greatest common divisor. Our research concern is on the identity to make it efficient for multiple users to interact at the same time. A key generation algorithm method can be used on remote data sensing, network authentication, and tracking schemes of public key revocation in order to process in a sequential pattern. By proposing this method, the main objective is to reduce the limitations on which it can be easily implemented in a wide range of dispersion to enhance the reliability. Table 6.1 gives the notation and descriptions used in the proposed work. Table 6.2 represents the names of the functions and their descriptions.

Table 6.1 Notation and descriptions of proposed work

Notation	Description
GK	Group key.
MSK	Master secret key.
Ω	Sharing network links to well-known group center.
δ	Set of attributes.
K	Entries to transmit to authenticators.
C	Cipher text for encryption of data.

Table 6.2 Function name and description of proposed work

Function name	Description
Setup()	This function is used for setting up a secured parameter for generating the input in a cyclical pattern.
Encrypt()	This function is used for encrypting the data by the predefined parameters declared in setup.
Decrypt()	This function is used to decrypt the data using following parameter C_r, L_i, R_e and private key.
Keygen()	This function is used to generate a private key using public key and shared secret key.

6.4 THE KEY GENERATION PROCEDURE

The key generation algorithm we use on this work is to make a pair of the group keys, either public or private, based on elliptic curves of linear or nonlinear. The following steps are to be followed:

- **Setup (1^n):** Initialization of the algorithm is used first to set up the specified parameter for generating the input values.
- **Encrypt (MSK):** Encrypt function is used to create a master secret key to give access of delivery in the allotted occurrence of members.
- **Decrypt (T, P_k):** Decryption process occurs on ending level of the cipher text to embed the data.
- **Keygen (C_r, L_i, R_e):** Proposed key gen algorithm is to be inherited at this stage whether the given condition is true otherwise the data will restart on the wrinkled setup of the parameters such as C_r, L_i, R_e for the group members to join or leave.

6.4.1 Proposed key distribution process

The proposed framework comes under three phases namely Group Center (GC) initialized, member join, and member left.

   GC Initialized: Initialization starts from selecting a number in which the number should be prime value such as x and y where x > y and $y \leq \lceil x/4 \rceil$ Value of "y" helps to define a group j_t^* (multiple group) and z is used to fix a threshold value based on α, where $\alpha = \delta + y$. The value δ will be a random element from the member group j_t^*.

6.4.1.1 Member join

When a new member joins in the multiple group for the first time the Group Key (GK) sends a secret key using the path of secure channel, which is known by the user V_j. The GC key should be used in order to protect the group's confidentiality by checking the condition in a random element in the group j_t^* and also to count the number of members by using $f_i > \alpha$. If the condition is not satisfied then the value of "δ" must be computed in such a way to achieve the said condition.

1) Set the GC value of a random number π *from* j_p^*.
2) Compute the GC from the shared key from $\beta = \gamma^x \bmod x$.
3) GC calculates: $\alpha_g = U_{n=1}^{j}(A_n \cap B_n)$.
4) After computing the GC from the keygen (ρ, α_r) by enhancing the sustaining algorithm for obtaining the required members in the group for C_r, L_i, R_e, such that $j + \rho * i + \alpha_g = c$.

5) GC distributes (γ, k, x, y, z) to the members in the group. User can join or leave as the mentioned method (γ, k, x, y, z) from GC, the user u_i, predicting the secret information for the cipher text for group analysis group key β.

6) Compute the μ using: $i \bmod t_{j_r} = r$.

7) Compute the μ *using ciphered value*: $n^{-1} + k_{r_i} = \mu$.

8) Now, the secret can be computed as: $\pi^{(y \times \omega) - c} \bmod a = \beta$.

Each individual leaf of the node is paired or associated with an adjacent group member and having a single node of a pair to public or private key is known as Key Encryption Key (KEK). As per the legacy control, the public key is divided into two parts: one is the current Group Key (GK) of the preceding location of cluster in the node, and the other is version information control. The public or private key can be represented as (C_j, F_j) for a coherent order of concurrency. The public key is identified as a tuple consisting of present data of GK and the node position in the cluster.

6.4.1.2 Member left

If a new member wishes to join or an existing member wants to leave the group in a multicast group, the proceeding patterns of GC are needed to distribute the new group key for the existing members with a minimum computational time. If a new member joins the existing multicast group for the group key of the old group, the old public key or group key is not known to the user of the previous communication. It helps to provide backward secrecy. Member-join operation and member-leave operation both have different impacts on the group. Whenever a member leaves the group, GC will start to avoid the use of an existing group's old key or the Sublevel Group Key (SGK) for encryption of a new group key. Since, the member knows the old key of GK/SGK, it is necessary for a member to know that the existing key will not work for the future multicast group as it performs re-key operations. Therefore, in our proposed work the user needs to create a future key for public group multicast. Hence, our work focuses on the transmitted key between the member reference and group members. However, it is necessary to analyze the existing patterns to provide a more optimistic method for the users to compute the key.

6.5 PROPOSED SCHEME FOR KEY GENERATION

Figure 6.4 represents the proposed architecture of secured key generation and distribution algorithm using Identity-Based Encryption (IBE) in a cloud environment. The process starts with the user registration by which the user generates the public key made available as public in the network, which is retained by the data owner. The trusted authority verifies the user by performing the validation process using the credentials. The data owner performs the encryption and uploads the data with the control policy metrics.

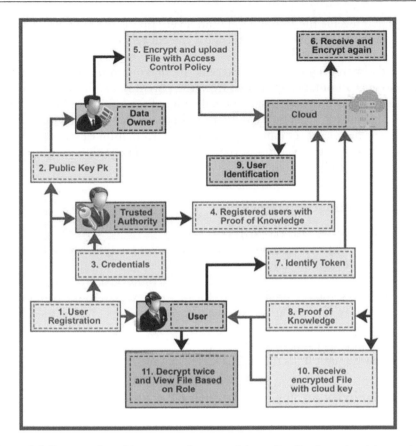

Figure 6.4 Proposed architecture of secured key distribution algorithm using identity-based encryption in cloud key updating algorithm.

The cloud storage receives the data from the owner and encrypts again. Therefore, here there is dual way of encryption in the proposed method. The user verifies the token using the keys. As the dual way of encryption, the proof of knowledge is also in dual way. The user again is identified. During post confirmation of identification, the encrypted file is received with the cloud key. At this final point, the user is able to perform dual decryption depending on the role.

Security and scalability are the foremost processes to be achieved in the proposed work for the distribution of the key by applying the scheme to cluster-based trees. It updates the information or existing pattern to recover the functionality of the SGK and GK for the sublevel trees.

1) Lowering the level of zeroth level ($0th$ level) cluster is the sub-group key.
2) Next level will be the first level (1st level) consists of private keys, β_μ in which $j = 1,2,3 \ldots .n$.

3) Final level is the second level (2nd level), that is the member's level. It consists N number of members for the clusters in group.

When the member joins, if this exceeds the maximum member size then a new node is automatically created from the parent node. For the secondary cluster of the tree for parameterizing, the GC of the key should be declined. If the managed key is not fixed, then it alternates the regional key for the restricted channel of n number of series in the formation of tress key based setup. The size of the N series is to be adjacent to the maximum members of the group of the key.

6.5.1 Key updating algorithm

1. Scale devices $\alpha_g(J_{1,4}) = \alpha_g(J_{1,4})/J_5$
2. Now it allows to compute the β_2^1 of the values in this section to join or leave a person in this section.
3. Now LC will compute the keygen values of keygen $(\rho, \alpha_g(J_{1,4}))$.
4. Now to setup the prefixed path for the (α, μ, x, y, z) to the members in the group that are already in the old group.
5. Computes f using $j \bmod j_{v_i} = f$.
6. Computes ρ using $f^{-1} \bmod j_{v_i} = \rho$.
7. Now the user finds the shared secret key. $\omega^{(y \times \rho)-c} \bmod a = \beta_2^1$

6.5.2 Security analysis for identity-based encryption

From the obtained information we can easily encrypt the ciphered message, which is denoted by T. Data may be taken as a private key, public key, or ciphered text. A private key is denoted by R, the encrypted algorithm is denoted by V, while cipher text is denoted by C.

$$T \rightarrow R, K, C_V(D)$$

$$K \rightarrow Keygen(R, maskey)$$

This work analyzes the computation path for the public key to be managed for the protocol by moving either forward or backward secrecy. Even though there is some computational path for the needs of protocol, the assumption is to be considered a probabilistic path of binomial distribution algorithm. Moreover, if the adversary is able to access the network, then it is possible for the adversary to insert, delete, update, and replace the data. Hence, the private key must be kept confidential.

6.5.2.1 Backward secrecy

The proposed technique prevents a new person for access to the old communication messages that are sent prior to joining in the group. In owing to create an established communication for the existing protocols to match the required field for the grouping partners, the computing methodology $T \to R, K, C_V$ is used. This makes it more complicated for the unknown members to access the information from the existing member in the group. The decryption process will be easier for the special character textures with respect to the analysis for the random value of the multiplicative group M_x^* of the axioms in the key.

6.5.2.2 Forward secrecy

The forward secrecy technique is used for preventing the member of a group who previously left the group on obtaining the present communication. It is automatically performed as early as the leave operation of the member happens. Whenever a member leaves a group, he/she tries to find the time sent by the existing members and prevent such entry from attackers and deny them the ciphered text for the users in the group $\alpha_g(J_{1,4}) = \alpha_g(J_{1,4})/J_5$. The updated key makes the group key inactive and access to group is denied for members who have left the group.

6.5.2.3 External user agent

In this proposed work, the key distributed initially prevents the attacker and tries to find the value of ρ. This ρ can be can be computed only by the authenticated users for every member who joins or leaves the group J_x. For an external agent, an opponent who is inactive but tries to obtain the secret key from the existing members in the chat by the method of random learning through the preferences of the user, carries the key, either a public or private key. If the size of J_x is greater, then the number of ways that the intruder tries also increases and the time to develop the key will be extended. Hence, it is a challenging task for an illegitimate user to gain access and to enter the current group. Therefore, the feasibility of access for the external agent is negated and our scheme is proposed for achieving such strong security. The proposed work takes less time to compute the secret key and does not allow access to it by an external member who is not a member of the current group. This helps to maintain a secret conversation in the group.

6.6 PERFORMANCE ANALYSIS OF THE PROPOSED IBE-BASED SYSTEM

As part of the system security, authentication is an important and inevitable step to be followed. There are two essential cases to assure authentication. Unauthorized users must be prevented from gaining access to the communication group. Figure 6.5 represents the authentication mechanism for a key management system for an invalid signature. Authorized users are verified for their legitimacy and then permitted to enter the system. Figure 6.6

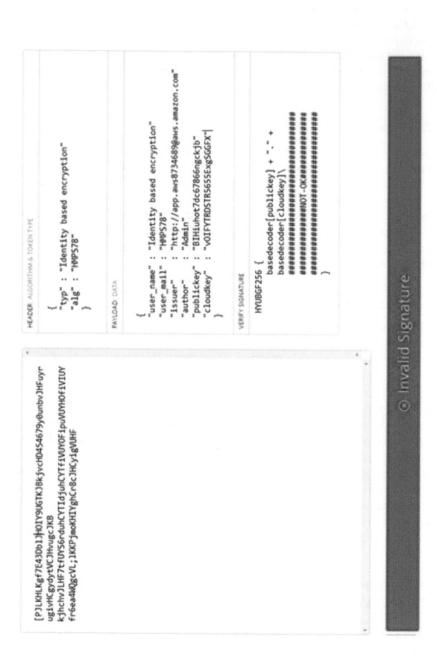

HEADER ALGORITHM & TOKEN TYPE

{
  "typ" : "Identity based encryption"
  "alg" : "HMPS78"
}

PAYLOAD DATA

{
  "user_name" : "Identity based encryption"
  "user_mail" : "HMPS78"
  "issuer"   : "http://app.aws8734689@aws.amazon.com"
  "author"   : "Admin"
  "publickey" : "BIHiuhot7dc67866ngckjb"
  "cloudkey" : "vOIFYTRDSTRS65SExgSGGFX"|
}

VERIFY SIGNATURE

HYUBGF256 {
    basedecoder[publickey] + "." +
    basedecoder[cloudkey]\
    ##########################NOT-OK##############
    ###
    ###
    }

[PJLKHLKgf7E43Db1JHOIY9U6TKJBkjvcH0454679y0umbvJHFuyr
ugivHCgydytVCJHvugcJKB
kjhchvJLHF7tfUYS6rduhCYTIdjuhCYTfiVUYOFipuVUYHOFiVIUY
fr6ea4WQgcVL;1KKPjmoKHYghCr8cJHCyigVUHF

Ⓘ Invalid Signature

Figure 6.5 Authentication for key management for an invalid signature.

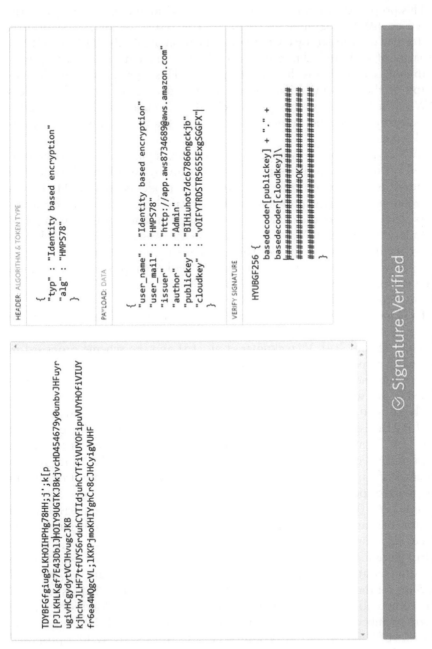

HEADER: ALGORITHM & TOKEN TYPE

{
  "typ" : "Identity based encryption"
  "alg" : "HMPS78"
}

PAYLOAD: DATA

{
  "user_name" : "Identity based encryption"
  "user_mail" : "HMPS78"
  "issuer"   : "http://app.aws8734689@aws.amazon.com"
  "author"   : "Admin"
  "publickey" : "BIHiuhot7dc67866ngckjb"
  "cloudkey" : "vOIFYTRDSTR565SExgSGGFX"|
}

VERIFY SIGNATURE

HYUBGF256 {
  basedecoder[publickey] + "." +
  basedecoder[cloudkey]\
  ################################
  #################OK#############
  ################################
  }

TDYBFGfgiug9LKHOIHPHg78HH;j';k[p
[PJLKHLKgf7E43Db1]H0IY9UGTKJBkjvcHD454679y0unbvJHFuyr
ugivHCgydytVCJHvugcJKB
kjhchvJLHF7tf0VS6rduhCYTIdjuhCYTfiVUY0FipuVUYHOfiVIUY
fr6ea4WQgcVL;1KKPjmokHIYghCr8cJHCyigVUHF

⊘ Signature Verified

Figure 6.6 Authentication for key management system for a valid signature.

represents the authentication mechanism for a key management system for a valid signature.

This proposed experiment is achieved on a GridSim Simulation platform based on JAVA programming language. The system simulation setup was performed on four laptops with the specification of P4 3.0 GHZ, with RAM capacity of 4GB and obtained this result. The implementation set up programming screen shot is shown in Figure 6.7. This represents the implementation of the authentication mechanism based on Amazon Web Services (AWS) which provides a base for the cloud environment and offers reliability, support for the increased size of the system, and less expensive distributed services.

AWS cryptography services are used for the implementation of the proposed key mechanism. The symmetric algorithm by an advanced encryption standard is used by utilizing Galois/Counter mode as AES-GCM. This is based upon solving the problems mathematically using the function parameters. The analysis of the data that were sent as messages is done using IBM QRadar Advisor with Watson. The reason for using this is the ability to prove the incidents as required. This tool has the capability to provide various information related to IPs. Figures 6.8 and 6.9 represent computation time comparisons when sending messages from a client to the cloud, at the group member and at the client side respectively.

The computation time for sending message from client to cloud at the group member for 21 messages incurs 0.19 ms, 0.14 ms and 0.10 ms for the schemes of Lim [14], Vijayakumar et al. [15] and the scheme proposed in this work respectively. For 33 messages it incurs 0.25 ms, 0.21 ms, 0.16 ms for the schemes of Lim [14], Vijayakumar et al. [15] and the scheme proposed in this work respectively.

The computation time for sending message from client to cloud at the client for 21 messages incurs 0.13 ms, 0.11 ms and 0.09 ms for the schemes of Lim [14], Vijayakumar et al. [15] and the scheme proposed in this work respectively. For 33 messages it incurs 0.2 ms, 0.18 ms and 0.14 ms for the schemes of Lim [14], Vijayakumar et al. [15] and the scheme proposed in this work respectively.

Figures 6.10 and 6.11 represent the computation time comparison when sending messages from the cloud to a server, at the group member and at the server side respectively.

In Figure 6.10, the computation time for sending message from client to cloud server at the group member side for 21 messages incurs 0.27 ms, and 0.25 ms for the schemes of Lim [14] and Vijayakumar et al [15] respectively. The computation time for sending message from client to cloud server at the group member side for 33 messages incurs 0.39 ms, and 0.33 ms for the schemes of Lim [14] and Vijayakumar et al. [15] respectively. Our proposed system does not incur any cost in this case.

In Figure 6.11, the computation time for sending messages from client to cloud server at the server side for 21 messages incurs 0.28 ms, and 0.23 ms

Figure 6.7 Implementation of authentication in AWS.

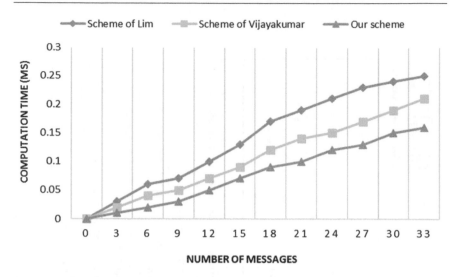

Figure 6.8 Comparison of computation time for sending a message from client to cloud on the group member side.

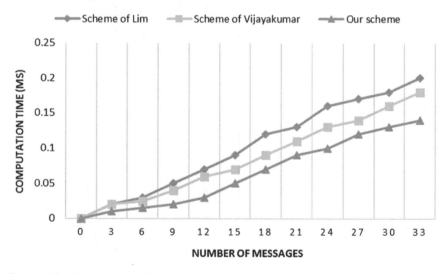

Figure 6.9 Comparison of computation time for sending a message from client to cloud on the client side.

and 0.17 ms for the schemes of Lim [14], Vijayakumar et al. [15] and our proposed work respectively. The computation time for sending messages from client to cloud server at the server side for 33 messages incurs 0.42 ms, and 0.37 ms and 0.25 ms for the schemes of Lim [14], Vijayakumar et al. [15] and our proposed work respectively.

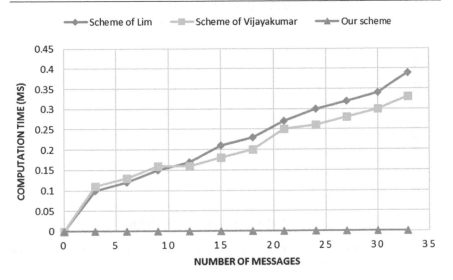

Figure 6.10 Comparison of computation time for sending a message from cloud to server on the group member side.

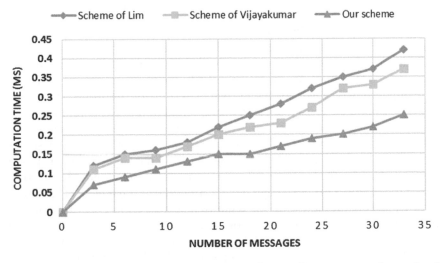

Figure 6.11 Comparison of computation time for sending a message from cloud to server on the server side.

Figure 6.12 shows the comparison of the computation time of the group member in key updating process in key management of our proposed system with the work proposed by Seo et al. (2015). In the scheme proposed by Seo et al. (2015), for a group size of 12, 18, 24, and 30 it incurs 0.06 ms, 0.08 ms, 0.11 ms, and 0.15 ms respectively. For the proposed system the computation time is invariant and it incurs 0.025 ms.

Figure 6.12 Comparison of computation time of the group members in a key updating process of key management.

6.7 CONCLUSION AND FUTURE WORK

In this chapter, we proposed a secured group key management algorithm for improving the security of identity-based encryption. This research work provides efficient key management, effectual encryption and decryption, and also an effective authentication process. The proposed work illustrates the protocol to achieve a successive method of a distributed keygen method of group members which creates a private key only for the group. The public keys are computed at users for enhancing mitigation of the communication costs for the user. The results prove that the proposed method is better than other competitive methods. The computation time for sending messages from client to cloud at the group member for 33 messages in the proposed system was computed and found improvements of 36% and 23.8% compared to the works proposed by Lim [14] and Vijayakumar et al. [15] respectively. The computation time for sending messages from client to cloud at the client for 33 messages in the proposed system was computed and found improvements of 30% and 22.22% compared to the works proposed by Lim [14] and Vijayakumar et al. [15] respectively. The computation time for sending messages from cloud to server at the server for 33 messages in the proposed system was computed and found improvements of 40.47% and 32.43% compared to the works proposed by Lim [14] and Vijayakumar et al. [15] respectively. Furthermore, the proposed research work with message transmission results in increasing security and efficiency in the key management protocol system. Finally, from the results of the experiment, we can observe that the computation time at the group member and client node in the various processes is much less than that of other well-known schemes.

Therefore, our algorithm can obtain better trade-offs between security and efficiency. Potential future works are as follows:

- For the centralized key distribution protocol using identity-based encryption, in future it could be worked to reduce the cluster of communication in reducing re-key messages for the workload of the group key.
- Creating and generating an evident proof for stateful one-to-many key dispersion that provides optimal and secure operations.

REFERENCES

1. Hardjono, Thomas, and Lakshminath R. Dondeti. *Multicast and Group Security*. Artech House, Boston, 2003.
2. Blundo, Carlo, and Antonella Cresti. "Space requirements for broadcast encryption." In Tor Helleseth (Ed.) *Work Shop on the Theory and Application of Cryptographic Techniques*, pp. 287–298. Springer, Berlin, Heidelberg, 1994.
3. Harn, Lein, and Guang Gong. "Conference key establishment protocol using a multivariate polynomial and its applications." *Security and Communication Networks* 8, no. 9 (2015): 1794–1800.
4. Naranjo, Juan Alvaro Muñoz, N. Antequera, Leocadio G. Casado, and Juan Antonio López-Ramos. "A suite of algorithms for key distribution and authentication in centralized secure multicast environments." *Journal of Computational and Applied Mathematics* 236, no. 12 (2012): 3042–3051.
5. Hwang, Jung Yeon, Su-Mi Lee, and Dong Hoon Lee. "Scalable key exchange transformation: from two-party to group." *Electronics Letters* 40, no. 12 (2004): 728–729.
6. Senan, Shayma, AishaHassan A. Hashim, Raihan Othman, Azeddine Messikh, and Akram M. Zeki. "Dynamic batch rekeying scheme using multiple logical key trees for secure multicast communication." In *2015 International Conference on Computing, Control, Networking, Electronics and Embedded Systems Engineering (ICCNEEE)*, pp. 47–51. IEEE, 2015.
7. Wallner, D., E. Harder, and R. Agee. "Key management for multicast: issues and architectures." *RFC – Informational, National Security Agency, (DoD, USA)*, pp. 1–23, (1999).
8. Gouda, Mohamed G., Chin-Tser Huang, and E. N. Elnozahy. "Key trees and the security of interval multicast." In *Proceedings 22nd International Conference on Distributed Computing Systems*, pp. 467–468. IEEE, 2002.
9. Zou, Xukai. "A dynamic conference scheme extension with efficient bursty operation." *Congressus Numerantium* 158 (2002): 83–92.
10. Mapoka, Trust T., Simon J. Shepherd, and Raed A. Abd-Alhameed. "A new multiple service key management scheme for secure wireless mobile multicast." *IEEE Transactions on Mobile Computing* 14, no. 8 (2014): 1545–1559.
11. Zhou, Zhibin, and Dijiang Huang. "An optimal key distribution scheme for secure multicastgroup communication." In *2010 Proceedings IEEE INFOCOM*, pp. 1–5. IEEE, 2010.

12. Liu, Jing, Yunyun Wu, Xuezheng Liu, Yunchun Zhang, Gang Xue, Wei Zhou, and Shaowen Yao. "On the (in) security of recent group key distribution protocols." *The Computer Journal* 60, no. 4 (2017): 507–526.
13. Seo, Seung-Hyun, Jongho Won, Salmin Sultana, and Elisa Bertino. "Effective key management in dynamic wireless sensor networks." *IEEE Transactions on Information Forensics and Security* 10, no. 2 (2014): 371–383.
14. Lim, Kiho. "Secure and authenticated message dissemination in vehicular ad hoc networks and an incentive-based architecture for vehicular cloud." (2016). [Doctoral dissertation, University of Kentucky, Lexington, Kentucky, United States].
15. Vijayakumar, Pandi, Maria Azees, Arputharaj Kannan, and Lazarus Jegatha Deborah. "Dual authentication and key management techniques for secure data transmission in vehicular ad hoc networks." *IEEE Transactions on Intelligent Transportation Systems* 17, no. 4 (2015): 1015–1028.

Chapter 7

Efficient key management and key distribution for online learning

V. Jeyalakshmi

College of Engineering Guindy, Anna University, Chennai, India

G. Ramesh

KLN College of Engineering and technology, Madurai, India

S. Rajkumar

PSNA college of Engineering and Technology, Dindigul, India

CONTENTS

Nowadays traditional blackboard teaching is rapidly transforming into online learning via smart devices. This online learning provides easy and efficient understanding by offering videos and animation in presentations.

DOI: 10.1201/9781003264538-7

E-learning is not only classroom learning it also includes live reading from the agricultural and medical fields of real-time value for prediction and decision making. This kind of e-learning should be efficient and secure for both learners and trainers. Secured e-learning should be provided by mutual authentication, confidentiality, integrity, and availability. These secured learning techniques all depend on keys for making encryption, envelope, and encapsulation. So, the key plays an important role in making efficient and secure learning. This chapter discusses key management and distribution in the online mode to support customer access with confidence and without any hesitation.

7.1 INTRODUCTION

Education is important to everyone. During the COVID-19 pandemic, e-learning played a vital role for remote learning: anyone, anywhere, at any time, or at any age could update their skills in all fields through self-paced videos or by online mode. Education sectors elevated themselves with new technologies, providing live teaching and group chatting, free apps, classrooms, and managing software. E-learning platforms like NPTEL, MOOC, edx, eskills India, Coursera, and MOODLE, Skills share, and so on offer flexible learning for the self-paced mode with accredited courses [1]. This fruitful online learning should be spread over till the rural is the achievement of digital India.

The transmission of source content, delivered without any data loss, without any data modification, and also without any network issues is a huge challenge. The education environment should also be trusted to protect the e-content from viruses, malware, spyware, and ransomware. So secured data transmission is more and more essential for today's technologies [2]. MS Teams, Google Classroom, and Zoom are secure sources for teachers and students to conduct online meetings and uploading. Generally, secured data involves integrity, confidentiality, authentication, and availability [3, 4]. It should be free from active and passive attacks. An active attack means the intruder can modify the content during transmission. In the case of a passive attack, the intruder can duplicate the theft data without any modification. Most secured systems are offered by the authentication process. The authentication process is verified by a password or key. The key is the fundamental component in cryptography developed by a mathematic algebraic expression [5].

7.1.1 Authentication

Authentication plays a vital role in internet access by username and password protection techniques, to confirm the identity of the originator of the actual message. It is responsible for delivering the message to the proper customer without any kind of intruder attack, and without undergoing any active and passive attacks. Message authentication protects the message and connection authentication checks the logical connection has not experienced any attacks from intruders [6]. Let us discuss both authentications.

7.1.1.1 Message authentication

Integrity is essential in delivering the original message between the users and also in storage. In the case of storage, the system should be reliable, and the document should be well protected. Today's online classes are successfully run by sharing more documents. The teacher can share the study material and the students can submit their assignments and assessments. In agriculture, plant status like moisture level, growth level, diseases and maturity can be remotely monitored by sensors. In the medical field, elderly home care patient reports are observed by health administration via the internet. During sharing and storing such data should be kept secure to protect it from active attack to prevent any modification, and also from passive attack to avoid the leakage of assessment marks/reports, or question papers. Users can sanitize the message before usage. In the case of mail or WhatsApp usage, social media provides secured end-to-end communications by AES encryption and decryption technique. In this way, users can enjoy sharing all kinds of information like text, image, audio, and video in a user-friendly and convenient mode.

Hence, the selection of the software platform, service provider, or operating system is also important for the safe journey of the message. The message should be confidential and maintain integrity to avoid disclosure, masquerade, modification, and repudiation [7].

Message authentication and digital signatures create very effective protection for the message. A message digest is created from the original message and covered with a digital signature and then passed to the receiver. The receiver can decrypt the message digest and compare it with the received digest by a verification algorithm for a confidentiality and integrity test.

The SHA algorithm works efficiently to secure the messages. Figure 7.1 shows the creation of a message digest like a fingerprint of the original message by the SHA (Secured Hash Algorithm) algorithm. This message digest is again covered with a digital signature by the DSS (Digital Signature Standard) algorithm then transmitted via a secured channel [8]. At the receiver, the verifier, as shown in Figure 7.2, verifies the created message digests from the received message against the decrypted received digest. If both are the same, then it identifies and ensures the message's integrity.

Figure 7.1 Creation of message digest.

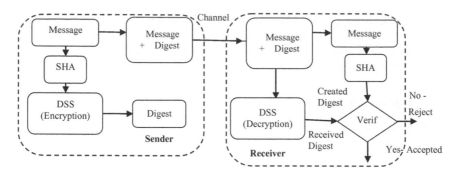

Figure 7.2 Message authentication process.

7.1.1.2 Connection (access) authentication

Authentication is the process of identifying and verifying the customer before providing access. Username and password processes are used for the connection authentication procedure. Each customer is required to identify and can perform access according to the permissions granted by the roles assigned server. In online classes, classroom entry is permitted with access control only. All students authenticated themselves to get permission to listen to the class and the same method is used to upload or download documents. TLS (Transport Layer Security)/SSL(Secured Socket Layer), PKI(Public Key Infrastructure) certificates, x.509 certificates and certificate authority are used for connection authentication [9].

Establishing a secure connection with authentication is important for users' confidence. It is mostly used by client-server application protocol. The server binds all clients' details and their requirements. Accordingly, client authentication by the server and server authentication by the client are applied with mutual authentication processed to ensure the originator. The client-server components use a security package, security context, session key, and context management, and application protocol is followed in the exchange of data [10].

E-learning is the help of electronic devices and internet technologies to deliver various solutions to enable learning and improve performance. The data should be available at all times without any denial of service. Guessing the administration's account passwords through brute force and social engineering is an access control attack [11]. Overloading of web servers or hacking the webserver to prevent access is denial of service.

7.1.2 Key generation and distribution

Key preparation is a process of generating a key to perform encryption at the sender side and decryption at the receiver side. Keys are used to protect the data in order to store and transfer in a secured manner. Mathematical expressions are used to generate the key. Cryptanalysis should be complicated, time-consuming, key meta-data and key life cycle for the key generation algorithm. The key should be periodically updated to prevent expiry [12]. There are two types of keys namely symmetric and asymmetric keys.

The same keys are used for both encryption and decryption algorithms as shown in Figure 7.3. Symmetric keys are mostly used with data at rest. The symmetric key-based cryptosystem is fast and efficient, but it suffers from exchanging of keys. Examples: DES, AES, RC4, and Blowfish

Different keys are used for both encryption and decryption algorithms as shown in Figure 7.4. The pair of keys, namely a private key and a public key, are created with mathematical expression. A public key is a common key anyone can decode to decrypt the original message. Asymmetric keys are most preferred for data at motion encryption. Examples: RSA, VPN network.

A master key is a non-crypt analyst and a very protective key shared by KDC to the end user. A session key is a temporary key shared between two end users for making a logical connection by the key distribution center. Session key = $N * (N - 1)/2$, where N is the master key. If selecting the master key $N = 4$, then it will generate six possible different session keys. Among these only one is provided to the requested users securely. The user transaction time is limited by session timeout.

Key distribution is of two kinds, based on the usage of keys. One is the symmetric key distribution used to distribute the key for the symmetric and asymmetric encryption process. The other is a public key distribution under asymmetric key encryption technique which have private and public keys. There four different distribution techniques. They are the public announcement of public keys, publicly available directory, public key authority, and public key certificates [13].

This introduction is followed by Section 7.2 which describes a literature survey of online authentication, and then Section 7.3 illustrates key encryption

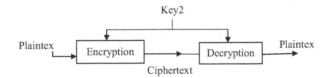

Figure 7.3 Symmetric keys.

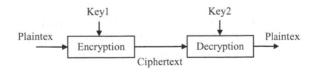

Figure 7.4 Asymmetric keys.

techniques for online architecture. Section 7.4 explains key management and distribution for online learning, and Section 7.5 shows methods for secured online learning. Section 7.6 illustrates and demonstrates the security system and the chapter concludes with future work in Section 7.7.

7.2 LITERATURE REVIEW

7.2.1 E-learning authentication

The trust authentication process depends on the server which is authorized to access the database. Trust authentication is very convenient for local connections suitable for TCP/IP connections on a single user workstation. Authentication with Generic Security Service Application Programming Interface (GSSAPI) is an industry standard protocol by single sign-in for automatic authentication [14]. This authentication itself is very secure and the transferring of the data is in unencrypted form. So, the SSL concept is used for exchanging data. Kerberos authentication is one of the industry-standard secure authentication systems mostly applied for distributed computing over a public network [15]. This technique is also supported by the SSL concept for carrying data between users. It is a third-party authentication process by single sign-in. It provides a secured service with centralized password storage.

Peer authentication is supported by local connections for providing access between the users with authentication by the server. Light Directory Access Protocol (LDAP) authentication is a authentication technique that depends on the password concept and its verification is done by the LDAP server [16]. It is used only to validate the user id and password pairs. It applies only to LDAP registered users in the database for authentication.

Remote Authentication Dial-In User Service (RADIUS) is a password verification technique utilized by a server for its regular users. This service is provided by rising access requests and an access response signal from the RADIUS server. The access process proceeds based on access response or access rejected with verification. This protocol is also used for authorization and accounting for remote applications [17, 18].

The Certificate Authentication (CA) method uses client certificate for authentication instead of the username and password concept. Usernames and their certificate mapping are used to allow database access. The x.509 certificate authentication is mostly used for client authentication and internal authentication of users for repeated usage of the network [19].

The Pluggable Authentication Modules (PAM) authentication method provides access by password with the PAM authentication concept. It is also used to validate only the username and password that are registered in the PAM. Salted Challenge Response Authentication Mechanism (SCRAM) authentication is mostly used to access the database.

Multitier Authentication is a multitier server used for some applications. Client identity is required for all tiers and then only allowed for access. The middle tier is a connection pooling that allows multiple users to access the data services without any additional connections.

Biomedical Authentication is where online exam frameworks are developed by face and fingerprint acknowledgment to verify and upload material to online mode. It eases to distinguish proof and access control [20].

7.3 KEY ENCRYPTION TECHNIQUES FOR ONLINE LEARNING

The key preparation and mode of delivering to the customer are essential. Both should be protective. Hence, some encryption techniques are listed for carrying online learning applications.

- **Data Encryption Key (DEK)** is a key used to encrypt and decrypt the data as shown in Figure 7.5 (e.g., sensor data).
- **Key Encryption Key (KEK)** is a key used to encrypt and decrypt the DEK. That is, encrypted data over coated or enveloped as shown in Figure 7.6 (e.g., medical data that should be protected and kept confidential).
- **Key Management API (KM API)** is an application interface designed to securely retrieve and pass along encryption keys from a key management server to the client requesting the keys [21]. API function is given in Figure 7.7. It consists of a queue manager for authority checks and also to make a network connection between user1 and user2 after verifying their user id and password. It also checks authority to access the resources.

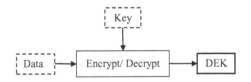

Figure 7.5 Preparation of DEK.

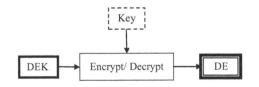

Figure 7.6 Preparation of KEK.

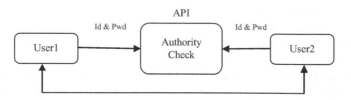

Figure 7.7 Key management API process.

- **Certificate Authority (CA)** is an entity that creates public and private keys, creates certificates, verifies certificates, and performs other PKI functions (e.g., Aadhar).
- **Public Key Infrastructure (PKI)** is a set of policies and processes in software and in workstations. It is related to an asymmetric key system consisting of message digests, digital signature, and encryption services [22]. A digital certificate is used to activate this service (e.g., employee id card).
- **Key Management System (KMS)**: XML KMS is proposed for trust-related decisions in XML encryption/ decryption. XKMS is jointly proposed by Microsoft, VeriSign, and web methods. This protocol is used for distribution. It consists of two parts, namely X-KISS (XML Key Information Service Specifications) and X-KRSS (XML Key Registration Service Specifications).
- **Transport Layer Security (TLS)** is a cryptographic protocol that provides security, through mutual authentication, for data-in-motion over a computer network.
- **NIST (National Institute of Standards and Technology)** defines crypto period as a pre-operational, operational, post-operational and deletion stage. It was created by Originator Usage Period (OUP) and Recipient Usage Period (RUP) whose period is the maximum that will be considered as the crypto period.
- **Secured Electronic Transaction (SET)** is an open encryption technique used for protecting credit/debit card online transactions. It was initiated jointly by Mastercard and Visa credit cards. It provides secured e-commerce transactions with authentication by digital certificate verification via the payment gateway.

Figure 7.8 shows an e-commerce transaction. Initially the cardholder was interested and initiated a request for the merchant to buy a product. At the same time the cardholder sends the merchant's certificate, the merchant sends the cardholder certificate to the certificate authority. Once the certificate authority provides clearance then the merchant will respond to the cardholder's request. Now the cardholder will share bank details. The bill amount is credited to the merchant account by a protected payment gateway service [23].

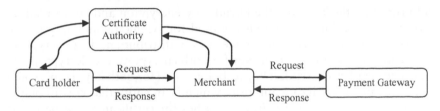

Figure 7.8 E-commerce transaction.

- **Pretty Good Privacy (PGP)** is a protocol mainly used for electronic mail. It is activated by username and password. The created email message is converted to a message digest by an SHA algorithm to get a digital signature, then compressed by an algorithm for reducing size. Following this it is encrypted, enveloped, and encoded to be transmitted in a secured manner.
- **Secure Multipurpose Internet Mail Extensions (S/MIME)**, like PGP, provides for digital signature and encryption of email messages. A digital standard signature, Diffie Hellman, RSA, and DES-3 of cryptographic algorithms are used to provide a secured transmission [24, 25].

7.4 KEY MANAGEMENT AND DISTRIBUTION FOR ONLINE LEARNING

Key management is about managing the key for the cryptosystem. It mainly focuses on generating, exchanging, and storing between users. Key management should be considered at physical security level and logical security level. Physical security provides security with the end user's equipment. In the case of logical security, some sets of protocols and sensors are used to ensure security. In this smart world, more challenges have to be faced to update system certificates or system keys, to update before the expiration time, to maintain malware protection, and also to identify any third party entry and to protect from intruders.

A centralized key management implementation system consists of equipment, policies, and process. The equipment should be able to act as secure servers that create, store, retrieve, and manage encryption keys. Its policies are the defined criteria for the handling of encryption keys, and its processes are inputs, activities, and outputs which all implement centralized key management.

7.4.1 Key distribution

Key distribution is the process of delivering both public and private keys between the end users. It is also responsible for protecting the keys during any exchange of the keys. So, many recent techniques support carrying and protecting the key from the intruder by encryption and encapsulation. Various key distribution methods are used for symmetric and asymmetric keys separately. In the case of symmetric key distribution, data encryption key techniques are used with the key for both encrypting and decrypting the data. The next key encryption key technique used for both keys is encrypted [26]. The third is certificate authority which is an entity that creates public and private keys, creates certificates, verifies the certificates, and performs the secured functions. The fourth is transport layer security performed with protocols to provide security through a mutual authentication process. Cryptography is used to protect online network applications like e-banking, e-commerce, and e-learning by key management systems. This means that KMS-related hardware, software, and processes exist at multiple locations.

The flowchart in Figure 7.9 shows the encryption key process. When a user needs to access the encrypted data, initially the user sends the request to the database, application, file system, or storage then sends a DEK retrieval request to the client (KM API). Next, the client (KM API) and KM verify each other's certificates by sending a certificate from a client (KM API) to the KM for verification. The KM then checks the certificate against CA for authentication. Once the client (KM API) certificate has been verified, the KM then sends its certificate to the client (KM API) for authentication and acceptance [27]. Once certificates have been accepted, a secure TLS connection is established between the client (KM API) and the KM. The KM then decrypts the requested DEK with the key. The KM sends the DEK to the client (KM API) over the encrypted TLS session. The client (KM API) then sends the DEK to the database, application, file system, or storage. The database may cache the DEK in temporary secure memory. The database, application, file system, or storage then sends the plain text information to the user.

7.4.2 Key distribution center (KDC)

A Key Distribution Center (KDC) is one of the systems responsible for providing keys to the users in a network in order to share any kind of data. Two users in a network mutually verify each other by getting the unique strong password from the KDC request. After successful key sharing, two users start to share their private and confidential messages securely or peacefully. This process will be followed every time when users wanted to communicate.

Each user has a separate secret key with KDC. When any user wants to start their communication, they will share their secret key with KDC. Then, KDC provides a session key to both for communication within the specified time as shown in Figure 7.10. Consider User A wants to share communication with User B. First User A sends its Secret key KA to KDC for communicating with User B. Now KDC sends User A's request to User B. If User B accepts User A's request, then KDC creates a session key and sends it to both. Now User A and User B will start transferring a message by the session

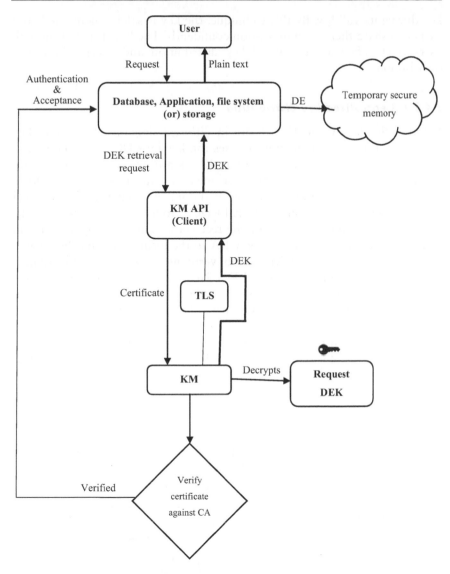

Figure 7.9 Encryption key process.

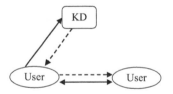

Figure 7.10 Key distribution center.

key during its validity. By this technique, the key is safely maintained, and users can share their communication confidently. The key distribution with users is classified as centralized key distribution and decentralized key distribution.

7.4.2.1 Centralized key distribution

When both User A and User B are in different domains then secret key sharing with KDC and creation of a session key by KDC are different and also time-consuming. Sometimes more KDCs are involved to allow communication between the users. Suppose one user wants to share from a local domain to another user in an international domain. Then, the order of local KDC, regional KDC and international KDC is followed for the sender side, and the same in reverse order for the receiver as shown in Figure 7.11. In this case, User A sends its secret key KA to the local KDC and then it will forward it to the regional KDC after verifying. Following verification, it is forwarded to the international KDC. Now the request of User A is forwarded to the regional KDC of User B, and then it is forwarded to the local KDC of User B to check its interest with User A. This kind of requesting, sharing of secret keys and creation of session keys with each KDC is time-consuming. Users also suffer from some relays time, and sessions out of any one of the KDC's session keys. Nevertheless, this is a standard, systematic, reliable, and secured key distribution system [28].

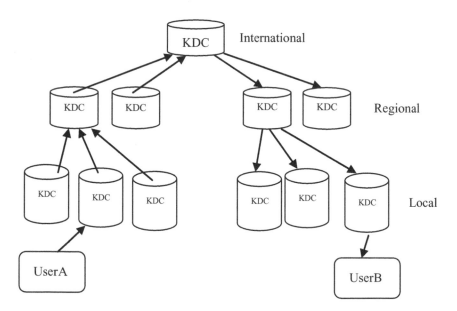

Figure 7.11 Centralized key distribution.

7.4.2.2 Decentralized key distribution

The decentralized key distribution system has no central authority to provide the key. The users can start the session and communicate between themselves by means of simple procedures. The system uses a session key and an encrypted master key. End users are 100% responsible for their own key management [29]. The organization requiring the use of encryption provides no support for handling key governance.

Figure 7.12 shows User A and User B who want to share their communication. First User A shares their id, key KA, and session with User B. Next User B checks User A's details then encrypts User B's key KB, along with User A's details, to send it as the encrypted master key. Now User A knows the master key and checks with the received key after decrypting. Based on this, User A generates a new session key to User B and both can communicate with each other until the session runs out.

7.4.3 Key distribution methods

Key distribution is of two kinds based on the usage of keys. One is symmetric key distribution, used to distribute the key for symmetric and asymmetric encryption processes. The other is public key distribution under asymmetric key encryption technique, which has private and public keys.

7.4.3.1 Distribution of public keys

The distribution of public keys is delivered in four ways. These are public-key announcement, publicly available directory, public-key authority, and public key certificate. Some mathematical expressions are used to create the key for encryption. That key should be complicated to decode, in order to consume more time for detecting and recovering the original key. The popular asymmetric schemes are in the RSA cipher algorithm and the Diffie-Hellman Key Exchange protocol, and learn how and why they work to secure communication. Online learning becomes efficient when secured keys are exchanged between the end users. The public announcement means that the key is publicly announced. The user can access their data using this public key,

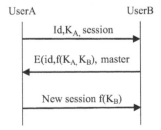

UserA   UserB

Id, K_A, session

$E(id, f(K_A, K_B))$, master

New session $f(K_B)$

Figure 7.12 Decentralized key distribution.

for example, E-Aadhar. A publicly available directory is a dynamic directory created for public keys. This is to be maintained and distributed by a trusted organization. The organization will maintain the directory with the registered username and key. This key can be updated at any time and also accessed for the mutual authentication process before starting sharing. This scheme is more secure. Public key authority technique provides more security through the control unit. It allows both users to share their keys to the control unit. It will verify first and then it allows the users to communicate. A public key certificate is a digital certificate created by the Certificate Authority (CA) which is the main unit between the users. When any one of the users wants to communicate, they should send user authority information to the CA. It will generate a new certificate based on the received information, with that key applicable only for the requested receiver. The same process has to be done for another user who wants to communicate.

7.4.3.2 Private key management

This is mainly for protecting, private keys and multiple key pairs. Some examples of keys are password protection, tokens, Biometrics, and smart cards.

7.4.3.3 Symmetric key distribution using symmetric encryption

This technique has four different ways to deliver the key among the users.

1. Physical delivery: a common key is delivered to the communicating users by physical mode, like asking a known person to deliver.
2. Third party: this is also a physical delivery mode to carry a common key. Here the third party is trusted to deliver the key. This kind of delivery has been followed in banks for providing debit/credit card PINs.
3. Encrypted key: when the same users want to communicate often, they will use the previous key in encrypted form. There is potential for leakage of the key because of the repeated usage.
4. Secured channel: this kind of delivery depends on a secured third party without physical mode. The common key is shared by One-Time Password (OTP) via mobile or mail which is the secured channel.

Today's online transactions and file transfer security are done by network-level and transport levels. At the network level, email security and IP (Internet Protocol) security protocols play a vital role. Email security is mainly used for message authentication. It consists of a set of algorithms used to provide secured service by DES (Decryption Encryption Standard), AES (Advanced Encryption Standard) and MD5 (Message Digest) algorithms for hashing. Two parties can establish secret communication by the asymmetric key algorithm for authentication and encryption. A set of protocols, based on a strong secret key can ensure secure communication. A trusted third party is considered to distribute and generate the key and certificate. PGP is one of the best protocols for providing secured email service. S/MIME protocol provides content compatibility between users.

IPsec consists of a set of protocols used to provide network-level security for a user's pocket. It provides more security service over the internet and also incorporates authentication and confidentiality for the user service. It consists of two main protocols namely Authentication Head (AH) protocol for source authentication, and Encapsulating Security Payload (ESP) protocol for source authentication, data integrity, and confidentiality of packets. A set of security policies are used between the users and the server to provide reliable service.

SSL and TLS is a transport-level security protocol that provides end-to-end user services which are reliable and securable. This protocol was established for compatibility, compression, standard keys for encryption, the best way of key exchange, along with authentication of service and confidentiality of the message [30]. Different cipher suites provide various secured services based on the customer's need. Internet Key Exchange (IKE) provides security, and protects against clogging attack and man-in-the-middle attack.

7.5 CRYPTOGRAPHIC TECHNIQUES FOR SECURED ONLINE LEARNING

In a symmetric key cryptosystem, linear and modular arithmetic with linear congruence procedure is used to select the proper number of keys, which makes it tough to decrypt. Generated keys are applied to either substitution or transposition cipher concepts for both block and steam ciphering. Diffusion and confusion relations are strictly followed in the assigning of keys for encryption and decryption.

$$\text{Encryption} : \text{Cipher} = \text{Plaintext.xor.f}(\text{key})$$

$$\text{Decryption} : \text{Plaintext} = \text{Cipher.xor.f}(\text{key})$$

The most standard forms of symmetric encryption methods are the Data Encryption Standard (DES) and the Advanced Encryption Standard (AES). Both have some sets of rounds for encryption to carry the data, and the reverse process with the same sets of rounds for decryption to recover the original message. They have a separate key generation algorithm developed with shifting, compressing, and expanding, along with round constants by an irreducible polynomial as shown in Figure 7.13. By increasing the rounds for generating keys these algorithms become very strong and also a big challenge for cryptanalysts. They follow the trapdoor one-way function to select

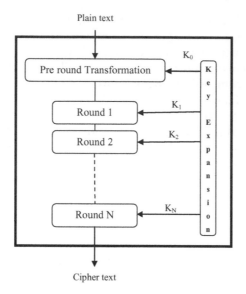

Figure 7.13 AES structure.

the key which leads to strong and efficient key generation, ensuring it is difficult to find and is also more time-consuming. Thus, the cryptanalyst would not be able to find the key within the specific time.

In an asymmetric key cryptosystem, keys are selected by mathematical calculations to get greater prime numbers. Prime numbers play an important role in encrypting and decrypting the message. The prime number selections are done by the Chinese Remainder Theorem (CRT), exponential and logarithmic algorithms. The CRT algorithm is executed by this linear concurrence equation $ax \equiv b$ *(mod n)*. In the case of two equivalences of the form

$$x \equiv b1(\mathrm{mod}\, n1)$$
$$x \equiv b2(\mathrm{mod}\, n2)$$

then the method demands that n1 and n2 are relatively prime, and this should solve that problem. Most standard algorithms for asymmetric key systems are RSA as shown in Figure 7.14 and Table 7.1 and Rabin cryptosystem. Biometric and digital signatures along with these are used to strengthen the asymmetric cryptosystem.

The Diffie-Hellman algorithm is used to establish a shared secret that can be used for secret communications while exchanging data over a public network using the elliptic curve to generate points and get the secret key using the parameters. it consists of four variables, two large prime numbers and two user constant values. User A and User B share their key with prime numbers as shown in Figure 7.15, common key established between the users.

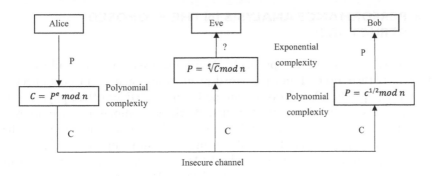

Figure 7.14 RSA key generation and sharing between users.

Table 7.1 RSA key generation procedure

Key generation	Encryption:
Select p, q of two large prime numbers, $p \neq q$.	Ciphertext: $C = P^e$ mod n
	Decryption:
Calculate $n = p \times q$	Plaintext: $M = C^d$ mod n
Calculate $\phi(n) = (p - 1)(q - 1)$	
Select constant e value. gcd $(\phi(n), e)) =$	Relationship between e and d is
1 & 1 < e < (n)	expressed as:
Calculate $d; d = e^{-1}$ mod (n)	e^d (mod (n)) = 1
Public Key, PU = {e, n}	e^d = 1 mod (n)
Private Key, PR = {d, n}	$d = e^{-1}$ mod (n)

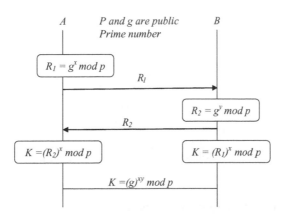

Figure 7.15 Diffie-Hellman algorithm.

7.6 PERFORMANCE ANALYSIS IN THE PROPOSED STRUCTURE

Edusat is a client server approach. Registered users only are allowed to access via their user id and password protection. Each client is connected with their specific IP address for online learning. TriNet offers payroll services, access to big-company benefits, workers' compensation, employer practices, liability insurance, and strategic HR support and services. The company also provides online tools for manager and employee self-service.

The Advanced Encryption Standard (AES) is a fast and secure form of encryption used for e-learning content sharing. When uploading the lecture e-notes, AES is used to encrypt and applied to the SHA algorithm to encapsulate the ciphertext which provides more security. To access the QP/ e-content, the user (student) gets the authentication via a key. The key is provided by the Diffie Hellman algorithm. Taking two large prime numbers along with their key creates a secret key generated then this is followed with the SHA algorithm added to envelop the session key which helps users to complete their access in safe mode.

The online contents (message) are encrypted by AES-256 then applied to the SHA algorithm to make a digest then upload as shown in Figure 7.16. The Diffie Hellman algorithm applied to share the key with the SHA algorithm to over protect the key for the secured transmission of text, image and video are simulated. The same concept is also applied in diagnosing the fruit ripening stage and maturity information shared with farmers. The same kind of procedure also applies to sharing medical information between doctors and patients. Table 7.2 and Figure 7.17 show the encryption and decryption time analysis for various data.

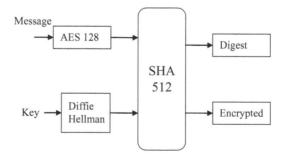

Figure 7.16 Proposed encryption structure.

Table 7.2 Encryption and decryption time analysis for various data

File size	Data	Encryption time (ms)	Decryption time (ms)
5 KB	Text	522	342
	Image	798	426
	Video	1024	598
50 KB	Text	3457	1745
	Image	4566	1936
	Video	7028	2478
5 MB	Text	8423	3467
	Image	11256	3896
	Video	17234	4584
50 MB	Text	42564	23753
	Image	57892	26894
	Video	83268	30146

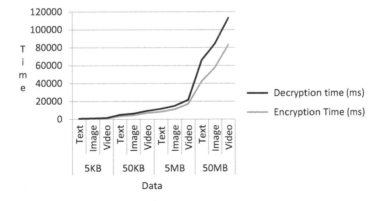

Figure 7.17 AES Cipher text and plain text conversion time chart.

7.7 CONCLUSION AND FUTURE WORK

For online learning, security over the internet is essential and must strengthen its protocol for key exchange services. Accordingly, some standard forms of key creation, key management, and key distribution are discussed in this chapter. Future internet technologies include the development of e-learning programs and personalized data sharing, and encourage students to be involved in the learning process. The Internet of Things will lead the learning process of sensor technologies for real-time learning remotely.

REFERENCES

1. Coman, Claudiu, Laurenţiu Gabriel Ţîru, Luiza Meseşan-Schmitz, Carmen Stanciu, and Maria Cristina Bularca, "Online Teaching and Learning in Higher Education during the Coronavirus Pandemic: Students' Perspective," *Sustainability*, 12(10367), 2020, pp. 1–24. doi: 10.3390/su122410367.
2. Leea, Aeri, and Jin-young Hanb, "Effective User Authentication System in an E-Learning Platform," *International Journal of Innovation, Creativity and Change*, 13(3), 2020, pp. 1101–1113.
3. Karthika, R., L. Jegatha Deborah, and P. Vijayakumar, "Intelligent E-learning System Based on Fuzzy Logic," *Neural Computing and Applications*, 32(12), 2020. pp. 7661–7670.
4. Masadeh, Shadi, Jamal Zraqou, and Mamoun Alazab, "A Novel Authentication and Authorization Model Based on Multiple Encryption Techniques for Adopting Secure E-Learning System," *Journal of Theoretical and Applied Information Technology*, 96, 2018, pp. 1529–1537.
5. Galbraith, Steven D., *Mathematics of Public Key Cryptography. Version 2.0*, Cambridge University Press, 2018.
6. Masadeh, Shadi R., Jamal S. Zraqou, and Moutaz Alazab, "A Novel Authentication And Authorization Model Based On Multiple Encryption Techniques For Adopting Secure E-Learning System," *Journal of Theoretical and Applied Information Technology*, 96(6), 2018, pp. 1529–1537.
7. Alwi, N., and I. Fan, "E-Learning and Information Security Management," *International Journal of Digital Society (IJDS)*, 1(2), 2010, pp. 148–156.
8. Kessier, Gary G., *An Overview of Cryptography*, Prineceton University Press, 2022.
9. Saleh, M. M., and F. A. Wahid, "A Review of Security Threats by the Unauthorized in the E-learning," *International Journal Computational Technology*, 14(11), 2015, pp. 6240–6243.
10. Vinoth Chakkaravarthy, G., and P. Ambiga, "Dynamic Key Management Schemes: A Survey," *Advances in Natural and Applied Sciences*, 8(17), 2012, pp. 1–8.
11. Qamar, Maryam, Mehwish Malik, Saadia Batool, Sidra Mehmood, Asad W. Malik, and Anis Rahman, "Centralized to Decentralized Social Networks," 2016. doi: 10.4018/978-1-4666-9767-6.ch003.
12. Raju, B., and C. Meenu, "A Survey on Efficient Group Key Management Schemes in Wireless Networks," *Indian Journal of Science and Technology*, 9(14), 2016, pp. 1–16.
13. Patil, Vijaya, Aditi Vedpathak, Pratiksha Shinde, Vishakha Vatandar, and Surekha Janrao, "E-learning system using cryptography and data mining techniques," *International Research Journal of Engineering and Technology (IRJET)*, 05(01), 2018, pp. 446–449.
14. Gautam, Amit, and Rakesh Kumar, "A Comprehensive Study On Key Management, Authentication And Trust Management Techniques In Wireless Sensor Networks," *SN Applied Sciences*, 3, 2021, p. 10. doi: 1007/s42452-020-04089-9. Atul Kahate, "Cryptography and Network Security, Second Edition, Tata McGraw Hill Pvt Ltd, 2010.
15. Banerjee, Amit, and Mahamudul Hasan, "Token-Based Authentication Techniques on Open Source Cloud Platforms," *Sistemas & Telemática*, 16(47), 2018, pp. 9–29. doi: https://doi.org/10.18046/syt.v16i47.3211.

16. Balaj, Yjvesa, *Token-Based vs Session-Based Authentication: A survey*, Market Technologies, 2017.
17. Astriani, Maria Seraphina, and Satrio Pradono, "E-School Implementation Using Radius Server And Authentication Mechanism," *ComTech*, 3(2), 2012, pp. 908–916.
18. Zink, Thomas, and Marcel Waldvogel, "X.509 User Certificate-based Two-Factor Authentication for Web Applications," 2017. doi: 10.13140/RG.2.2. 31620.94083.
19. Kashyap Ramgopal, "Biometric Authentication Techniques and E-Learning," *Biometric Authentication in Online Learning Environments*, 2019, p. 30. doi: 10.4018/978-1-5225-7724-9.ch010.
20. Dammak, Maissa, Sidi-Mohammed Senouci, Mohamed Ayoub Messous, Mohamed Houcine Elhdhili, and Christophe Gransart, "Decentralized Lightweight Group Key Management for Dynamic Access Control in IoT Environments," *IEEE Transactions on Network and Service Management*, 17(3), 2020, pp. 1742–1757.
21. Mahfouth, Amjad, "The Authentication Techniques in Distributed E-Learning between Universities in Avicenna Virtual Campus Network," *IJCSI International Journal of Computer Science Issues*, 9(3), 2012, p. 2.
22. Gerck, Ed, "Overview of Certification Systems: X.509, PKIX, CA, PGP & SKIP," *The Bell Newsletter*, 1, 2000, p. 8. 10.13140/RG.2.1.1274.2489.
23. Zivi, Afshin, Gholamreza Farahani, and Kooroush Manochehri, "The Role of SSL/TLS, IPsec & IKEv2 Protocols in Security of E-learning System's Communications, A Study & Simulation Approach," *International Journal of Computer Trends and Technology*, 50(1), 2017, pp. 20–33.
24. Lal, Nilesh A., "A Review of Encryption Algorithms-RSA And Diffie-Hellman," *International Journal Of Scientific & Technology Research*, 6(07), 2017, pp. 84–87.
25. Vijayakumar, P., Bose Sundan, and Kannan Arputharaj, "Centralized Key Distribution Protocol Using the Greatest Common Divisor Method," *Computers & Mathematics with Applications*, 65, 2013, pp. 1360–1368. doi: 10. 1016/j.camwa.2012.01.038.
26. Davis, Michael A.," Physical and Logical Security Convergence," *Information Week reports*, 2012.
27. Tabassum, Tamanna, Sk Alamgir Hossain, Md Anisur Rahman, Mohammed Alhamid, and M. Hossain, "An Efficient Key Management Technique for the Internet of Things," *Sensors*, 20(2049), 2020. doi: 10.3390/s20072049.
28. Lavanya, Raja, K. Sundarakantham, and S. Mercy Shalinie, "Cost Effective Decentralized Key Management Framework for IoT," *Computer Systems Science & Engineering, CSSE*, 41(3), 2022, pp. 1057–1070. doi: 10.32604/ csse.2022.021052.
29. Dammak, M., O. R. M. Boudia, M. A. Messous, S. M. Senouci, and C. Gransart, "Decentralized Lightweight Group Key Management for Dynamic Access Control in IoT Environments," *IEEE Transactions on Network and Service Management*, 17(3), 2020, pp. 1742–1757.
30. Al-Janabi, Sufyan, and Mohammed Ibrahim, "Secure E-Mail System Using S/MIME and IB-PKC" 2006.

Chapter 8

An efficient privacy preserving and public auditing data integrity verification protocol for cloud-based online learning environments

L. Jegatha Deborah, S. Milton Ganesh, and P. Vijayakumar

University College of Engineering, Tindivanam, India

CONTENTS

Ever since the onset of COVID-19, governments and educational organizations have understood the significance of e-learning education systems for continuing education during lockdown periods. This paradigm shift has come with noticeable needs for security procedures for efficient integrity verification for the e-learning contents uploaded to the cloud storage servers. In spite of many works in the past, the need for computationally efficient protocol is still a concern. The research in this chapter is one of the pioneering attempts in data integrity verification for e-learning scenarios and it strives to address the issues of e-learning data integrity verification in three contexts. First is the invention of a novel integrity verification mechanism utilizing the security strength of elliptic curve cryptography. The second context is that of careful design of the protocol with lesser numbers of computationally expensive operations to suit diverse devices. The third context focuses on enabling support for public auditing mechanisms for the proposed protocol. This research work has been implemented using the pbc library 0.5.12 and the results suggest that the proposed protocol is better than previous works in terms of computational and communication overheads.

8.1 INTRODUCTION

Since the dawn of 2020 cloud storage in the twentieth century, e-learning systems have made several leaps beyond the imagination, crossing the barriers of intercollegiate education, national, and international education systems. This strategic shift has come with many security vulnerabilities in data storage and management in the cloud storage servers, as mentioned by Vijayakumar et al. [1, 2]. In a very short period due to COVID-19, online education platforms such as BYJU's Learning have acquired Aakash Educational Services Limited in 2021, WhiteHatJr in September 2020, and US-based Osmo in January 2019 making this e-learning industry a multi-billion dollar business in its scale. Such is the boom, with acquisitions by e-learning platform giants such as Udemy, SkillShare, MasterClass, Coursera, EdX, Udacity, Pluralsight, and others. Hence, many research works in e-learning contexts are being proposed by various authors [3, 4].

Verification of the integrity of the e-learning data uploaded to the cloud servers is of significant concern. But, since e-learning users utilize varying devices ranging from desktop computers to mobile phones, there is an unquenched thirst for integrity verification schemes with augmented performance improvements. Many famous works have been proposed by authors in the recent past with unsatisfied requirements for computationally efficient protocols [5–7].

In an e-learning environment, the contents of the e-learning system such as teaching materials, lecture notes, e-books, exercises, and examination question papers are stored in cloud storage servers. A course instructor or a teacher might upload the teaching materials to the private or public cloud server of the educational system to share them with the students and other teachers during the online learning management process [8]. But, since this industry has become a multi-billion dollar business, it is possible that, competitors or hackers might indulge in modifying or erasing sensitive e-learning materials in the cloud servers. If the data loss is not immediately addressed, many issues in the education system might later arise [9, 10]. During an online examination, a student may try to modify the online question paper or a competitor may erase the students' feedback and answers on an e-learning platform. Hence, ensuring the data uploaded to the cloud server remains intact is of utmost concern during this boom in e-learning environments.

The organization of the chapter is as follows. Section 8.2 describes various important works on data auditing, identifies gaps, and helps in fixing the objectives of this research work. Section 8.3 shows the design of the proposed protocol. Section 8.4 performs security analysis, and section 8.5 compares the proposed protocol, based on the results. Section 8.6 presents the conclusions of this research work.

8.2 LITERATURE SURVEY

The need for integrity verification has been present since the invention of cloud storage in the early 2000s. Education systems make use of cloud storage technology for providing seamless e-learning crossing international barriers. Under this compelling scenario, it is very unfortunate that only a very few works for integrity verification of e-learning contents in cloud storage have been proposed. This section provides an overview of the relevant works in integrity verification, identifies the gaps in them, and paves the way for fixing objectives for research needs.

One of the very early works on the auditing of outsourced data was carried out by Schwartz and Miller [11]. To reduce the network bandwidth, they made use of algebraic structures, for example, a 32 bit signature and a 64 bit signature are susceptible for collision with a probability of 232 and 264 respectively. But, later protocols reduced the bandwidth better than this work. Another pioneering and state-of-the-art work on data auditing, based on the concept of Provable Data Possession (PDP), emerged from Ateniese et al. [12]. The authors put forward two schemes based on reducing the server workload on disk input output operations. These schemes had a constant size for request/response messages during auditing. But, these schemes required clients to possess metadata for auditing purposes.

Hao et al. [13] improved the data integrity checking protocol proposed by Sebe et al. [14] with support for both static data verification and data dynamics. A significant contribution lies in avoiding the third party auditor during public data verification with improved performance, as in Sebe et al. [14]. Gopinath and Geetha [15] proposed an auditing service based on secure hash function SHA-256 for e-learning systems for distributed storage-based applications. The learning materials were erasure coded data, and, when uploaded to cloud servers, the audit scheme could not only find the modified blocks but could also perform quick error correction as well. But, this work was not secure as hash codes are prone to birthday attacks.

Zhu et al. [16] claimed their work to be efficient in terms of computational, communication, and storage overheads using a probabilistic query-based approach and by periodic audits on the remote data. The constant size of communication overheads and the use of an index hash table for data dynamic operations were salient features of this work. But, present day works show more computational efficiency than this work. Liu et al. [17] contributed a very useful research work with focus on efficient auditing of both static and dynamic data stored in the cloud servers. The use of the

Merkle Hash Tree and storing block indexes in multiple levels in the tree prevented invalid data blocks to generate valid signatures.

In 2016, Saxen and Dey [18] invented a novel Paillier Homomorphic Cryptography (PHC), called Cloud Audit, for auditing purposes. The use of homomorphic tags together with using Paillier cryptography generated unique verifiable codes for each data block. The work was implemented using Hadoop clustering and a MapReduce framework. One notable contribution based on elliptic curve cryptography was from Yu et al. [19] in 2017. They designed a protocol for data integrity verification based on user identity and using key-homomorphic cryptographic methods to avoid the complex public key cryptography. The work ensures zero knowledge data privacy from the Third Party Auditor (TPA), but, with relatively more computational and communication overheads.

Tan et al. [20] discussed the pros and cons of the two audit methods PDP and PoR (Proof of Retrievability) for cloud storage. The authors claimed that PoR performed well as it could support both data recovery and data auditing. They analysed various PoR based audit schemes from 2013 to 2016, and suggested that the designers of the auditing protocols should make use of Software Defined Networking (SDN), machine learning and artificial intelligence concepts.

The authors Ganesh and Manikandan [21] identified the gaps in auditing works based on identity-based schemes, PDP schemes, multi-cloud storage schemes, batch-auditing schemes, and data dynamics. They claimed that, an authentication-based efficient audit scheme is in demand for mobile-based data integrity applications. In this line, the authors proposed an authentication-based remote data verification protocol [22] with support for data dynamics and with improved computational overheads. Hence, the objectives of the proposed work in this chapter are:

    i. To carefully design the protocol with improved computational overhead.
   ii. To provide support for public auditing.
  iii. To preserve the data privacy from the TPA during auditing.

8.3 THE PROPOSED PROTOCOL

This consists of signature generation, proof request, proof generation, and proof verification phases. The proposed protocol is based on elliptic curve cryptography using the bilinear pairing properties as mentioned by the authors in [23, 24].

8.3.1 System initialization

Private Key Generator (PKG) initializes the system using two cyclic groups G_1, G_2 of order q such that the problem of ECDLP is intractable in Z_q^*.

Let q be large prime number, g be a generator or the primitive element of G_1 and $H(.) \to Z_q^*$ be a relevant hash function for the purpose of integrity verification. Let $e(.,.)$ be a specific pairing operation from $G_1 \to G_2$. With this initial setup, PKG randomly selects the private key $\alpha \epsilon Z_q^*$ and computes the public key g^α in which given g^α, finding the value of the private key α is an Elliptic Curve Discrete Logarithm Problem (ECDLP). At last, PKG publishes the parameters $G_1, q, g, H(.), e(.,.), g^\alpha$ and keeps α as a secret for enabling the support for public audit situations.

8.3.2 Signature generation phase

A teacher wants to upload e-learning content such as e-books, audio and video lectures, PowerPoint presentations, examination question papers, and other learning materials to the cloud server from where they can be accessed by the corresponding students who undertake that course. Since a teacher might teach some specific courses remotely to students from diverse universities and even from multiple countries, the teacher, to ensure the integrity of the data, divides each of the files F into different blocks as $F = b_1, b_2, b_3, ..., b_n$ such that each of the blocks is $b_i \epsilon Z_q^*$. Then, the teacher generates the signatures $Sig = s_1, s_2, s_3, ..., s_n$ for all of the blocks.

Let us assume that, s_i refers to the signature of the block b_i. The signature s_i is generated as

$$s_i = \left(g^\alpha\right)^{b_i} \cdot H(i \parallel b_i)^r$$
$$= g^{\alpha \cdot b_i} \cdot H(i \parallel b_i)^r$$

Here, g^α is the public key from the PKG, r refers to the random number from Z_q^* which is used as the teacher's private key, that is $r \epsilon Z_q^*$ and $H(i \parallel b_i)$ refers to the hash of the block number i and the data block b_i for which the signature is being generated. For all the blocks of the file F, the parameter r is unaltered during the signature generation process.

Also, the teacher T_i computes the public key of the user g^r. Then, T_i uploads the blocks $F = b_1, b_2, b_3, ..., b_n$ and their signatures $Sig = s_1, s_2, s_3, ..., s_n$ as $\{F, Sig\}$ to the Cloud Server (CS). Moreover, for each block $\{i\}_{i=1}^n$ of the file F, the teacher T_i sends the hash value $HV_i = H(i \parallel b_i)$ of all the blocks and g^r to the TPA to be used during the integrity verification.

8.3.3 Proof request phase

In this competitive and advertisement-friendly world, competitors are trying to lure customers to their e-learning content management systems. In such a scenario, it is possible that they may hire hackers and attackers to intrude into the system and put the video lectures, learning materials of different kinds, and especially question papers during online exams under jeopardy in an attempt to spoil the integrity of the organization which supports e-learning. Hence, it is mandatory for a teacher, or the administrator of the e-learning organization to verify the integrity of the data uploaded to a cloud server.

Under such a scenario, the course instructor requests the TPA for audit verification of the file F under consideration. Subsequently, the TPA, on behalf of the user, based on the sensitivity of the data, random selects only c blocks $\{i\}_{i=1}^c$ out of n blocks $\{i\}_{i=1}^n$ of the file F such that $c < n$ for the integrity verification process. Also, for each block number to be audited, the TPA randomly selects an integer $v_i \epsilon Z_q^*$ which is represented as $\{v_i\}_{i=1}^c$. Finally, TPA sends the block numbers from $1,2,\ldots,c$ and the respective $v_1, v_2, \ldots, v_c$ as filename, $\{i, v_i\}_{i=1}^c$ to the CS as the audit proof request.

8.3.4 Proof generation phase

On receiving Fname, $\{i, v_i\}_{i=1}^c$ from the TPA, CS understands that, the file to be audited is represented by the filename Fname and the blocks to be verified are represented by $\{i\}_{i=1}^c$. In this regard, for each block in $\{i\}_{i=1}^c$, CS retrieves the data block b_i and its signature s_i from its elastic storage servers and computes the following two items.

$$\sigma = \prod_{i=1}^{n} (s_i)^{v_i}$$

$$\lambda = \sum_{i=1}^{n} b_i \times v_i$$

Then, the CS sends the two items $\{\sigma, \lambda\}$ to the TPA, as a proof of data stored in its servers.

8.3.5 Proof verification phase

For the proof of storage $\{\sigma, \lambda\}$ from the CS, TPA does the audit verification of data for the file F uploaded to the CS by the user during the signature generation phase as

$$e(\sigma, g) \overset{?}{=} e\left(g^{\alpha, \lambda}, g\right) \times e\left(\prod_{i=1}^{C} H(i \parallel b_i)^{v_i}, g^r\right).$$

If the L.H.S and the R.H.S of this equation are same, then, the TPA responds with the audit status as success to the teacher T_i who requested integrity verification for the file F. If L.H.S $\neq$ R.H.S, then, the TPA sends the audit failure status to the user.

8.4 SECURITY ANALYSIS

8.4.1 Support for public auditing

A teacher T_i uploads the data blocks $\{b_i\}_{i=1}^n$ and their corresponding signatures $\{s_i\}_{i=1}^n$ to the CS. During the signature generation phase, for the block b_i, the signature was computed as $s_i = g^{\alpha.b_i}.H(i \parallel b_i)^r$ in which g^α is the public key of the PKG, r is the private key of the teacher T_i for the file F. Based on the request for audit from a T_i, TPA does the audit using the mathematical equation $e(\sigma,g) \overset{?}{=} e(g^{\alpha.\lambda},g).e(\prod_{i=1}^c H(i \parallel b_i)^{v_i},g^r)$ in which g^r is the public key of the teacher T_i who generated the signatures and g^α is the public key of the PKG. Based on the hardness of the ECDLP problem, it is infeasible for an attacker to recover the value of α given g^α and to recover the value of r given g^r. Moreover, the TPA possessing the public parameters g^α, g^r of the PKG and the teacher T_i, does the auditing on behalf of the user.

8.4.2 Completeness

The proposed work for audit verification is complete only if the mathematical equation used for the verification purpose $e(\sigma,g) \overset{?}{=} e(g^{\alpha.\lambda},g).$ $e(\prod_{i=1}^c H(i \parallel b_i)^{v_i},g^r)$ does have a valid mathematical proof. It is given as follows.

$$e(\sigma,g) = e\left(\prod_{i=1}^n (s_i)^{v_i},g\right)$$

$$= e\left(\prod_{i=1}^n \left[g^{\alpha.b_i} \cdot H(i \parallel b_i)^r\right]^{v_i},g\right)$$

$$= e\left(\prod_{i=1}^n \left[g^{\alpha.b_i.v_i} \cdot H(i \parallel b_i)^{r.v_i}\right],g\right)$$

$$= e\left(\prod_{i=1}^n \left[g^{\alpha.b_i.v_i}\right],g\right) \cdot e\left(\prod_{i=1}^n \left[H(i \parallel b_i)^{r.v_i}\right].g\right)$$

$$= e\left(g^{\alpha.\sum_{i=1}^n b_i.v_i},g\right) \cdot e\left(\prod_{i=1}^n H(i \parallel b_i)^{v_i},g^r\right)$$

$$= e\left(g^{\alpha.\lambda},g\right) \cdot e\left(\prod_{i=1}^n H(i \parallel b_i)^{v_i},g^r\right)$$

8.4.3 Preservation of data privacy from TPA

A TPA does the audit verification for data in the CS based on the request from a Data Owner (DO). It is to be noted that the TPA gets possession of parameters under three circumstances. First, during the signature generation phase, the DO receives only the hash values $\{H_i\}_{i=1}^{n}$ of the blocks $\{b_i\}_{i=1}^{n}$ and the user public key g^r. Second, as part of proof request phase, TPA randomly selects c block numbers $\{i\}_{i=1}^{c}$ and sends $\{,i,v_i\}_{i=1}^{c}$ for each of the block b_i to be verified. Third, as a response to the request for proof of data in the CS, it receives $\{\sigma,\lambda\}$ from the CS in which $\sigma = \prod_{i=1}^{n}(s_i)^{v_i}$ and $\lambda = \sum_{i=1}^{n} b_i.v_i$. From these values such as $\{H_i\}_{i=1}^{n}, g^r, \{,i,v_i\}_{i=1}^{c}, \sigma = \prod_{i=1}^{n}(s_i)^{v_i}, \lambda = \sum_{i=1}^{n} b_i.v_i$, the TPA can elicit neither the value of any data block b_i nor the value of signature s_i of any of the data block $\{b_i\}_{i=1}^{n}$ of the file F uploaded to the CS by the DO. Thus, as it is intended only for auditing purposes, the proposed work restricts the role of the TPA only to the auditing process and elegantly preserves the privacy of both data and the signatures from it.

8.5 ANALYSIS OF PERFORMANCE

The proposed protocol for data integrity verification for the data stored in the cloud servers pertaining to e-learning environments is compared with relevant works such as Zhu et al. [16] and Yu et al. [19].

The proposed protocol has been implemented using Pairing Based Cryptography (PBC) library version 0.5.12 and Cygwin tool running on top of Windows 7 operating system powered by Core i3 processor with 4 GB of primary memory. The C programming environment was chosen for implementation in the computer to compare the computational capabilities of the algorithms under comparison. Let us assume that $T_H, T_P, T_{PM}, T_{PA}, T_E, T_M, T_A$ represent the computational cost for one hash operation, one pairing operation, one point multiplication operation, one point addition operation, one point exponentiation operation, one integer multiplication operation, and one integer addition operation respectively.

For the proof verification phase, the proposed protocol incurs a computation overhead of three pairing operations, two exponentiation operations, c times the cost of one hash operation, and one point addition operation. The improvement in the performance of the proposed protocol can be attributed to the fact that the hash operation alone increases linearly with the number of blocks. Other operations such as three pairing operations, two exponentiation operations and one point addition operation are constant under any number of blocks. Compared to Yu et al.'s [19] scheme, the proposed work eliminates the computation of one exponentiation operation and one pairing operation for each of the block under auditing. Similarly, compared to Zhu et al.'s [16] scheme, the proposed work is designed to avoid c times the

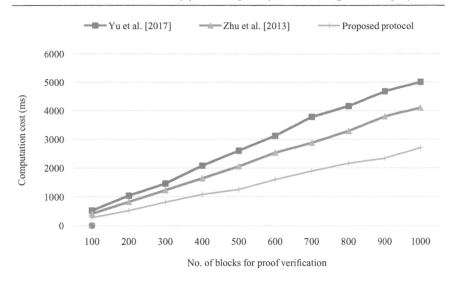

Figure 8.1 Computation cost comparison for proof verification.

cost of two exponentiation operations. Accordingly, the improvement in the performance during proof verification is depicted in Figure 8.1. For 100 blocks of proof verification, the proposed work incurs a 247 ms, 139 ms less computational overhead than the Yu et al. [19] and Zhu et al. [16] schemes.

8.6 CONCLUSION

A novel data integrity verification protocol with support for public auditing has been proposed in this chapter. Each of the processes involving signature generation, proof generation, and proof verification has been designed to incur relatively fewer computational and communication overheads. The proposed work shows significant computational improvement during the proof verification process compared with the Yu et al. [19] and Zhu et al. [16] schemes. This is due to the fact that the increase in computational cost with increase in the number of audit blocks is based only on the number of hash operations. Other computationally expensive operations such as pairing, exponentiation, point multiplication, and point addition are tactically avoided during this phase. Apart from this, the integrity verification protocol ensures data privacy from the third party auditor, making it a highly appropriate work for adaptation in e-learning environments.

REFERENCES

1. Vijayakumar, P., Chang, V., Deborah, L. J., and Rawal B. S. 2018. Key management and key distribution for secure group communication in mobile and cloud network. *Future Generation Computer Systems*, 84: 123–125.
2. Vijayakumar, P., Ganesh, S. M., Deborah, L. J., Islam, S. K. H., Hassan, M. M., Alelaiwi, A., and Fortino, G. 2019. MGPV: A novel and efficient scheme for secure data sharing among mobile users in the public cloud. *Future Generation Computer Systems*, 95: 560–569.
3. Deborah, L. J., Karthika, R., Vijayakumar, P., Rawal, B. S., and Wang, Y. 2019. Secure online examination system for e-learning. *2019 IEEE Canadian Conference of Electrical and Computer Engineering CCECE*, pp. 1–4.
4. Karthika, R., Deborah, L. J., and Vijayakumar, P. 2020. Intelligent e-learning system based on fuzzy logic. *Neural Computer Applications*, 32(12): 7661–7670.
5. Wang, H., Zhang, J., Lin, Y., and Huang, H. 2021. ZSS signature based data integrity verification for mobile edge computing. *2021 IEEE/ACM 21st International Symposium on Cluster, Cloud and Internet Computing (CCGrid)*.
6. Li, X., Chen, L., and Gao, J. 2021. An efficient data auditing protocol with a novel sampling verification algorithm. *IEEE Access*, 9: 95194–95207.
7. Mohammed, A. T., and Mohammed, B. A. 2020. Security architectures for sensitive data in cloud computing. *ICEMIS'20: Proceedings of the 6th International Conference on Engineering & MIS*, pp. 1–6.
8. Shi, Y., Yang, H. H., Yang, Z., and Wu, D. Trends of cloud computing in education. *International Conference on Hybrid Learning and Continuing Education (ICHL 2014)*, Springer, pp. 116–128.
9. Shaikh, F. B., and Haider, S. 2011. Security threats in cloud computing. *2011 International Conference for Internet Technology and Secured Transactions*, pp. 214–219.
10. Costinela-Luminiţa, C., and Nicoleta-Magdalena, C. 2012. E-learning security vulnerabilities, *Procedia - Social and Behavioral Sciences*, 46: 2297–2301.
11. Schwartz, T. S. J., and Miller, E. L. 2006. Store, forget, and check: Using algebraic signatures to check remotely administered storage. *Proceedings of ICDCS'06*. IEEE Computer Society.
12. Ateniese, G., Burns, R., Curtmola, R., Herring, J., Kissner, L., Perterson, Z., and Song, D. 2007. Provable data possession at untrusted stores. *Proceedings of the 14th ACM Conference on Computer and Commununications Security*, pp. 598–609.
13. Hao, Z., Zhong, S., and Yu, N. 2011. A privacy-preserving remote data integrity checking protocol with data dynamics and public verifiability. *IEEE Transactions on Knowledge and Data Engineering*, 23(9): 1432–1437.
14. Sebe, F., Domingo-Ferrer, J., Martinez-Balleste, A., Deswarte, Y., and Quisquater, J. J. 2008. Efficient remote data possession checking in critical information infrastructures. *IEEE Transactions on Knowledge and Data Engineering*, 8: 1034–1038.
15. Gopinath, R., and Geetha, B. G. 2013. An e-learning system based on secure data storage services in cloud computing. *International Journal of Information Technology and Web Engineering*, 8(2): 1–17.

16. Zhu, Y., Ahn, G. J., Hu, H., Yau, S. S., An, H. G., and Hu, C. J. 2013. Dynamic audit services for outsourced storages in clouds. *IEEE Transactions on Services Computing*, 6(2): 227–238.
17. Liu, C., Ranjan, R., Yang, C., Zhang, X., Wang, L., and Chen, J. 2015. MuR-DPA: Top-down levelled multi-replica Merkle Hash tree based secure public auditing for dynamic big data storage on cloud. *IEEE Transactions on Computers*, 64(9): 2609–2622.
18. Saxena, R., and Dey, S. 2016. Cloud audit: A data integrity verification approach for cloud computing. *Procedia Computer Science, Elsevier*, 89: 142–151.
19. Yu, Y., Au, M. H., Ateniese, G., Huang, X., Susilo, W., Dai, Y., and Min, G. 2017. Identity-based remote data integrity checking with perfect data privacy preserving for cloud storage. *IEEE Transactions on Information Forensics and Security*, 12(4): 767–778.
20. Tan, Choon Beng, Hijazi, Mohd Hanafi Ahmad, Lim, Yuto, and Gani, Abdullah. 2018. A survey on proof of retrievability for cloud data integrity and availability: Cloud storage state-of-the-art, issues, solutions and future trends. *Journal of Network and Computer Applications*, 110: 75–86.
21. Ganesh, M., and Manikandan, S. 2019. A survey on various integrity verification schemes on the data outsourced to cloud storage. *10th International Conference on Applications and Techniques in Information Security (ATIS)*, Thanjavur, India. 2019.
22. Ganesh, M., and Manikandan, S. P. 2020. An efficient integrity verification and authentication scheme over the remote data in the public clouds for mobile users. *Security and Communication Networks*, 2020: 1–13.
23. Vijayakumar, P., Azees, M., Kozlov, S. A., Rodrigues, J. J. P. C. 2021. An Anonymous batch authentication and key exchange protocols for 6G enabled VANETs. *IEEE Transactions on Intelligent Transportation Systems*, 23: 1–9.
24. Vijayakumar, P., Obaidat, M. S., Azees, M., Islam, S. K. H., and Kumar, N. 2019. Efficient and secure anonymous authentication with location privacy for IoT-based WBANs. *IEEE Transactions on Industrial Informatics*, 16: 4.

Chapter 9

A novel secure e-learning model for accurate recommendations of learning objects

R. Karthika

University College of Engineering Tindivanam, Tindivanam, India

S.C. Rajkumar

Anna University Regional Campus Madurai, Madurai, India

L. Jegatha Deborah

University College of Engineering Tindivanam, Tindivanam, India

S. Geetha

Government College for Women (A), Kumbakonam, India

CONTENTS

Since the COVID-19 pandemic situation, secure e-learning recommendation systems are the preferred mode of learning. They enable time and location-independent learning. Even though both institutions and students accept the use of technology in their educational processes, personalized course learning materials based on each student's learning preferences are not without limits and security problems. No-blockchain recommendation engines, including collaborative and content-based filtering, may now better focus their recommendations by incorporating information about the users and

DOI: 10.1201/9781003264538-9

the content they're looking at. There is no consideration for the preferences of students, such as their preferred methods of learning, which will help to ensure the accuracy and security of course learning materials. Thus, in order to address these issues and enhance the consistency, security, and quality of recommendation systems, we propose an innovative secure decision support algorithm that incorporates ratings and learning styles in order to securely deliver courses as learning objects. Additionally, the proposed work focuses on enhancing security while conducting online courses and assessments through the use of a novel secure learning algorithm. This contributes to the enhancement of the secure and predictive rating of learning objects and recommends to the e-learner the most highly rated learning objects. Furthermore, the experiment showed that integrating collaborative filtering and content-based filtering techniques to develop our suggested secure hybrid algorithm resulted in a more accurate predictions for e-learning purposes.

9.1 INTRODUCTION

Secure online education has become an accomplished need in today's world because it provides learners with excellent learning experiences compared with other learning management systems. The adaptive educational system is a topic-based personalization approach to guide the e-learner with learning materials. The topic-based personalization for content modeling and student modeling is done with the help of a quiz guide [1]. The e-learner's preferences and interests change in the developing environment. The learning material provided in the adaptive educational system may not satisfy individual needs [2, 3]. This leads to an increase in the dropout rate of e-learners. A survey was conducted for identifying the e-learner dropout rate in online programs and this was accomplished by collecting details of the students who dropped out. Moreover, the reason for e-learners dropping out varies for each individual [4]. Participation, submission of response papers, scoring, and publication of results are all required. Some users may undertake deception attacks, such as leaking and manipulating test papers, impersonating another person to take an examination, or altering answer sheets after submission, in order to acquire more course credits. As a result, it is critical to pay close attention to the security of online tests.

In this modern era, powered by abundant information on the internet, filtering and prioritizing the appropriate information according to the user preference is the need of the hour. The user gives feedback on products or movies as reviews or ratings. The information given by the user as feedback is used by recommendation systems (RS) [5, 6]. Amazon recommends a product to its user and Netflix recommends a movie to its users by applying the recommendation system technique [7, 8]. RS can predict the user's preference for a product or a movie depending upon the user's profile information. Content-based filtering, collaborative filtering, and hybrid filtering are all forms of recommendation systems. [9].

Content-based filtering recommends an item to the users using their profile information [10]. User profiles are updated by storing the attributes of the items of interest to the user. An item is recommended by comparing the user profile with the content or attributes of the item. In contrast to content-based methods, collaborative filtering does not use the profile information for recommending an item [11–13, 35–40]. As a result, it recommends an item based on other people's opinions about the product. Users' feedback or ratings for the items are saved in a matrix known as the user-item matrix, which is used in collaborative filtering. Content-based and collaborative filtering are combined in a hybrid filtering system. The hybrid method gives accurate and effective recommendations as it can rule out the demerits of one RS with another RS [14, 15].

Memory-based and model-based approaches are subclasses of collaborative filtering. Cooperative filtering can be accomplished in two ways: item-based, and user-centered. In order to predict whether an item will be preferred by a user, most of the collaborative filtering RS use an explicit feedback matrix, or an implicit feedback matrix [16]. The user's preferences for an item are stored in a matrix. In the real scenario, either only a few users give feedback for the majority of items, or the majority of users give their feedback only for a few items. Hence the feedback matrix is very sparse. The performance of the RS is degraded due to this sparsity problem. Users and items alike are affected by the problem of sparsity. Items are recommended to the users based on user feedback in a user-centered approach. But since the feedback is given only for few items, we cannot predict the user's preference which leads to the sparsity problem. Similarly, in an item-based approach, users are recommended for the items.

The secure e-learning recommender system as shown in Figure 9.1 is most widely used when compared to the learning management systems (LMS) since the former considers the learning style which improves the e-learners' performance. Here the learning objects are represented as items and the e-learners act as users. Learning objects refer to the different formats of the e-learning contents, namely text documents, PowerPoint slides, video lectures, and others. The Felder-Silverman Learning Style Model (FSLSM), which is used to determine a student's learning style, is utilized to calculate this recommender system's learning style recommendations. Students' preferred learning styles must be taken into consideration while designing an online course [17].

E-learners have various choices in learning such as with whom to learn, how to learn, and what to learn. As a result, learning style has a significant impact in an e-learning context. Learners' learning styles and learning object profiles are used to create an e-learning recommender system. The learning style vector is calculated using index learning style questionnaires, that contain 44 questions. Active, introspective, visual, verbal, sequential, global,

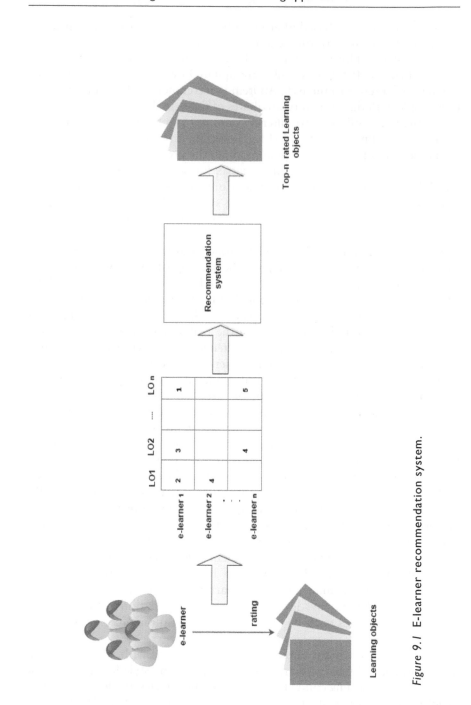

Figure 9.1 E-learner recommendation system.

sensing, and intuitive learning styles were calculated using the questionnaire [18]. The subject expert or the instructor creates the learning object profile vector.

The proposed work focuses on clustering the learning style and learning object profile vectors using a Density-Based Spatial Clustering of Applications with Noise (DBSCAN) algorithm. The hybrid filter recommendation technique is used to recommend the most highly rated learning objects to e-learners after clustering the learning style and learning object profile vectors. The proposed work considers the e-learner learning style as well as the ratings given by the e-learner for the learning objects. In order to improve the learning abilities of students, this research examines how best to recommend courses to students according to their preferred learning style by:

1. Clustering the learning style and learning object profile vector using a DBSCAN algorithm.
2. Using a hybrid filtering recommendation algorithm, to direct e-learners to the most highly rated learning items.
3. Enhancing the accuracy of clustering learning style and learning object vectors which, in turn, precisely recommends the top highly rated learning objects to the e-learners.

The rest of this proposed work has been given in such a way that Section 9.2 provides previous related works by other authors, Section 9.3 gives the architecture of the proposed research work, Section 9.4 presents the performance analysis and finally Section 9.5 concludes the proposed work.

9.2 RELATED WORKS

Recommendation systems based on the learner's shifting learning style have been proposed by Nafea et al. [20]. Through a questionnaire, the Felder-Silverman Learning Style Model (FSLSM) is used to identify learners' preferences and develop their profiles. The index learning style (ILS) questionnaire is divided into four dimensions. Based on the answers given by the learners, their learning style profiles are dynamically updated. The learner need not respond to all the questions, which saves time in building the learner profile.

Barragans-Martınez et al. [10] present a blockchain-based platform to help students in need of financial assistance. Imran et al. [15] proposed a personalized learning object recommender system (PLORS) that provides recommendations for learning objects to learners and assists them in selecting the learning objects that are most appropriate for their needs and preferences. The recommendation system considers the learning objects that are known and familiar to the learner as well as known to other learners who have the same profile. This helps in enhancing the performance of the learning and guides the learner to successfully complete the course with utmost satisfaction.

El Bachari et al. [16] focus on the design, implementation and evaluation of a personalized education framework based on learner performance using the Myers-Briggs indicator types (MBIT) tool. For example, the MBIT can be used to test extroversion vs introversion; sense and intuition; thinking and feeling; as well as judging and perceiving. There are a total of 16 possible combinations of these preferences, which are represented by a person's propensity on four different scales. Using this technique, teachers are able to match the learning type of each student to the right teaching method. Nevertheless, it is still difficult to create four versions of the same course to meet the personal learning process.

Deborah et al. [22] focuses on the programming tutoring system (Protus) for recommendations which can systematically adjust to the preferences and intelligence levels of learners. The Aprioiriall algorithm is used for examining the preferences of the learner and frequent pattern mining is done. The collaborative filtering recommendation is preferred to recommend the learners based on their preferences and intelligence level. Karthika [23] suggests a personalized e-learning material recommendation system. This system recommends the learning contents to the learners who may have various skill sets, preferences, and learning styles. Moreover, it gathers learner information, and recognizes learner preferences. It selects the learning content based on the above criteria and finally recommends the learning content to the learner.

Hence, previous works conducted by researchers focus on traditional recommendation algorithms which do not take into account the learning process. They also do not take into account the learner's learning style and other important aspects of the learning objects. Due to the limitations in time to complete the course, the learners may not give ratings to the learning objects and this results in a data sparsity problem. To overcome this, the proposed work implements the hybrid filtering recommendation to precisely predict the ratings of learning objects and to recommend the top highly rated learning objects to the e-learners.

The proposed system creates a secure e-learning environment and considers the following research to learn about various security attacks, techniques, and approaches for better implementation. Such Distributed Denial-of-Service (DDoS) attacks prevention use a combined statistical-based approach [25–26], a lightweight and robust secure key establishment protocol [27–31], the monarch butterfly optimization algorithm [28], boosting-based DDoS Detection [36], a ResNet model [41–43], an ensemble machine learning approach for classification [44], an infrastructure-based authentication method [45], or a Gaussian Distribution-Based Machine Learning Scheme for Anomaly Detection [46–56].

9.3 PROPOSED FRAMEWORK

Figure 9.2 depicts the suggested system's architecture. The FSLSM model is used to generate the e-learning learner's style vector and the learning content's learning object profile vector. The DBSCAN technique is used to cluster the learning style and learning object profile vectors. The hybrid filtering algorithm is used to predict the rating of the learning objects using learner profile and object profile.

9.3.1 Learning style

Based on the results of the dynamic learning style questionnaire, the adaptive learner profile is generated. Initially the e-learner must register with the learner portal. Once the registration process is completed, e-learners can enter into the system with the login credentials assigned to them. Later, they enter their personal details such as name, address, course registered, and so on and this information is updated in the learner profile database. Next, the e-learners must retrieve the index learning style (ILS) questionnaire which is already stored in the database and answer the questionnaire. The questionnaire's purpose is to discover a person's preferred method of learning and their interests. Felder and Silverman first came up with this concept.

Information processing, information perception, information input, and information interpretation are all considered when constructing the 44 items that make up the index learning style (ILS) questionnaire. Active and reflective learning styles are part of the information processing dimension. Physical experimentation, group work, and understanding how things function are favorites of the active learner. Reflective learners want to learn on their own and to consider their options carefully before acting. Sequential and global learning styles are part of the information understanding dimension. Global learners prefer a more methodical approach to learning and want to view the broad picture first before getting down to the nitty-gritty, while sequential learners prefer a more haphazard approach. Visual and verbal learning styles are both included in the input component of the information system. The verbal learner loves to hear or read material and look for explanations with words, while the visual learner prefers graphs, pictures, and diagrams. The dimensions of information perception include sensing and intuitive learning styles. In contrast to an intuitive learner, who likes conceptual and theoretical knowledge, a sensing learner prefers concrete, practical, and procedural information.

When the e-learner completes the questionnaire, the system keeps track of the responses 'a' and 'b' and uses this information to determine the learning style. Once you've figured out the difference between the two counts, you can proceed to the next step. From 1 to 10, an e-preference learner's score can be assigned. E-learners have a minor bias for one dimension if their

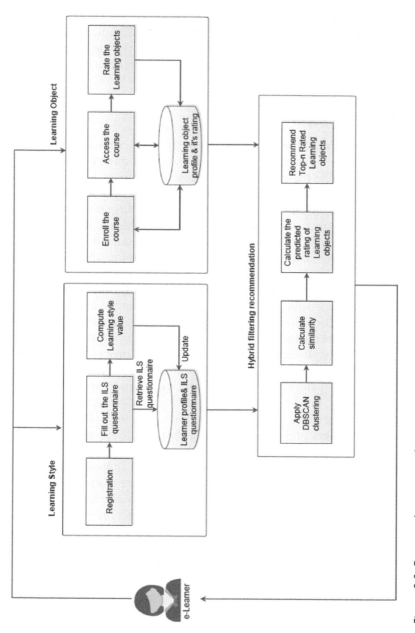

Figure 9.2 Proposed system architecture.

score is 1–3. This means that if e-learners score between 5 and 7, then they prefer some aspect of e-learning above others. There is a considerable preference for one dimension if the learner scores are between 9 and 11. Afterwards, the learning style vector is kept in a learner profile database.

9.3.2 Learning object

An educational institution develops a course management system (CMS) and the instructors play the role of managing and maintaining the courses. Learner profiles consists of their learning styles, goals, prior knowledge, abilities, and interests. The learning object profile database consists of different types of courses offered in the e-learning system. Each and every e-learner should enroll on the course based on their interests. Various units of the course are broken down into sub-units, and each sub-unit is further broken down into individual sections. Commentary, content objects, self-assessment tests, and discussion forums are only some of the learning objects that may be found in each area. Additional reading material, animations, exercises, and examples are also included. In the commentary, the e-learner gets a clear idea about the unit. In real-life applications, the e-learner can apply the concepts read to real-life situations. Animation methods have the units explained in multimedia format (picture, video and so on). In the discussion forum e-learners can have discussions on any topics that they were not clear about.

The e-learners can access the course based on their preferences and interests. Each e- learner's behavior is tracked in the learning object profile database, and data for e-learners with comparable behavior is accessed to create the tailored learning object recommendation. This refers to the information gathered about the learning object visited by each learner and the time spent on each learning object. The e-learners were asked to score each learning object on a five-level rating system after finishing the course. The rating given by the e-learner for each learning object was updated in the learner object profile database.

9.3.3 Hybrid filtering recommendation

The rating of the learning object is predicted by the hybrid filtering recommendation algorithm. Hybrid filtering is a combination of content-based and collaborative filtering suggestions to improve the prediction of learning object ratings and to recommend the top n-highest rated learning objects to e-learners. In the previous works, clustering the e-learners, learning style, and learning object profile vector were done by the k-means algorithm. In our proposed work, the DBSCAN clustering algorithm is used instead of k-means, since the number of clusters need not be given by the user, and it can form clusters of any arbitrary shape. Moreover, the DBSCAN algorithm reduces the computational complexity and improves the clustering accuracy. The DBSCAN clustering algorithm is given below [24].

DBSCAN: the algorithm

- To get started, pick a random point P on the coordinate plane.
- EPs and MinPts must be less than or equal to 1 at all locations in P.
- If P is the central point, then a cluster is produced.
- DBSCAN goes on to the next point because no points in the database can be density-reachable from P.
- The process should be repeated until all of the issues have been addressed, and then the process should be completed.

The hybrid filtering recommendation algorithm to recommend the top highly rated learning objects is given below.

The Hybrid filtering algorithm

- Let S be the learning style vector of the active student and O be the learning object profile.
- Let γ be the weight of collaborative filtering and $(1-\gamma)$ be the weight of content-based filtering in the hybrid filtering model and the value of γ lies between 0 and 1.
- Apply DBSCAN algorithm to cluster the e-learners learning style and learning objects.
- Select non-similarity (NS) the closest cluster to S using cosine similarity.

$$C(x,y) = \frac{x.y}{\|x\| . \|y\|} \tag{9.1}$$

- Let θ be the set of all learning objects rated by S.
- Apply DBSCAN algorithm to cluster θ.
- For each O, y:
- Assume NO the closest cluster to O using cosine similarity as in Equation (9.1).
- Let M be the set of the top-n closest element to S in NS that have rated y using Pearson correlation.

$$P(x,y) = \frac{\Sigma_{i=1}^{n}(x_i - \bar{x})(y_i - \bar{y})}{\sqrt{\Sigma_{i=1}^{n}(x_i - \bar{x})^2}\sqrt{\Sigma_{i=1}^{n}(y_i - \bar{y})^2}} \tag{9.2}$$

- Let N be the set of the top-n closest element to x in N, O using Pearson correlation as in Equation (9.2).
- If $\|M\| = 0$ and $\|N\| > 0$, then calculate the predicted rating for y as in Equation (9.3).

$$r_1(S,y) = \frac{\Sigma_{l \in M} P(S,l) \times r(l,y)}{\Sigma_{u \in M} P(S,l)} \tag{9.3}$$

- Where $r_1(S,y)$ represents the predicted rating value of the learning object y for the active e-learner S. $P(S,l)$ implies the pearson correlation coefficient between to e-learner vectors S and l. $r(l,y)$ implies the actual rating of learning object by the e-learner l.
- $\|M\| > 0$ and $\|N\| = 0$, then calculate the predicted rating for y as in Equation (9.9.4).

$$r_3(S,y) = \frac{\Sigma_{l \in N} P(y,l) \times r(S,l)}{\Sigma_{l \in N} P(y,l)} \tag{9.4}$$

- Where $r_3(S,y)$ represents the predicted rating value of the learning object y for the active e-learner S. $P(y,l)$ implies the pearson correlation coefficient between the learning objects y and l. $r(S,l)$ implies the actual rating of learning object by the active e-learner S and l.
- If $\|M\| > 0$ and $\|N\| > 0$, then calculate the predicted rating for y as in Equation (9.5)

$$r(S,y) - \gamma \times r_1(S,y) + (1-\gamma) \times r_3(S,y) \tag{9.5}$$

- Where $r_1(S,y)$ and $r_3(S,y)$ represent the predicted rating value of the learning object y for the active e-learner S.
- $\|M\| = 0$ and $\|N\| = 0$, then calculate the predicted rating for y as in Equation (9.6).

$$r(S,y) = int(0.5 + P(S,l) \times 5) \tag{9.6}$$

- Where $r(S,y)$ represents the predicted rating value for the unrated learning object y for the active e-learner S. Recommend top-n highly rated Os.

9.3.4 Secure online evaluation platform

This section includes the system model, security model, and design goals. Assembling the system's model uses the consortium blockchain. Table 9.1 shows the six types of entities and the notations that go along with each of them.

Data suppliers must submit their data on or before the deadline set by the organization. Whether they are graduate students or professors, their data may eventually be available in an online environment. Students provide the

Table 9.1 Precision

K	K-means	AFC	DBSCAN
2	0.782	0.705	0.865
3	0.812	0.725	0.906
4	0.802	0.733	0.881
5	0.813	0.711	0.895
6	0.822	0.728	0.927
7	0.838	0.749	0.882
8	0.829	0.767	0.892
9	0.849	0.745	0.898
10	0.852	0.755	0.889

answers, while teachers provide the grades. Proof of authenticity is provided by storing ciphertext files on the blockchain. This system is equipped to respond to user requests for data. The requests come from a variety of sources, including students, teachers, and educational management organizations. The establishment and operation of blockchain nodes has been undertaken by a number of recognized organizations, In addition to educational administration divisions and educational alliances. A record of evidence relating to the data they publish is kept by them.

1. In a distributed storage system (DSS), encrypted data is kept safe and secure.
2. In addition to an online classroom and an exam, The proposed system features has a number of service interfaces.
3. Key distribution authorities (KA), registration authorities (RA), authentication authorities (AA), and educational administration (EA) departments are all examples of authorities.
4. Key distribution is handled by KAs following an investigation. AAs are responsible for verifying the identities of users when they log in. In the event of examination-related disputes or concerns, exam assistants (EAs) are the ones to turn to. There are three steps to the system's operation:

   i. During the registration procedure, data providers and data requesters set up their own fuzzy vaults in order to authenticate with an RA.
   ii. During the login process, the AA receives the user's face features. This passes authentication once the private polynomial is located in the vault.
   iii. During the data upload phase, EP receives information from a student. Cryptographic ciphertext from the answer sheet is saved

in a DSS, and the proof pieces are stored in the blockchain. The results are submitted in the same manner by a teacher. Through the EP, users can obtain ciphertext from a DSS and then decrypt it. The plaintext is obtained when their attributes fits the decryption policy. The EA combines data from a DSS and evidence on the blockchain to make a conclusion when there is a disagreement.

9.3.5 Formalization of the security model

When assessing dangers, it is critical to distinguish between internal and external threats. External attacks include eavesdropping, forgeries, and replay. It's possible that data requestors and data suppliers want access to information they don't have a right to. EPs may alter data for a variety of reasons, including financial gain, equipment malfunction, or managerial directive. The biometric templates used by an AA may allow an attacker to obtain a picture of a user's face.

Teachers' exam papers can only be utilized by their pupils for a limited period of time. Educators have the right to go through students' answers with their students. Teachers and EAs have access to their colleagues' exam scores. The regulations in effect when ciphertext providers generate their data can restrict access to their data.

Tamper resistance is required for online examination systems. Changes can only be made to data that has already been input into the computer system. This will have a negative impact on the educational system's impartiality if it is not implemented.

A multi-authority system has many advantages, including the elimination or decrease of a single point of failure [57]. For a variety of reasons, data is exchanged between organizations. Multiple authorities from different domains issue an attribute key to avoid a single point of failure and to enhance system security.

To decrypt a communication, two or more people will try to combine their own keys in order for the decryption. This is called collusion. According to the approach, the combined keys must fail to decrypt the correct plaintext.

When it comes to resolving disagreements, it is crucial to keep a watch out for people who are impersonating students or professors. Has the answer sheet been tampered with by an outside invader, a student, or an employee of the company?.. This results in the creation of a fuzzy vault as shown:

A polynomial with a degree lower than 1 can be obtained using algorithm 3. An estimation of the user's own face features is used in this scenario.

$$a = W^T * I. \tag{9.7}$$

Here, I is the vector corresponding to the user's face.

(1) Calculates the feature coding $\left(i, a^i, f(ai)\right)_{1 \le i \le t}$, where a_i is the ith dimension feature of a.
(2) Randomly generates r–t chaff points $\left(j\%t + 1, x_j, y_j\right)_{1 \le j \le r-t}$, which satisfy

$$\left\{\left(i, a_i\right)\right\}_{1 \le i \le t} \cap \left\{\left(j\%t + 1, x_j\right)\right\}_{1 \le i \le r-t} = \varnothing, y_j \ne f\left(x_j\right). \tag{9.8}$$

Here, r is the fuzzy vault size.
User scrambles the r points and then obtains the fuzzy vault.

$$V = \left\{\left(d, x_m, y_m\right)_{1 \le d \le t, 1 \le m \le r}\right\}. \tag{9.9}$$

where x_m is the dth dimension feature of the face space. The user sends V to the AA.

For each user, PKI also provides a private key pair (Private Key Prik and Public Key Pubk) in addition to a vault (V). The user's global identity and blockchain account address are referred to as Pubk. Attribute keys must be requested from the KAs by the user as well. If he is able to apply for the key of the attribute i the KA, which is accountable for the attribute i

$$(3) \text{ computesk}_{i,\text{Pubk}} = g^{\alpha^i} H\left(\text{Pubk}\right)^{y_i}. \tag{9.10}$$

and issues it to the user

9.4 PERFORMANCE ANALYSIS

The clustering accuracy was evaluated in terms of precision, recall, and the F-measure by conducting a performance analysis. DBSCAN's clustering algorithm is superior to K-means and other clustering algorithms in terms of accuracy. The experimental analysis was done for 100 students = studying computer science and engineering in University College of Engineering Tindivanam. MOODLE was used to construct an online course on 'Database Management Systems'. Each of the 30 subjects in the online course had a minimum of ten separate learning objects to illustrate it. The students were given the Index Learning Style questionnaire and from the answers given by the students, their learning style was evaluated and updated in the learners' profile database.

After enrolling on the course, the students accessed the course and rated the learning objects on a scale of 1–5 where 5 represents 'very useful' in their learning process and 1 is 'useless'. The ratings given by the students were updated in the learning object profile database. To cluster the e-learners learning style profile vector and learning object profile vector, the proposed work used DBSCAN clustering algorithm. The clustering accuracy was evaluated in terms of precision, recall and F-measure as given in Equations (9.11)–(9.13) and compared with the other existing works such as K-means and AFC.

$$\text{Precision} = \frac{\text{No. of relevant learning style } or \text{ } learning \text{ } objects \text{ } generated}{\text{Total no. of learning style } or \text{ } learning \text{ } objects} \quad (9.11)$$

$$\text{Recall} = \frac{\text{No. of relevant learning style } or \text{ } learning \text{ } objects \text{ } generated}{\text{Total no. of relevant learning style } or \text{ } learning \text{ } objects} \quad (9.12)$$

$$\text{F} - \text{measure} = 2 * \frac{\text{Precision} * \text{Recall}}{\text{Precision} + \text{Recall}} \quad (9.13)$$

The comparison between the DBSCAN and other clustering algorithms are shown in Table 9.1 for precision, Table 9.2 for recall and Table 9.3 for

Table 9.2 Recall

K	K-means	AFC	DBSCAN
2	0.785	0.652	0.884
3	0.779	0.673	0.867
4	0.782	0.668	0.877
5	0.852	0.695	0.885
6	0.868	0.685	0.892
7	0.867	0.675	0.901
8	0.861	0.662	0.941
9	0.876	0.682	0.945
10	0.877	0.695	0.942

Table 9.3 F-measure

K	K-means	AFC	DBSCAN
2	0.784	0.639	0.871
3	0.783	0.638	0.865
4	0.812	0.686	0.891
5	0.841	0.678	0.882
6	0.866	0.637	0.893
7	0.859	0.646	0.923
8	0.851	0.657	0.916
9	0.855	0.654	0.877
10	0.832	0.643	0.868

F-measure. The graphs shown in Figures 9.3–9.5 depict that the DBSCAN algorithm outperforms the other two clustering algorithms and hence it enhances the clustering accuracy.

After clustering the e-learners' learning styles and learning objects profile vector, a hybrid recommendation algorithm is applied to predict the rating of learning objects and recommend the top highly rated learning objects.

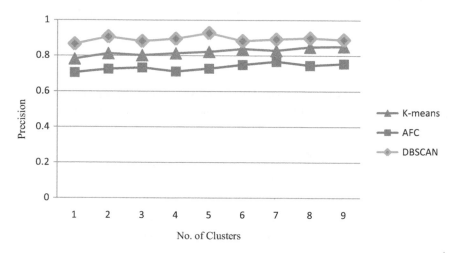

Figure 9.3 Precision.

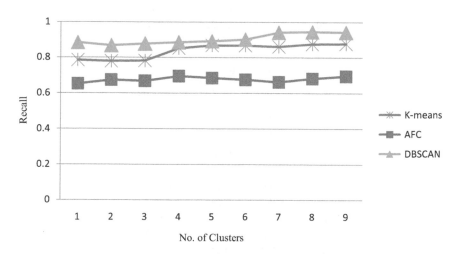

Figure 9.4 Recall.

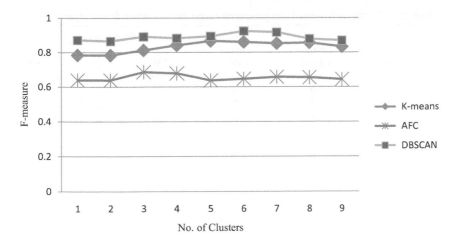

Figure 9.5 F-measure.

According to Equations (9.13) and (9.14), the accuracy of prediction is evaluated by comparing the results of mean absolute error (MAE) with the results of collaborative and content-based filtering (9.15) [25].

$$\text{MAE} = \frac{1}{n}\sum\nolimits_{i=1}^{n} |ar_i - pr_i| \tag{9.14}$$

$$\text{RMSE} = \sqrt{\frac{1}{n}\Sigma_{i=1}^{n}\left(ar_i - pr_i\right)^2} \tag{9.15}$$

Where, ar_i the learning object's actual e-learner rating and pr_i represents the e-expected learner's rating of the content.

Table 9.4 shows the anticipated rating of the proposed method compared to collaborative filtering and content-based recommendation algorithms. Figure 9.6. illustrates the accuracy of e-learner recommendation algorithms.

Table 9.4 Actual and predicted rating of recommendation algorithms

E-learner ID	Learning object ID	Actual rating	Predicted rating		
			CBF	CF	HF
I	I	2	I	2	2
2	2	4	3	3	4
3	3	2	2	3	2
4	4	5	2	3	5
5	5	2	3	3	2

(Continued)

Table 9.4 (Continued) Actual and predicted rating of recommendation algorithms

E-learner ID	Learning object ID	Actual rating	Predicted rating		
			CBF	CF	HF
6	6	3	2	2	3
7	7	2	2	2	2
8	8	4	4	4	4
9	9	4	2	2	4
10	10	5	4	4	4

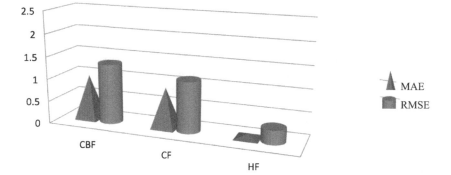

Figure 9.6 Accuracy of e-learner recommendation algorithms.

9.5 CONCLUSION

The proposed research work focused on improving the clustering accuracy by using DBSCAN clustering algorithm to cluster the e-learners' learning styles and learning objects vector. This accuracy in clustering helps in recommending the top highly rated learning objects to e-learners, thereby improving the performance of the e-learner in completing their course. When compared to collaborative and content-based filters, the suggested hybrid filtering recommendation performs better in predicting learning object ratings than the other two methods. We propose a decentralized, open, and unforgeable online examination system based on blockchain technology. In the proposed system, a blockchain network is established to securely preserve evidence of data uploads by a collection of organizations. A Data Security System (DSS) is used to store all encrypted data and no other organization is permitted to tamper with the uploaded data.

REFERENCES

1. Sosnovsky, S. and Brusilovsky, P. (2015). Evaluation of topic-based adaptation and student modeling in quiz guide. *User Modeling and User Adapted Interaction*, 25(4): 371–424.
2. Vu, P., Fredrickson, S., and Moore, C. (2016). *Handbook of Research on Innovative Pedagogies and Technologies for Online Learning in Higher Education*. IGI Global, Hershey, Pennsylvania.
3. Ghauth, K. I. and Abdullah, N. A. (2010). Learning materials recommendation using good learners' ratings and content-based filtering. *Educational Technology Research and Development*, 58(6): 711–727.
4. Bennane, A. et al. (2013). Adaptive educational software by applying reinforcement learning. *Informatics in Education-An International Journal*, 12(1): 13–27.
5. Bobadilla, J., Ortega, F., Hernando, A., and Gutierrez, A. (2013). Recommender systems survey. *Knowledge Based Systems*, 46: 109–132.
6. Adomavicius, G. and Tuzhilin, A. (2005). Toward the next generation of recommender systems: A survey of the state-of-the-art and possible extensions. *IEEE Transactions on Knowledge and Data Engineering*, 17(6): 734–749.
7. Linden, G., Smith, B., and York, J. (2003). Amazon.com recommendations: Item-to-item collaborative filtering. *IEEE Internet Computing*, 7(1): 76–80.
8. Li, W.-J. and Yeung, D.-Y. (2011) Social relations model for collaborative filtering. *Proceedings of AAAI Conference on Artificial Intelligence*, p. 1.
9. Burke, R. D. (2002). Hybrid recommender systems: Survey and experiments. *User Modeling and User Adapted Interaction*, 12(4): 331–370.
10. Barragans-Martınez, B., Costa-Montenegro, E., Burguillo-Rial, J. C., Rey-Lopez, M., Mikic-Fonte, F. A., and Peleteiro-Ramallo, A. (2010). A hybrid content-based and item-based collaborative filtering approach to recommend TV programs enhanced with singular value decomposition. *Information Sciences*, 180(22): 4290–4311.
11. Hu, Y., Koren, Y., and Volinsky, C. (2008). Collaborative filtering for implicit feedback datasets. *Proceedings of IEEE International Conference on Data Mining*, pp. 263–272.
12. Niesler, A. and Wydmuch, G. (2009). User profiling in intelligent tutoring systems based on myers-briggs personality types. *Proceedings of the International Multiconference of Engineers and Computer Scientists*, vol 1, pp. 18–20.
13. Nafea, S. M., Siewe, F., and He, Y. (2019). A novel algorithm for course learning object recommendation based on student learning styles. *2019 International Conference on Innovative Trends in Computer Engineering (ITCE)*, pp. 192–201.
14. Nafea, S. M., Siewe, F., and He, Y. (2018). Ulearn: Personalised learner's profile based on dynamic learning style questionnaire. *Proceedings of SAI Intelligent Systems Conference*, pp. 1105–1124.
15. Imran, H., Belghis-Zadeh, M., Chang, T.-W., and Graf, S. (2016). PLORS:Apersonalized learning object recommender system. *Vietnam Journal of Computer Science*, 3(1): 3–13.
16. El Bachari, E., Abelwahed, E. H., and El Adnani, M. (2012), An adaptive teaching strategy modeling in e learning using learners. *International Journal of Web Science*, 1: 257–274.

17. Klanja-Mili¢evi¢, A., Vesin, B., Ivanovi¢, M., and Budimac, Z. (2011). E-Learning personalization based on hybrid recommendation strategyand learning style identification. *Computers & Education*, 56(3): 885–899.
18. Lu, J. (2004). A personalized e-learning material recommender system. *Proceedings of the International Conference on Information Technology Application*. Sydney, NSW, Australia: Macquarie Scientific, pp. 374–379.
19. Patnaik, S. (2016). An efficient and scalable density-based clustering algorithm for normalize data. *2nd International Conference on Intelligent Computing, Communication & Convergence (ICCC-2016)*, pp. 136–141.
20. Nafea, S. M., Siewe, F., and He, Y. (2019). On recommendation of learning objects using Felder-Silverman learning style model. *IEEE Access*, 7: 163034–163048.
21. Karthika, R., Deborah, L. J., Vijayakumar, P., and Audithan, S. (2017). *Grouping Users for Quick Recommendations of Text Documents Based on Deep Neural Network*. Book Chapter, Springer International Publishing, Midtown Manhattan, New York City.
22. Deborah, L. J., Sathiyaseelan, R., Audithan, S., and Vijayakumar, P. (2015). Fuzzy-logic based learning style prediction in e-learning using web interface information. *Sadhana*, 40: 379–394.
23. Karthika, R., Jegatha Deborah, L., and Vijayakumar, P. 2020. Intelligent e-learning system based on fuzzy logic. *Neural Computer Applications*, 32(12): 7661–7670. doi: 10.1007/s00521-019-04087-y.
24. Deborah, J., Karthika, R., Vijayakumar, P., Rawal, B. S., and Wang, Y. 2019. Secure online examination system for e-learning. *2019 IEEE Canadian Conference of Electrical and Computer Engineering (CCECE)*, pp. 1–4. doi: 10.1109/CCECE43985.2019.9052408.
25. Gupta, B. B., Misra, M., and Joshi, R. C. (2012). An ISP level solution to combat DDoS attacks using combined statistical based approach. arXiv preprint arXiv:1203.2400.
26. Mishra, A., Gupta, B. B., and Joshi, R. C. (2011). A comparative study of distributed denial of service attacks, intrusion tolerance and mitigation techniques. *2011 European Intelligence and Security Informatics Conference*, pp. 286–289. IEEE.
27. Masud, M., Gaba, G. S., Alqahtani, S., Muhammad, G., Gupta, B. B., Kumar, P., and Ghoneim, A. (2020). A lightweight and robust secure key establishment protocol for internet of medical things in COVID-19 patients care. *IEEE Internet of Things Journal*, 8(21): 15694–15703.
28. Alweshah, M., Khalaileh, S. A., Gupta, B. B., Almomani, A., Hammouri, A. I., and Al-Betar, M. A. (2020). The monarch butterfly optimization algorithm for solving feature selection problems. *Neural Computing and Applications*, 34: 11267–11281.
29. Gupta, B. B., Joshi, R. C., and Misra, M. (2012). ANN based scheme to predict number of Zombies in a DDoS attack. *International Journal of Network Security*, 14(2): 61–70.
30. Mishra, A., Gupta, N., and Gupta, B. B. (2021). Defense mechanisms against DDoS attack based on entropy in SDN-cloud using POX controller. *Telecommunication Systems*, 77(1): 47–62.
31. Manasrah, A. M., Aldomi, A., and Gupta, B. B. (2019). An optimized service broker routing policy based on differential evolution algorithm in fog/cloud environment. *Cluster Computing*, 22(1): 1639–1653.

32. Gupta, B. B., Joshi, R. C., and Misra, M. (2009). Defending against distributed denial of service attacks: Issues and challenges. *Information Security Journal: A Global Perspective*, 18(5): 224–247.

33. Sahoo, S. R. and Gupta, B. B. (2021). Multiple features based approach for automatic fake news detection on social networks using deep learning. *Applied Soft Computing*, 100: 106983.

34. Ren, P., Xiao, Y., Chang, X., Huang, P. Y., Li, Z., Gupta, B. B., Chen, X., and Wang, X. (2021). A survey of deep active learning, *ACM Computing Surveys (CSUR)*, 54(9): 1–40.

35. Prathiba, S. B., Raja, G., Bashir, A. K., et al. (2021). SDN-assisted safety message dissemination framework for vehicular critical energy infrastructure. *IEEE Transactions on Industrial Informatics*, 18(5): 3510–3518.

36. Cvitić, I., Peraković, D., Gupta, B., and Choo, K. K. R. (2021). Boosting-based DDoS detection in internet of things systems. *IEEE Internet of Things Journal*, 9(3): 2109–2123.

37. Gupta, B. B., Li, K. C., Leung, V. C., Psannis, K. E., and Yamaguchi, S. (2021). Blockchain-assisted secure fine-grained searchable encryption for a cloud-based healthcare cyber-physical system. *IEEE/CAA Journal of Automatica Sinica*, 8(12): 1877–1890.

38. Zhou, Z., Gaurav, A., Gupta, B. B., Lytras, M. D., and Razzak, I. (2021). A fine-grained access control and security approach for intelligent vehicular transport in 6g communication system. *IEEE Transactions on Intelligent Transportation Systems*, 23(7): 9726–9735.

39. Kaur, M., Singh, D., Kumar, V., Gupta, B. B., and Abd El-Latif, A. A. (2021). Secure and energy efficient-based E-health care framework for green internet of things. *IEEE Transactions on Green Communications and Networking*, 5(3): 1223–1231.

40. Poonia, V., Goyal, M. K., Gupta, B. B., Gupta, A. K., Jha, S., and Das, J. (2021). Drought occurrence in different river basins of India and blockchain technology based framework for disaster management. *Journal of Cleaner Production*, 312: 127737.

41. Nguyen, G. N., Le Viet, N. H., Elhoseny, M., Shankar, K., Gupta, B. B., and Abd El-Latif, A. A. (2021). Secure blockchain enabled Cyber–physical systems in healthcare using deep belief network with ResNet model. *Journal of Parallel and Distributed Computing*, 153: 150–160.

42. Elgendy, I. A., Zhang, W. Z., He, H., Gupta, B. B., El-Latif, A., and Ahmed, A. (2021). Joint computation offloading and task caching for multi-user and multi-task MEC systems: Reinforcement learning-based algorithms. *Wireless Networks*, 27(3): 2023–2038.

43. Hammad, M., Alkinani, M. H., Gupta, B. B., El-Latif, A., and Ahmed, A. (2021). Myocardial infarction detection based on deep neural network on imbalanced data. *Multimedia Systems*, 28: 1373–1385.

44. Jian, S., Huijie, Y., Vijayakumar P., and Neeraj, K. 2021. A privacy-preserving and untraceable group data sharing scheme in cloud computing. *IEEE Transactions on Dependable and Secure Computing, IEEE*, 19(4): 2198–2210.

45. Xia, X., Ji, S., Vijayakumar, P., Shen, J., and Rodrigues, J. J. 2021. An efficient anonymous authentication and key agreement scheme with privacy-preserving for smart cities. *International Journal of Distributed Sensor Networks*, 17(6): 155014772110268.

46. Wang, C., Shen, J., Vijayakumar, P., Liu, Q., and Ji, S. 2021. Ultra-reliable secure data aggregation scheme with low latency for isolated terminals in 5G and beyond defined stins. *Computer Standards & Interfaces, North-Holland*, 77: 103512.
47. Lu, J., Shen, J., Vijayakumar, P., and Gupta, B. B. 2021. Blockchain-based secure data storage protocol for sensors in the industrial internet of things. *IEEE Transactions on Industrial Informatics*, 18(8): 5422–5431.
48. Yang, H., Shen, J., Zhou, T., Ji, S., and Vijayakumar, P. 2021. A flexible and privacy-preserving collaborative filtering scheme in cloud computing or VANETs. *ACM Transactions on Internet Technology (TOIT)*, 22(2): 1–19.
49. Wang, C., Shen, J., Vijayakumar, P., and Gupta, B. B. 2021. Attribute-based secure data aggregation for isolated IoT-enabled maritime transportation systems. *IEEE Transactions on Intelligent Transportation Systems*. doi: 10.1109/TITS.2021.3127436.
50. Zhiyan, X., He, D., Vijayakumar, P., Gupta, B., and Shen, J. 2021. Certificateless public auditing scheme with data privacy and dynamics in group user model of cloud-assisted medical WSNs. *IEEE Journal of Biomedical and Health Informatics*. doi: 10.1109/JBHI.2021.3128775.
51. Lee, M. T. and Suh, I. (2022). Understanding the effects of environment, social, and governance conduct on financial performance: Arguments for a process and integrated modelling approach. *Sustainable Technology and Entrepreneurship*, 1(1): 100004. doi: 10.1016/j.stae.2022.100004.
52. de Castro-Pardo, M., Fernández Martínez, P., and Pérez Zabaleta, A. (2022). An initial assessment of water security in Europe using a DEA approach. *Sustainable Technology and Entrepreneurship*, 1(1): 100002. doi: 10.1016/j.stae.2022.100002.
53. Bai, S. and Khoja, S. A. (2021). Hybrid query execution on linked data with complete results. *International Journal on Semantic Web and Information Systems (IJSWIS)*, 17(1): 25–49. doi: 10.4018/IJSWIS.2021010102.
54. Choi, J. and Lim, S. (2021). Interactive E-textbook platform based on block editing model in crowdsourcing E-learning environments. *International Journal on Semantic Web and Information Systems (IJSWIS)*, 17(1): 50–66. doi: 10.4018/IJSWIS.2021010103.
55. Cheng, Y., Zhang, X., Wang, X., Zhao, H., Yu, Y., Wang, X., and Ordoñez de Pablos, P. (2021). Rethinking the development of technology-enhanced learning and the role of cognitive computing. *International Journal on Semantic Web and Information Systems (IJSWIS)*, 17(1): 67–96. doi: 10.4018/IJSWIS.2021010104.
56. Tiwari, R. K. and Kumar, R. (2021). A robust and efficient MCDM-based framework for cloud service selection using modified TOPSIS. *International Journal of Cloud Applications and Computing (IJCAC)*, 11(1): 21–51. doi: 10.4018/IJCAC.2021010102.
57. Dwivedi, R. K., Kumar, R., and Buyya, R. (2021). Gaussian distribution-based machine learning scheme for anomaly detection in healthcare sensor cloud. *International Journal of Cloud Applications and Computing (IJCAC)*, 11(1): 52–72. doi: 10.4018/IJCAC.2021010103.

Chapter 10

Efficient key management and key distribution schemes for online learning

Fahmina Taranum

Muffakham Jah College of Engineering and Technology, Hyderabad, India

K.S. Niraja

BVRIT Hyderabad College of Engineering for Women, Hyderabad, India

CONTENTS

In the current situation of a pandemic, the trend of using an online mode of education has drasticallyrisen . The need to experiment with multiple presentation and meeting modes have led to exploration of multiple solutions for transmitting data in a fast and secured manner. The idea is to get good performance efficiency for data such as textual, audio or video, along with secured transmission. To make transmission secure some key management and distribution techniques can be deployed. The current solutions used to schedule online classes, video conferencing, online meetings, webinars, and screen or application-sharing includes Zoom, Google Meet,

DOI: 10.1201/9781003264538-10

Microsoft Teams, Cisco Webex, and Zoho Meeting. These enterprising solutions promise secure access using sharing links in a private mode with the participants or audience. The aim of this chapter is to discuss different possible solutions to make online teaching or learning mode more secure, by applying multiple key management strategies. The purpose of the proposal is to improve public awareness of key distribution schemes and make the online learning process secure and efficient.

10.1 INTRODUCTION

10.1.1 Standards

Issues with manual key management are that it can be time-consuming, expensive, and unreliable, as well as having a slow threat response, and being error prone. To reduce the impact of these challenges, the proposal is to work with non-manual approaches. Some standards are defined by the National Institute of Standards and Technology (NIST) to protect the keys used for encryption and decryption rather than working on protection of the algorithm. Compliance regulation bodies like the Pharmacy Council of India (PCI) provide Quality & Reliable safety instructions, while Global Experience for Indian Companies Doing Business (GDPR) in collaboration with Europe's union has defined new data privacy and security law for large business organizations around the world. Google and Facebook are included in this compliance. The Health Insurance Portability and Accountability Act (HIPAA) defines data protection for huge data storage like cloud services [1], for example Amazon web services. The California Consumer Privacy Act (CCPA) has also defined privacy rights for consumer security and protection. The Service Organization Control 2 (SOC2) is a demonstration based on the examiner standards board of the American Institute of Certified Public Accountants' (AICPA), which is used to observe the existing trust services and their compliance with measures for defending against cyberattacks and duplicating data.

10.1.2 Approaches

Trust principles followed by SOC2 certification include: integrity, confidentiality, availability, and privacy. These are the approaches used to manage online transmission in a secured and efficient manner. These approaches are depicted in Figure 10.1.

Security for disseminated data. Use some approaches to transmit data in a confidential way. Some supportive approaches include:

i. Providing public or private privileges to group members for transmitted data.
ii. Sharing data using links.

Creating groups like Google classroom or Zoom meetings to post the information.

Encryption
2-factor autentication
Access control

2-factor authentication
Intrusion detection
Firewall

Performance monitor
Disaster recovery
Security handling

Process monitoring
Quality assurance

Encryption
Access control
Application firewall

Figure 10.1 Stages of SOC2.

10.1.3 Learning

Learning can be made effective by using different parameters as listed below. The features that support online learning include:

i. Unlimited permission to access e-learning resources.
ii. Systematized content shared in varied modes.
iii. Open or privileged access to resources shared.
iv. Ease of evaluation of the exam with returned response option.
v. Option to generate .CSV file for huge sizes of data.
vi. Support for assessment tools like multiple choice, match the sentences, and others.
vii. Support to frame user defined formula to generate the required weighted score.
viii. Support to generate reports and data analytics.

10.1.4 Efficient learning approaches

Online training can be an efficient and productive way for professional engineers to complete their continuing education requirements while saving time and money. The system needs to be effective to provide learners with online classrooms or mobile access to classrooms to help them to access the material posted in the class, and allow the learners interact and acquire understanding in a collaborative atmosphere.

i. **How to study efficiently online**
   • Go with group study and share ideas.
   • Attend class and explore the content to extract more knowledge.

- Follow and concentrate on the planned schedule.
- Turn off distractions and rewind lectures to understand difficult concepts.
- Use books to explore more and justify the content.
- Maintain and manage time properly.
- Revise and explore the difficult content.
- Access your knowledge.

ii. **Understand online learning practices and target some expectations**
- Be committed to justify yourself to learned approaches.
- Be an active learner and communicate in virtual class.
- Work efficiently and perfectly.
- Be adaptive and technology savvy.
- Keep to targets to complete your assessment or assignments on time.
- Be sincere, hardworking, and self-disciplined.

iii. **Facilities and resources**
- Use a reliable and authentic internet connection.
- Keep a dedicated and separate space to study.
- Identify and target your learning motto, objectives, and goals.
- Construct a study plan and maintainproper management of the schedule.
- Be a learner and participate in online deliberations.
- Stay engaged and active.

iv. **Student-friendly approach to teaching**
- Read students' faces and gauge their understanding, followed by posting questions on topics covered.
- Complete assessments to know the learning capability and ability of students.
- Make your class interactive and take timely feedback to improve your sessions.
- Maintain synchronization in content delivery and teach the approaches using practical examples.
- Highlight important concepts by using expressions, examples, images, videos, or realistic solutions.

v. **Familiarity with remote teaching tools**
- Explore the tools, techniques, platforms, and strategies freely available for demonstrating online sessions and select the appropriate tool based on your requirements. Follow up by instructing the students with the working principles of the selected tool.

vi. **Using channels based on social media**
- Popularity and leverage on the session can be increased by using social media channels.

- For example: channels used to keep connected include Facebook, Twitter [5] LinkedIn, and WhatsApp, among others.
- Permit the creation of exclusive groups or communities among teachers.
- Communicate, share, and continue your presence after online class hours to clarify doubts.
- Share and stock important relevant information, presentations, notes, and resources related to lessons.
- Conduct group quizzes and assessments.
- Encourage students to maintain group interaction among themselves.
- Conduct live events such as seminars, webinars, and presentations using Facebook or Instagram Live.

10.2 FEEDBACK SYSTEM

To maintain a balanced and planned approach for teaching and learning, adapt the feedback system. Feedback can be conducted after completion of each chapter or content segment to measure the ability of the students to understand, and furthermore to help to identify candidates having difficulties. Special classes or attention must be given to overcome any difficulty experienced by students in understanding the concepts. To improve the learning atmosphere or ambience, a survey conducted on graduating students and alumni can be an added input, as depicted in Figure 10.2.

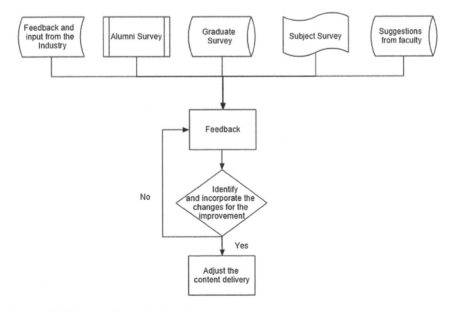

Figure 10.2 Inputs for a feedback system.

Reviews of planning concepts can be collected from other course coordinators teaching the same subjects. Some input from industry can be applied to make teaching improvements using some practical tools to target the future requirements.

10.3 E-LEARNING WITH DIGITAL EDUCATIONAL TOOLS

Due to the present pandemic situation, many approaches are being explored and experimented with to make learning easy and convenient. Difficulties that arise can be dealt with by utilizing practical approaches, with tools like Wacom, Jamboard, Whiteboard, and Geometry Pad Tool. Other tools used in e-learning include the following:

a. **Kahoot** is based on queries posted by the teacher after liaison to analyze learner level of understanding during any discussions, sessions or lessons conducted.

b. **Animoto** helps to create high-quality short videos using any gadget like a mobile device or ipad. These inspire students and assist in the delivery of academic lessons.

c. **Storybird** helps to communicate ideas using storytelling. A special graphical user interface is used by the instructor to interact in an artistic way, viz. using books online through a simple and easy interface.

d. **ClassDojo** is a tool used to improve student behavior by rewarding students with points for reacting and being receptive during the classes, and also by taking immediate feedback.

e. **cK-12** is a website with free e-learning resources or e-books to ease the financial burden of academic books for the students.

f. **TED-Ed** is an educational platform used by teachers, students, and animators to expand knowledge and share ideas in order to learn in collaborative manner

g. **Thinglink** allows educators to work with realism by creating an interactive image with audio and popping with texts and comments. This makes learning easy with websites or on social networks, such as Twitter and Facebook.

h. **Projeqt** is tool to design multimedia presentations, which helps in creating dynamic slides with embedded hyperlinks, videos, interactive maps, Twitter timelines, and audio material. Presentation are shared with the students to make learning easy and interesting. However, to avoid difficulty in playing the presentations they must be made adaptable to different gadgets.

i. **Socrative** is designed by a collection of entrepreneurs and engineers passionate about education and games used to create an interactive approach to education. Students solve problems using their gadgets and submit the responses on completion of the course.

j. **Edmodo** a tool disseminated on social media to connect learners and teachers. Teaching is delivered in groups and administered by super peers. An additional facility here is to post students' grades to their parent's email ids or contact numbers. This platform allows teachers and students to share and explore references and educational material.

10.4 FREE E-LEARNING COURSES

These are provided by government organizations like ATAL, NPTEL, SWAYAM, Coursera, and ALISON, among others. Free and paid learning academies include Udemy, edX, Udacity, LinkedIn Learning, General Assembly, and Skill Share, to name a few. NPTEL is an educational initiative, working in collaboration with IISc. Bangalore and 7 IITs (Bombay, Delhi, Guwahati, Kanpur, Kharagpur, Madras, and Roorkee) to encourage excellence in education through e-learning methods. ALISON has a wide range of free sample classes on knowledge, science, financial literacy, languages, and entrepreneurship as well as personal and soft skills. ATAL provides services to improve teaching skills by learning through faculty development programs based on new and emerging areas. Application of information and communication technology (ICT) helps to promote modern computing. Most countries are using ICT e-learning approaches in the current situation, so as to prevent students from being disadvantaged during the pandemic. With increasing demand and need for online classes to maintain social distance, the utilization of these supportive tools is rapidly escalating. The modern world is now adopting modern technology, which allows distance learning and helps to develop more efficient teaching methods.

10.5 PLANNING AND SCHEDULING A COURSE

Many of the courses currently available are commercial. Advertisements for them are created with great talent by experts to attract and sometimes mislead the crowd. Care must be taken to select a course which is both beneficial and economic. The learner must plan the course before starting to deliver it. Some examples to demonstrate this are listed in Figures 10.3 and 10.4. The parameters used to schedule a course must be set in advance, and monitoring the system on a timely basis helps to improve the performance. Figure 10.3 shows the week time on Y-axis and parameters of planning.

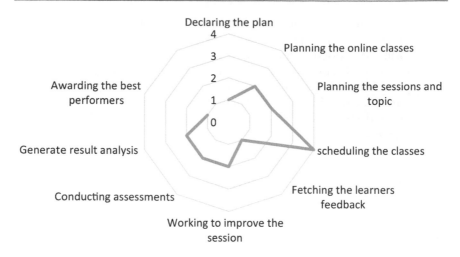

Figure 10.3 Planning a course.

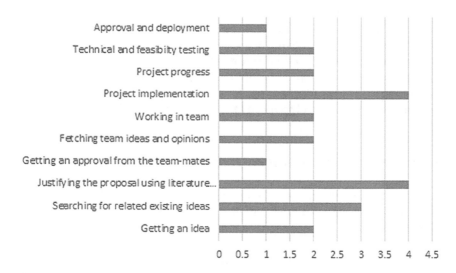

Figure 10.4 Planning a project.

Planning before the commencement of the semester for scheduling the classes should cover the content of the selected course. Some crucial things to do prior to the start of the semester are as follows.

  i. Prepare the teaching schedule, ideally spread over 12–13 weeks of classwork.
 ii. Place the teaching schedule.
iii. Order textbooks/reference books for the course.
 iv. Develop valid and reliable methods to evaluate course learning outcomes.
  v. Intimate the specific requirements for the course for attainment of the course outcomes.
 vi. Plan a project/mini project/ R & D project and submit details to the module coordinator as shown in Figure 10.5.

The following tasks should be completed preferably at the end of the semester:

  i. Administering student evaluation forms after completion of the course.
 ii. Carrying out assessments as per laid down norms and storing the information.
iii. Carrying out annual course review and providing written inputs for e-assessments for the learners.
 iv. Presenting an assessment of student capabilities and highlighting areas of possible learning difficulties.
  v. Providing appropriate introduction as necessary to the new staff involved in teaching the module.

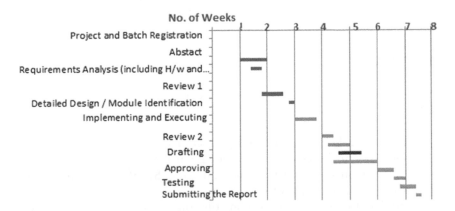

Figure 10.5 Rubrics for project evaluation.

vi. Reviewing and ratifying the teaching schedule, course outcomes, course files, lab manuals, and proposed teaching and assessment strategies.

vii. Addressing the classes and communicating clearly with the students about the relevance of the course.

viii. Providing the students with the expected application of the knowledge and skills gained throughout the module.

ix. Briefing the students about opportunities for employment and higher studies, in diverse areas of the course.

x. Monitoring the coverage of the course.

xi. Obtaining oral feedback from students to ascertain the strengths and weaknesses of the teaching team vis. a vis. appropriateness of course material and attainment of course concepts.

xii. Devising and implementing suitable strategies to overcome shortcomings in the delivery of the courses.

xiii. Reviewing assignments and other planned activities for attainment of course outcomes.

xiv. Reviewing pedagogical initiatives by course coordinators: Formative assessment is assigned constantly throughout the course using tutorials, quizzes, classroom problem solving, class tests, group assignments, university examinations, laboratory records, regular experiment performance, laboratory class tests, and laboratory viva voce. Summative assessment is a comprehensive evaluation conducted at the end of the course.

10.6 CHALLENGES

You will face challenges. Successful online learning demands a different set of skills than traditional classroom environments, with the added challenge of not sharing the same space with your students.

10.7 TOOLS

The following tools may be used to facilitate technological aspects in e-learning:

a. Bookmark helps resources for your course.

b. Do not fear the Google search engine: it is very unlikely you are the first person to face a technological issue. See if others online have shared or resolved your issue.

c. Find a "buddy," either someone on your course or in your life who can be a reliable source of support, both technical and personal.

d. Training programs or academic courses. Perhaps consider sitting in a classroom or lecture hall with fellow students, listening to an instructor.

10.8 ONLINE LEARNING – PROS AND CONS

Benefits of online learning include sessions that can be attended from anywhere, and study time that is flexible. Online learning is getting more and more popular, and for good reason.

There are also some drawbacks with online learning, such as students having more freedom, more distractions, and less contact with their peers.

10.9 FIVE KEY SUCCESS FACTORS FOR ONLINE STUDYING

All in all, there seem to be five key success factors with regard to online studying. These are cognitive factors, social factors, the role of the instructor, self-regulated learning skills, and the platform's ease of use.

10.10 TIPS TO ENGAGE LEARNERS FOR ONLINE AND HYBRID EDUCATION

Strategy 1: Offer open choices for accepting participation from learners, using planning with registrations
   a. Promoting collaborative documentation with in-depth exploration from all group members.
   b. Polling to collect the responses and feedback for evaluating the learner's capability and improving the delivery strategies.
   c. Creating forums to deal with queries.

Strategy 2: Use noticeable intellectual themes and protocols to organize interactions
   a. Self-governing reflection: Encourage cognitive and goal setting approaches.
   b. Facilitate connection among students to interact and share their ideas.
   c. Conduct group evaluation by assigning work in groups.

Strategy 3: Raise opinions and expressions through presentations of learning
   a. Showcase the exhibits to audience.
   b. Share and plan an improvement using a feedback system.

    c. Be positive to the input collected from learners and work on that to improve the delivery mechanisms.

10.11 SIX WAYS TO MOVE BEYOND CLASS WORK

    a. Be open and adaptive to change.
    b. Be open to learning and improving.
    c. Be realistic and practical.
    d. Rethink and interpret the role of content,
    e. Devise careful planning with intention.
    f. Be clear and precise.
    g. Be interactive.

10.12 PANDEMIC WITH INTELLIGENT E-LEARNING REQUIREMENT

The COVID-19 pandemic has raised requirements for online e-learning. The whole world is struggling to fight the pandemic and, simultaneously, experimentation in using new devices or electronic gadgets to facilitate e-learning continues. This emergency has trained people to use the latest technologies integrated with many secure, intelligent, and fuzzy-logic-based systems. In one example, the facility in Google Classroom to conduct a quiz with Google Forms helps the instructor and reduces the work of evaluation to a large extent as it is auto-calculated based on the key provided while setting the quiz.

10.13 LITERATURE SURVEY

The study of the approaches used has been made with available research on these strategies. The authors have demonstrated analysis of the effects of COVID-19 and the need to pursue online modes of education, along with their adverse effects. The website listed in [3] gives more details of the advantages and disadvantages of online learning. The final conclusion is a comparison of physical and virtual classrooms. In [2] the perspective of the author is to highlight the problems in covid and few suggestions to help students to study in the pandemic.

The study in [4] explores the use of electronic learning in some Egyptian universities. The aim was to use latest technologies and multimedia techniques to make online learning effective.

This article [6] highlights the demands and requirements of online learning in a pandemic that has lasted for over two years. Innovative and pedagogical approaches are used to strengthen the teaching.

The effectiveness of e-learning is justified by the author, who has used review papers to show the effectiveness of e-learning in this article [7].

Article [8] discusses using the latest technologies to improve the application of e-learning approaches in higher studies.

The purpose of the author in [9] is to suggest some blended techniques to make e-learning effective. An analysis is made in [10] by the authors, using both qualitative and quantitative studies in an integrative study used for evaluating the outcomes of correspondent learning in nursing education.

Several reviews and studies are considered as meta-studies on the effectiveness of e-learning using quantitates approaches in [11].

The authors in [12] have tried to distinguish the pros and cons of face-to-face learning. New initiatives in approaches to electronic learning are highlighted.

10.14 CONCLUSIONS

Even though the demand for online education has been high in this present situation of the COVID-19 pandemic, and many strategies have been designed and adopted, it can never replace all of the benefits of physical education. The debate is still open with regard to the pros and cons of physical and virtual classrooms. The advances in technology invented to cater to the customer's need, starting with the link-sharing approach to schedule a Google or Zoom meeting, have helped to maintain secured systems. However, the point-to-point and easy communication of the physical classroom management remains always efficient.

REFERENCES

1. Gaurav, A., Psannis, K., and Peraković, D. (2022). Security of cloud-based medical internet of things (MIoTs): A survey. *International Journal of Software Science and Computational Intelligence (IJSSCI)*, 14(1), pp. 1–16, 2022.
2. Khalid, M., Taranum, F., Nikhat, R., Farooqi, M. R., and Arshad Khan, M. (2022). Automatic real-time medical mask detection using deep learning to fight COVID-19. *Computer Systems Science and Engineering*, 42(3), pp. 1181–1198.
3. https://elearningindustry.com/mobile-learning-advantages-disadvantages.
4. El-Seoud, S. A., Taj-Eddin, I. A. T. F., Seddiek, N., Mohamed, M., and Nosseir, A. E-learning and students' motivation: A research study on the effect of e-learning on higher education, M. University in Egypt. *International Journal of Emerging Technologies in Learning*, 9(4), pp. 20–26. doi: 10.3991/ijet. v9i4.3465
5. Sahoo, S. R. and Gupta, B. B. (2019). Hybrid approach for detection of malicious profiles in twitter. *Computers & Electrical Engineering*, 76, pp. 65–81.

6. Dhawan, S. (2020). Online learning: A panacea in the time of COVID-19 crisis. *Journal of Educational Technology Systems*, 49(1), pp. 5–22, 2020.
7. Noesgaard, S. S. and Ørngreen, R. (2015). An explorative and integrative review of the definitions, methodologies and factors that promote e-learning effectiveness. *The Electronic Journal of e-Learning*, 13(4), pp. 278–290.
8. El-Seoud, S., Seddiek, N., Taj-Eddin, I., Ghenghesh, P., and ElKhouly, M. (2013). The effect of E-learning on learner's motivation: A case study on evaluating E-learning and its effect on Egyptian higher education, *The International Conference on E-Learning in the Workplace 2013* New York, NY, USA, ISBN: 978-0-9827670-3-0.
9. Means, B., Toyama, Y., Murphy, R., and Baki, M. (2013). The effectiveness of online and blended learning: A meta-analysis of the empirical literature. *Teachers College Record*, 115(3). doi: 10.1177/01614681131150030.
10. Patterson, B. J., Krouse, A. M., and Roy L. (2012). Student outcomes of distance learning in nursing education: An integrative review. *Computers, Informatics, Nursing*, 30(9), pp. 475–488.
11. Veneri, D. (2011). The role and effectiveness of computer-assisted learning in physical therapy education: A systematic review. *Physiotherapy Theory and Practice*, 27(4), pp. 287–298.
12. Maloney, S., Haas, R., Keating, J. L., Molloy, E., Jolly, B., Sims, J., Morgan, P., and Haines, T. (2012). Effectiveness of web-based versus face-to-face delivery of education in prescription of falls-prevention exercise to health professionals: Randomized trial. *Journal of Medical Internet Research*, 13(4), doi: 10.2196/jmir.1680.

Chapter 11

Secure virtual learning using blockchain technology

K.R. Karthick and J. Satheeshkumar

Anna University Regional Campus Madurai, Keelakuilkudi, Madurai, India

CONTENTS

A blockchain is a data structure composed of sequential blocks of data. It is characterized by its modularity, dependability, data sharing, security, and other features. It's been used in a wide range of fields, including digital currency, smart contracts, credit encryption, and so on. Due to the obvious advancement of internet technology, virtual learning, a novel educational modality, has risen in popularity. Educators' data protection is still of concern in this educational format, as is the credibility of the courses, and as are credit and credential authenticity. This article highlights the major technological

DOI: 10.1201/9781003264538-11

ideas and functionality of blockchain technology, drawing on recent literature and case studies, and recommends a blockchain-based remedy to virtual academia's problems. Learning records can be spread and trusted, digital certificates can be trusted, smart contracts can be used to share learning resources, and data encryption can be deployed to conform with intellectual property laws. Incorporating blockchain technology into the growth of online education, according to the research, is a promising trend.

11.1 INTRODUCTION

Online education has grown considerably since the turn of the century as a result of the rapid development of internet technology. Use of the internet to educate and learn quickly by exploiting data and information and web-based technologies is known as online learning. Students have access to high-quality teaching activities whenever and wherever they want, thanks to using the internet as a medium.

Online education can be broken down into a variety of categories, such as: occupational training, assessment and certification training, personal skills acquisition, curriculum, education programs, and elementary and high school education (kindergarten through 12th grade). These are all significant characteristics of education. New Oriental, Xuersi, and Hujiang are traditional education firms. Online education platforms are cropping up all across China with the support of players like traditional internet giants Net Ease and Tencent. Massive open online courses (MOOCs) have also received a lot of attention recently.

Massive open online courses (MOOCs) have their roots in the United States and companies like Coursera, Udacity, and edX have facilitated their development [4]. Since 2012, a number of major American universities have started offering free online courses. MOOCs, which are geared toward higher education, are distinguished by their high-quality instructional design and lack of central administration. Although online education is extremely popular, the current forms and systems have many flaws when compared to a digital internet that is becoming increasingly free and open. For example, official accreditation and public acknowledgement are lacking for the learning process and outcomes of MOOCs. To elaborate, because lectures and information protection are entirely reliant on learners, intellectual property cannot be effectively safeguarded on a unified virtual learning platform; the Web is open, and data might well be manipulated, and no sophisticated cross-platform technique exists for adequate sharing of curriculum materials. To ensure that formative assessments and results are authentic, a distributed and reliable data storage technique that tracks students' progress makes all learning data publicly available, and in order to ensure data security [6] non-tamperability must be developed. A wide range of online education-related challenges, including poor certification, lack of recognition, and insecure data, could be addressed with the implementation of blockchain technology. As of right now, financial services, the internet, and the Internet of Things (IoT) all employ this technology. Wallet, liquidity exchange, trade, and e-cash are all standard accounting solutions. Agreements that are really productive ranging from equities and stocks to bank lending, can be enforced electronically without any need for interpersonal interactions.

- This technology has also been utilized in the educational area, but only as a test case. For example, Mike Sharple's idea of creating a "knowledge currency" using the blockchain to store educational data.
- According to some studies, possible applications of blockchain include credit or debit card authorization, secure data encoding, and shared storage devices.
- Blockchain-based and Mozilla's accessible credential, the MIT Lab developed a digital learning certification method.
- Blockchain technology has also been deployed for designing products in the manufacturing industry. Sony Academy is an organization that specializes in education.
- Sony Corporation in Japan has designed a blockchain infrastructure system that allows open and safe sharing of online programs and data without exposing them to the education management authorities, therefore attaining education's fairness and digitalization. The University of London's financial risk management postgraduates can employ blockchain technology to validate the veracity of their educational credentials.
- Therefore, the key features of blockchain technology, as well as its deployment to online learning, are explored in this research with the purpose of building a safe online learning environment that is both open and reliable. Because of the findings of the study, the decentralizing of online education becomes a truth.

11.2 OVERVIEW OF BLOCKCHAIN TECHNOLOGY

In his dissertation "BTC: A Peer-to-Peer Electronic Cash System," a person using the identity Satoshi Nakamoto pioneered the idea of blockchain in 2008. Nakamoto [1] did not mention a blockchain in his work, despite the fact that he suggested the bitcoin system in this article. Instead, the data structures that preserve the history of the bitcoin ledger of transactions are referred to as the block and chain. A "block" is a unit of distributed data, whereas a "chain" is a temporal sequence of blocks structured using encryption primitives. When a block and a chain are combined, they constitute a kind of ledger of transactions. In a broader sense, blockchain technology refers to distributed accounting methods that utilize distributed consensus on the blockchain, agreements, privacy and confidentiality parameters, mentoring (peer-to-peer) transmission, and mentor (peer-to-peer) communication are all enhanced. In order to use blockchain technology, you

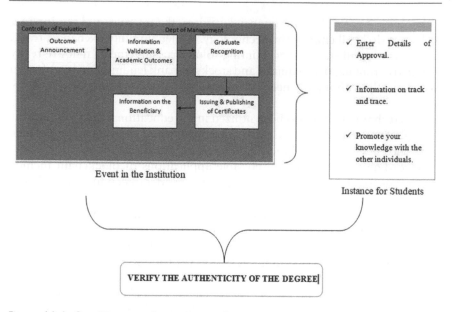

Figure 11.1 Certificate authenticity verification.

need to understand three basic concepts: transactions, blocks, and chains. When an item is added or removed from the ledger, the transaction status changes. The unit keeps track of the success rates of all operations all through their duration. The chain is a collection of blocks that represents all changes in the ledger state in a chronological order. The following describes how blockchain technology is implemented. To begin, the network requires a distributed ledger that only allows new data to be added. As a consequence, no data can be erased from the ledger, and the data remains unchanged. As shown in Figure 11.1, a series of blocks is established, with each block keeping the Checksum of something from it. For each new ledger entry, the entire system will keep a record, and link it to the chain using cryptography's elliptic curve digital signature algorithm (ECDSA). Thus, the information is impenetrable in the event of forgery. Data on all transactions is being broadcast and confirmed by all networks nodes at the same time, making it impossible to delete. As a result, blockchain technology has a distributed, decentralized data storage structure. Through the use of cryptographic algorithms, this technology assures that the data connected with every transaction cannot be changed and can be traced back to its source. The dispersed data storage and communal maintenance of the network preserve the network's distributed and decentralized character. In comparison to centralized databases, where an assault on a single node can have a significant impact on the entire network, blockchain technology reduces the possibility of data loss. There are many advantages for using blockchain technology over other methods like centralization and trust, as listed below.

It is decentralized: It is not necessary to have a central node to monitor it; because the blockchain is based on a modular, global network, it can store metadata. The trust system allows network nodes to exchange data directly, which increases the efficiency of data exchange. Meanwhile, even if one node is destroyed, the data on the entire network will remain unaffected.

De-trusted: Based on a checksum value, a chained block is created and then it uses an asymmetric digital signature to ensure transaction security [7], using the digital signature generated by the blockchain. No third-party oversight is required, so the nodes can safely conduct transactions.

Reliable: As a result of the blockchain database's distributed storage model, each node has a copy of all transaction data. This mode of storage guards against data corruption. Furthermore, all transaction data is recorded using timestamps and can be traced back to its original location, proving that the data has not been tampered with.

Collectively maintained: All nodes in the network contribute to the maintenance of the blockchain data. When a node fails, the entire network suffers because it is not included in the maintenance.

Privacy safe: It's possible to send data using a digital signature algorithm without disclosing the identity of any nodes. In the transmission process, the user is completely unnoticeable. The blockchain technology offers an ideal solution to the issues with online education because of its high credibility and security. In particular, the blockchain can provide non-tamperable and extensive teaching documentation for virtual classrooms without the requirement for third-party scrutiny, and ensure that course credits are awarded equitably. Additionally, smart contracts can assist educators by enhancing the efficiency of course sharing.

11.3 FIVE THINGS ABOUT BLOCKCHAIN TECHNOLOGY

Don't call it "the" blockchain

First ever thing to understand about blockchains is that there are many different types. Blockchains are global accounting systems of transactions that are autonomous and unchangeable. Blockchains are most commonly used to manage bitcoin events, but they are also used to track lending, financial rewards, agreements, health information, and even suffrage [2].

Security, transparency: the network's run by us

A blockchain system does not have a centralized authority. Peer-to-peer networks let computers trade regarding inclusion in the digital ledger, and events should be verified. Every node in the chain has a ledger of transactions and may rely on the authenticity of the signatures on other nodes copies. They add new blocks of data to the chain after wrapping up the most recent transactions [2]. A computer model "HASH" of the current block as well as the previous block in the chain is included in each block along with the transaction data. Hashes or digests are short digital representations of big amounts of data. Remodeling or fabricating a transaction in a previous block would change its hash, necessitating all following blocks' hashes to be recalculated to hide the change. It would be incredibly difficult to do this until all of the honest actors had contributed new, valid transactions to the chain's terminus.

Big business is taking an interest in blockchain technology

Initially, anti-establishment graphs wanting autonomy from central supervision were mentioned in blockchain technology [2], but it's quickly becoming part of the establishment.

No third party in between

There is no need for an intermediary or a third-party agency in a blockchain system because the computers that comprise it contribute to and guarantee the ledger's integrity in contributing to its content. The new tech is attracting lenders and commodity exchanges because of this, but it's also becoming a hindrance as the volume of traffic increases [2]. The number of BTC transactions last month on the 500 largest quantum computers in the world was so high that the infrastructure took up to 30 minutes to certify that some of them had been entered in the database, due to the fact that BTC mining is claimed to have more computing power than the combined processing speed of all other forms of payment.

Programmable money

Blockchains can be used to store a record of what should happen in the future, rather than what has already occurred. Companies like the Ethereum Foundation use blockchain for storing and processing technology "smart contracts" that are executed on a pay-per-use basis by the blockchain network's participating computers [2]. It may respond to transactions by collecting, holding, or sending data or by transmitting the blockchain's virtual money, as needed. The blockchain that stores the contracts ensures their immutability.

11.4 APPLICATION OF BLOCKCHAIN TECHNOLOGY IN ONLINE EDUCATION

Like we said earlier, the blockchain's technical features can help us come up with new ideas for improving online education. The following aspects of online education are targeted by this chapter's implementation of blockchain technology.

11.4.1 Full record of learning trajectory

Using a distributed database and timestamps, the blockchain keeps track of the order in which data blocks were added to the chain over time. It's impossible to remove newly created data blocks. To make fraud more difficult, the cryptographic algorithm is used to protect data from tampering. The majority of online education platforms are currently decentralized, resulting in a wide range of course options of varying quality. What's more, because there's no centralized certification system, the learning outcomes aren't recognized by the general public. Online education, unsurprisingly, has failed to produce positive results. The blockchain's chronological data recording is an excellent method for documenting online education students' progress.

Educational information such as academic tasks, assignment materials, and exam scores can be saved chronologically on the blockchain, with each record being time stamped. Data accuracy is ensured by using tools to effectively record approach, which removes threats such as manipulation and deletion. Because of the blockchain's openness, data dictionary, and collaborative maintenance, academic systems and organization would be able to track students' knowledge routes across regions and duration. As a result, the system will run smoothly and efficiently, with low operational costs. The learning data of educators is well-documented, and blockchain-based learning record prevents manipulation and deletion, ensuring that pupil's educational data is accurate. Simultaneously, encrypted learning data may be disseminated across the network and simply accessed by the organization, confirming its accuracy. Based on blockchain filament information, the organization can learn more about the students' understanding level and authenticate their metadata. As a result, blockchain technology may effectively combat academic credential theft and other forms of academic dishonesty, as well as create a reliable forum, educational systems, and academics.

11.4.2 Certification of academic results that may be trusted

Even after completing a few courses, students are unenthusiastic about online education platforms since the learning outcomes are neither officially acknowledged nor formally approved. This can be attributed to the fact that certification of learning outcomes has been slow to come about. Third-party agencies currently conduct online education certification inefficiently. This mode of operation will be insufficient in the future due to the expected growth of online education. For students who are looking for work, the certificates they have earned can be found in the student's education platform or school, where they can be checked by potential employers. However, blockchain technology offers a solution that is both quick and intuitive for scholastic accreditation, in particular, a form of certified of learning outcomes. Even if students' certificates are misplaced, they can still be verified. Cryptography on the blockchain uses an asymmetric encryption algorithm to protect the integrity of the data. It is possible to design a system of certification for learning outcomes based on this premise. For starters, using blockchain technology, student learning data is recorded by the online education platform or issuing organization, including their basic contact and academic information (such as grades and course information), on a central database. This involves using the platform or organization's private key to encrypt the data. The pupils and other network users are subsequently given the encrypted digital certificates. If this is the case, the employer can undertake Checksum validation on the digital certificates using the site or company's key pair.

11.4.3 Educational information is distributed in a distributed mode

There are numerous online education platforms currently available that offer a variety of courses with comprehensive curricula. Regrettably, due to limitations such as instructional mode, trademark, as well as other criteria, the courses are not universally accessible across platforms. The user experience for people taking various sorts of courses is unsatisfactory since they must log into many platforms. Similarly, collegiate education finds it challenging to study information from other universities or disciplines. Many advanced course contents are squandered due to a lack of unified and optimal exploitation. With the rise of collaborative consumption (for example, shared bikes), society is screaming for more optimizing of resources. The future of educational growth is an indication of resource sharing. Online instructors can exchange resources thanks to the usage of blockchain technology. A consensus mechanism is a software system built on top of a cryptographic security measure, and this is how most individuals use blockchain technology. It is capable of completing complex transaction operations without the involvement of a human. In addition, the system allows for the execution and verification of programs automatically. The transaction process can be expedited, digitized, and distributed using smart contract technology, all while improving transaction security.

A smart contract paves the way for the creation of a massive online educational resource sharing platform. The online education platform can efficiently and accurately complete course purchase, settlement, and acceptance on the basis of smart contracts without incurring any labor charges. Students can access the resources of different platforms by just logging into one node in the blockchain network, thanks to blockchain's shared memory and communal administration. Data security is ensured because even if individual nodes are damaged in an attack, the education resource data will remain valid. Additionally, employing blockchain technology, widespread data systems such as Wiki, R&D institutions, academic journals, and other tutorials may be consolidated to the blockchain network, resulting in a worldwide knowledge base. These knowledge resources are available to all blockchain nodes. This makes learning much more efficient and adds a lot to the learning materials.

11.5 ACADEMIC ISSUES AROUND THE WORLD

Most industrialized nations place a high value on education as a means of growth, which is why they devote considerable time and resources to it. This is due to the fact that advancement in any field is dependent on education. Despite recent advances in technology and its benefits to education, the development of human resources through learning still has to be a priority. It's important for researchers to pay attention to the following topics in education.

Abuse of educational degrees
First and foremost in education is the detection of false educational qualifications and degrees. According to an internet report, for as little as $4,000, fraudulent degrees are being offered in Malaysia. Another report states that one out of every twenty potential job hopefuls in Malaysia has a forged degree. Other sources also highlight this issue currently in Malaysia. All of the evidence points to this as a pressing issue in educational reform that must be addressed immediately. As is customary, many businesses ask that a candidate submit official documentation of their academic accomplishments before they may be considered for a position or additional education opportunities. Although this does not completely eliminate fraud, it greatly minimizes the likelihood of it occurring. Credential verification can be time- and money- consuming for both academic institutions and private sector employers. Because of this, it is a major issue in education.

Incapability of learners to choose an appropriate profession
Additionally, students are often unable to determine the right job route for themselves. Students social, economic, and mental well-being suffer when they are unable to make an informed decision about their academic major. For individuals who make poor decisions, this will not only have a negative influence on them, but will also have a negative impact on the quality of their work. The absence of high-quality labor is a hindrance to social progress. Students need to know how to select the right option when it comes to their future education.

Learners from non-homogeneous teams
Some pupils have a higher IQ and are able to understand the topics presented effortlessly. However, there is a group of pupils that aren't as quick to grasp new concepts. For teachers and facilitators, dealing with a classroom full of students with a wide range of cognitive capacities can be particularly taxing.

Illegal online distribution of academic content infringing copyright
When it comes to academia, plagiarism has become a most pressing issue. Online dissemination of copyrighted material is simple. This results in copyright infringement and puts an individual's intellectual property at risk.

11.6 TRANSITION LEARNING USING BLOCKCHAIN POSSIBILITIES

Numerous educational issues can be addressed using the blockchain's tracing and tracking capabilities. Education difficulties that were described in Section 11.4 are further addressed in this section [3].

11.6.1 Decentralized degree verification system

A blockchain-based verification method can be used to combat the threat of fake degree fraud. The system will include a barcode or QR code that can be scanned by stakeholders to obtain information about the degree. Academic transcripts [3], as well as their issuer and date of issue will be included in this information. Additionally, it will save higher education authorities time and money by eliminating the need to perform degree verification. Aside from that, the system will safeguard a candidate's academic qualifications. The degree holder won't have to worry about losing the original document. Individuals can also utilize this method to complete various types of short courses and educational certifications. In Figure 11.1 below, a potential model for such a system may be seen, as depicted from the viewpoints of various stakeholders such as students, employers, and accreditors.

11.6.2 Assisting students in keeping track of their academic progress

There are numerous advantages to storing student performance on a blockchain. Tracking student progress from Montessori to high school will aid data analytics in determining the areas in which a student has excelled and where they have struggled. As a result, this will assist students and their families better understand their potential [3]. In every industry, the number of successful professionals will rise as more students choose career choices based on their IQ. All sectors of society will benefit from this rise in production. Furthermore, teachers and pioneers will be able to classify individuals into classes and activities according to their talents as a result of the analysis. An improved and more competent learning environment can be achieved by grouping pupils according to their ability. If you're interested in a system like this, see Figure 11.2.

11.6.3 Computer program for managing intellectual property rights

It is possible to limit the spread of copyrighted information on the internet using blockchain technology. Secure storing of data in a chain is a primary purpose of this technology. Consequently, the chain's data cannot

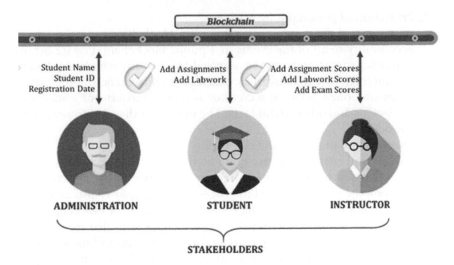

Figure 11.2 Blockchain based stakeholders communication.

be tampered with, as it is protected by powerful encryption techniques. Academic resources will be available, but they will be safe and unalterable thanks to this technology. Access to content can be readily restricted by the owner thanks to a chain of events tracking every use. Tracking usage and proving ownership are both simple tasks that may be done online.

11.7 DISCOURSE AND CHALLENGES OF BLOCKCHAIN INTEGRATION IN EDUCATION

When it comes to improving public education, the use of blockchain technology offers a lot of promise [3]. The foundation of any nation's progress is a well-funded and widely available educational system. Thus, as mentioned in this chapter, blockchain networks have the potential to increase everyone's access to quality education and related activities. Even though blockchain technology has the potential to transform education, there are a number of hurdles that must be overcome before the technology can be implemented [3]. These difficulties include but are not confined to:

1. Modifications to student records
   The data on the blockchain is immutable by design, meaning that once it is on the chain, it cannot be changed. Immutability is a double-edged sword when it comes to the implementation of blockchain in the education sector. As a result, students may not be able to change their educational records for legitimate reasons.

2. Protection of personal information

A centralized database implies that all a blockchain's members have accessibility to all of the events in a public blockchain. Private details and college transcripts can be accessed by anybody who has access to the internet. This creates privacy issues for consumers. Another effect of missing one's personal secret key is one can assert one's academic credentials and other useful facts. The gravity of this situation must be considered.

3. Phenomenon of scaling and complexity

Storage and energy costs are quite high for most blockchains because the full blockchain must be stored on each node in the network and the compute power required to process cryptography is also extremely high. In addition to increasing the scalability issue of blockchain networks, storing large amounts of student data will also increase the price. Computational complexity is also a significant technical impediment. As an example, the conventional solid evidence consensus protocol wastes energy and has low transaction speed, reducing the availability for use in public universities where it would incur extra costs.

11.8 VARIOUS OTHER USES OF BLOCKCHAIN TECHNOLOGY

11.8.1 Ethereum

Bitcoin and other crypto currencies have become a popular application area for the blockchain. Diverse digital currencies have risen to prominence since the first carrier bitcoin was created. An incredible $6,300 per BTC is currently the value of bitcoin because of its privacy and verifiability, as well as decentralization and consensus procedures. Some newer coins have also developed, and they now make up the current flourishing crypto currency industry. Blockchains for smart contracts, such as Ethereum [2] have been around for a few years now. As contracts evolve, blockchain technology can be deployed to a larger range of business scenarios such as contract processing and ownership changes. In addition to crypto currencies, the blockchain is increasingly employed in financial services, such as stock exchanges, cross-border payments, repurchase agreements, and digital identities [2].

Consequently, blockchain applications are more vulnerable to assault than traditional financial institutions. There is also a privacy feature built into the blockchain. Data is traditionally stored on a central server, and the system operator is responsible for ensuring the security of that data. Data in blockchain-based apps is available to all participants and can be restored to a previous state at any time. For financial institutions, even though "pseudo-anonymity" exists in blockchains in some financial business situations, this paradigm is too simple to suit the needs of complicated financial services.

11.8.2 Health care

Similarly, the healthcare industry is poised to invest in blockchain technology if new business cases develop. New business models and disintermediation, among others, are of tremendous interest to healthcare businesses that use blockchain technology [2]. Healthcare IT has been stymied by the problem of fragmented medical records due to the movement of patients between medical facilities. Recording transactions is easier with the help of the blockchain. Personal health records can be tracked by combining fragmented healthcare records on the blockchain. Access to medical records raises a number of ethical concerns. In order to build a foundation for high integrity tracking, it's a big challenge to use this program. Costs associated with history-based diagnosis are exacerbated by privacy concerns and the inherent complexity of medical information. There are many advantages to using a blockchain-based system for tracking the movement of services and money. An artificial intelligence-blockchain combination could help solve healthcare issues. However, in order to realize these magnificent ideals, there are obstacles from regulatory and privacy issues as well as technical ones, such as the need to access and store data on the blockchain.

11.8.3 Marketing

As a distributed, immutable, and open ledger, the blockchain is well-suited to the digital advertising supply chain's unique set of requirements. Advertising fraud, inefficiency, and transparency have always been fundamental problems for digital advertisers to address. Improved efficiency and transparency [2], reduced expenses, and prevention of fraud can be achieved with the use of blockchains. Some applications have been built with the intention of being tested by the general population. There is an open-source project called Ads.txt Plus that aims to uncover programmatic supply chain fraud by identifying and exposing rogue sellers and resellers. A (multichannel video programming distributors (MVPD) [2] is using blockchain platforms in premium digital channels and video supply chains, where marketers, programmers and operators can utilize smart contracts to plan, target, and report on ad buys across digital, broadcast, and streaming. As well as making quantifiable measures better, a better user experience can be achieved through the use of the blockchain. In the light of the blockchain, marketers may now create customer profiles straight from customers and obtain all the information they are prepared to offer in a single move. Interacting directly with clients means brands can take use of their data because there is no middleman. You don't have to shell out cash or tokens in order to be a customer. Additionally, you can charge for your time and focus. An effective marketing strategy can be improved by including all of the factors above. Digital advertising will benefit immensely from the creation of a distributed, decentralized, and Turing complete blockchain network.

11.8.4 Protecting one's intellectual property rights

Regular copyright disputes have accompanied the internet's growth, for example, Napster and Grokster, which are peer-to-peer file-sharing programs; however copyrights aren't usually respected on the internet. Copyrights are frequently overlooked or even attacked when viewed from the standpoint of a file owner. As a result, illicit and unauthorized file sharing and consumption of protected content are persistent issues. The advent of blockchain technology has shed some light on this problem. Blockchain is a distributed, decentralized digital ledger of records. To maintain consistency across all copies, this network updates and reconciles all its copies on a regular basis to ensure that each file's copy exists in every location. The blockchain is not controlled by a single machine or entity. It's nearly impossible to alter or corrupt due to the lack of a central storage site. All changes made to the ledger, starting with the basic entry, can never be reversed. As a result, anytime a copyrighted material is illegally utilized, a digital ledger including the owner's details as well as a detailed transaction history is made really public and easily provable. As an illustration, consider the use of photos found on the internet. One of the largest issues in copyright protection is enforcing control over the usage of photographs by those who post them online. In order to protect photographers' intellectual property, platforms are emerging that allow their photographs to be uploaded to a blockchain, where they may be authenticated and a way to prevent unauthorized usage is provided. There are, however, some limitations to copyright protection with blockchain technology. Initial authentication [5] for uploads is one of the issues that has to be addressed.

11.8.5 Applications in community

Money lending that is not traditional: Agreements, which are just the next information systems designed to resolve outstanding debts, get the ability to uplift traditional loan arrangements. As a result of high loan interest and the mortgage of commodities, the value of items mortgaged is generally greater than the loan amount in the traditional lending relationship. Borrowers can protect themselves from discounts on actual goods by using virtual assets as collateral, and they can also lower the interest rate on their loans by doing so. Credit and employment history aren't required to secure a loan, so there is no need to fill out a lengthy application. On the blockchain, everyone may see and utilize the information about the asset.

Automobile/cell phone: An automobile key with an anti-theft technology, for example, can only be enabled by selecting the appropriate protocol on the key. Unless you input the valid password, the cell phone will not function. To preserve rights, they are all engaged to encrypting technologies. Because the key is held in a physical container, it cannot be easily transferred or reproduced in the original form of intelligent property. For this issue, the blockchain ledger provides a solution by allowing miners to duplicate and replace lost protocols.

Soundtrack on the blockchain: Music publishers have been hampered by copyright concerns in both the record age and the digital music era. To remedy this issue, a traceable music copyright database can be created using blockchain and smart contracts. In addition, you can pay money to both the copyright owner and the musician in real time as consumer behavior changes. Music fans have the option of paying in digital currency.

Governance on the blockchain: In the 2016 US Election, both Republicans and Democrats challenged the ballot system's trustworthiness. Because of the blockchain and smart contracts, everyone can see how their vote is being counted and the overall statistical process. In addition, the government spends a considerable percentage of its annual budget verifying the flow of funds, and blockchain technology can greatly simplify the process. The blockchain can be self-managed by offering a platform for businesses, foundations, government institutions, and ordinary individuals. Through blockchain, individuals may ensure that their wishes are carried out.

11.9 CONCLUSIONS AND RECOMMENDATIONS

Because of the advent of virtual learning and digitization a new method of knowledge acquisition has developed. Regrettably, there are still issues with virtual classrooms, such as a lack of result certification, inadequate privacy, and no way for safely exchanging knowledge. Blockchain has gained considerable acceptance as a new computer system because of its decentralized, trustworthy, and reliable properties. As a result, similar transactions are made using blockchain technology and virtual classrooms to address these problems, leading to the creation of a distributed and smart online education network that also distributes information. According to the outcomes of a recent study, online learning is on the upswing.

Since advancement in other fields is dependent on education, most industrialized countries place a high value on it. Technology has improved greatly, but growth via learning should take priority and blockchain facilitates this. We can foresee how the education sector will benefit from blockchain technology in the same way that other industries have already done. In spite of its enormous educational potential, it will be intriguing to see how this technology is put into practice. Blockchain technology has been adopted by a number of countries to strengthen their educational institutions. Schools and other educational institutions must, however, take into account the possible issues that blockchain technology may bring before using it in their programs. When it comes to educational applications of technology, researchers should focus on providing feasible solutions to the current difficulties.

REFERENCES

1. Nakamoto, S. (2008) Bitcoin: A Peer-to-Peer Electronic Cash System. Volume: 2 Issue: 8. https://bitcoin.org/bitcoin.pdf
2. Sun, Han, Wang, Xiaquoe, and Wang, Xinge. (2018). Applications of block chain technology in online education. *International Journal of Emerging Technologies in Learning (iJET)*, 13(10), 252.
3. Capace, Guendaliana. (2020). Blockchain technology: Redefining trust for digital certificates. *Sustainability*, 12(21), 8952.
4. Alammary, A., Alhazmi, S., Almasri, M. and Gillani, S. 2019. Blockchain-based applications in education. *Applied Sciences*, MDPI.
5. Tewari, A. and Gupta, B. B. (2020). Secure timestamp-based mutual authentication protocol for iot devices using rfid tags. *International Journal on Semantic Web and Information Systems (IJSWIS)*, 16(3), 20–34.
6. Gaurav, A., Psannis, K., and Peraković, D. (2022). Security of cloud-based medical internet of things (MIoTs): A survey. *International Journal of Software Science and Computational Intelligence (IJSSCI)*, 14(1), 1–16.
7. Gupta, B. B., Misra, M., and Joshi, R. C. (2008). An ISP level solution to combat DDoS attacks using combined statistical based approach. *JIAS*, 3(2), 102–110.

Chapter 12

A robust mutual and batch authentication scheme based on ECC for online learning in Industry 4.0

Arun Sekar Rajasekaran

KPR Institute of Engineering and Technology, Coimbatore, India

Azees Maria

VIT-AP University, Inavolu, Beside AP Secretariat, Amaravathi 522237, India

P. Vijayakumar

University College of Engineering, Tindivanam, India

CONTENTS

DOI: 10.1201/9781003264538-12

Online learning is growing rapidly due to the emergence of the fourth industrial revolution (Industry 4.0). Using different online tools, instructors can efficiently deliver their content to learners. Furthermore, the content is available to learners at any time and from any location. Thus, online learning is a mutual benefit for both learners and instructors. Since content sharing occurs online, an efficient mechanism for securely transferring information content to entities is required. Hence, a lightweight authentication scheme for online learning is proposed. Moreover, the proposed scheme employs elliptic curve cryptography (ECC) of shorter key size, which provides performance benefits such as low computational and communication cost with equivalent security. Further, an efficient batch authentication is also incorporated for efficient transfer of information to a large number of learners due to the advancement in industry 4.0.

12.1 INTRODUCTION

Online education has become an emerging concept in recent years. With the advancement in Industry 4.0, online education has seen tremendous growth. During the current pandemic situation, it was reported that nearly 1.2 million children were out of the classroom. Due to this scenario, the mode of teaching has changed drastically and almost everything has changed to online mode (e-learning). In e-learning methodology, teaching is carried out remotely and mainly through digital platforms. Distance education forms the root cause for the emergence of online education. Advancement in digital technologies has paved the way for virtual classroom sessions, and delivery of online materials, and so on.

Nowadays, online learning has become an integral part of higher education. This is mainly due to the development of new online professional and degree courses. Recently, developments in higher education are attributable to two factors, namely online degree courses and online learning. As a result, learners can enhance their knowledge without going to colleges or educational centers. Moreover, several colleges have incorporated online courses in their curricula, which makes it more flexible for remote learners.

The main purpose of online education is to help learners who have work or other commitments during school/college hours. However, online learners should consider whether to choose specific full-time or part-time tracks. The number of courses in the particular track, the minimum credit points to be obtained, the order of the courses to be completed, and the maximum duration of the courses should all be ascertained by online learners. Moreover, some degree courses will allow learners to take many courses per term, but there will be a certain credit limit. The full-time track helps learners to complete their courses in a specific period without any time delay. On the other hand, the part-time track allows learners to take only a few courses per term but the completion of the course will also take a long time. Specifically, the goal of this chapter is to explore the consequences of recent trends and characteristics connected to digital transformation in the sphere of education and future jobs with the progress of Industry 4.0 [1]. To satisfy the demands of industry and technology within Industry 4.0, learners will need to undertake radical challenges. There are several challenges when we move towards online blended learning with the encroachment of Industry 4.0. The internet and advancements in technology are the two major paradigms in online teaching. Though this is a major hurdle for learners in underdeveloped countries, even learners in developed countries also face some issues regarding online teaching.

Online education may be of two types, namely synchronous mode and asynchronous mode. In the synchronous mode of online education, the learner receives the information without any delay from the instructor, so it is like live broadcasting. It makes the learner believe that, as in offline mode, they can interact with the instructor live. Here, there may be a possibility that an intruder could interrupt and damage the system or change the content of the delivery/materials. In the asynchronous mode of education, the sessions are recorded previously and kept securely. Whenever the learner is willing to access the learning materials, he/she can access them from a secure online platform. There is more flexibility for learners to engage with online teaching in asynchronous mode. Here, the learners are provided with credentials to access secure online materials or recorded sessions.

Moreover, digital platforms are used to stream lectures and online materials in online learning. In today's world, computer-based teaching is a common practice. Most higher education and training is supported by the computer technology of Industry 4.0 [2]. The important parameter in online teaching mode is the internet. Both learner and instructor should have a good laptop or desktop with high configuration and internet connectivity. However, the internet connectivity used for online education must be secure. Therefore, security [3] plays an important role. There are many roles played by the instructor for checking the authenticity of the learner. (1) The instructor should provide the necessary platform for the authenticated learner. (2) Moreover, the instructor checks and monitors the activities of the authenticated learner. (3) In addition, the instructor provides explanations and clarifications for the learner in case of any disagreement.

In Industry 4.0, communication of information is the basic feature. Though in online education pedagogy, transfer of information takes place through a wireless medium, important security parameters such as authenticity, integrity, non-repudiation, confidentiality, and privacy are to be preserved [4]. Moreover, with the development of Industry 4.0, there has been a rapid advancement in the internet which plays a major role in online education learning. Thus, Industry 4.0 should be integrated with online education to improve the efficiency and quality of education. Hence, for an effective transfer of information between the instructor and learner, a lightweight anonymous authentication scheme based on elliptic curve cryptography (ECC) with a low computational cost is proposed in this chapter.

Our contributions here are:

1. To develop the learner's anonymous authentication scheme by the instructor during the certificate generation to reduce the computational cost.
2. To develop the instructor's anonymous authentication scheme by the learner during the certificate generation to reduce the computational cost.
3. To ensure data integrity with minimum certificate verification cost.
4. To ensure the exchange of online delivery content (lectures/materials) with minimum communication cost.

The chapter is organized as follows. The related works concerning ECC, authentication and privacy are discussed in Section 12.2. Section 12.3 explains the basic preliminaries regarding ECC, bilinear pairing, and system description. The planned methodology is explained in section 12.4. Section 12.5 describes the security analysis. The performance investigation is elucidated in Section 12.6, and Section 12.7 concludes this work.

12.2 RELATED WORKS

Due to the rapid development in technology, humans are moving towards online education to enhance their knowledge, but the main drawback is the security concerns when information content is exchanged through a wireless medium. Even though many works have been proposed to enhance security needed [5], they are mainly based on public-key cryptosystems like Rivest, Shamir and Adleman algorithm (RSA) and digital signature algorithm (DSA), and so on. Here, in this work, security [6] is enhanced by using public key elliptic curve cryptosystems. In [7], Kanda et al. describe the various issues related to authentication and hardware requirements. In [8], Louw et al. focus on security requirements like privacy, authentication, and impersonation attack. Several schemes based on ECC are introduced to enhance secure communication between two different entities. An encryption scheme based on ECC is developed by Koblitz et al. [9]. Here, a generated shared key is used to encrypt the message. Encryption computation is the main drawback of this work. Moreover, this work does not give a clear view regarding how the information is transferred on to the elliptic curve (EC). This work describes the encoding process of converting the plain text to ASCII and mapping these values to EC. Here a common ASCII table is shared, and it is easy for an intruder to learn the transmitted information from the cipher text. Tiwari and Kim [10] propose an ECC method based on DNA. Pseudorandom data is used, and the mapping is also random. Here, both the source and receiver should agree before encryption and decryption. There is a possibility of encryption flaws and attacks in this scheme. Singh et al. [11] propose an image encryption scheme based on ECC. Here, the pixel value in the image depends on the key size. An increase in the pixel value increases the key size which in turn increases the computation and storage overhead.

Roy et al. [12] propose reverse mapping concept in ECC. The encryption steps involved in this scheme for the ciphertext are not mentioned. Moreover, there is a possibility of chosen plain text attack in this scheme. Lee and Kim [13] propose an attack-resistant OTP scheme. This work is based on the bilinear pairing method. However, the computational overhead of this method is high and not suited for a wireless environment. Ahmed et al. [14] propose a hash function-based multifactor authentication scheme. A preset key and the idea of OTP are used to calculate every hash function. However, a succession of each hash function leads to significant overhead computing. Chen et al. [15] propose a fingerprint radiofrequency mutual authentication scheme. The approach proposed is an authentication system for the physical layer. However, in this work a pattern detection algorithm is used that incurs high computational overhead.

Shivraj et al. [16] suggest an identity-based ECC lightweight one-time password (OTP) scheme. This method is based on a simple Diffie–Hellman key exchange. In this work, the problem of the infinity point occurs during key generation and there is no method to prevent it. In [17], Amin et al. discuss a user knowledge-profile-based authentication technique. User authentication is based on the user's personal and academic information, but this scheme doesn't provide enough security for personal/academic data. Memon et al. [18] discuss the various threats to security in the process of e-learning. Further, research has been done in the human-oriented online education system on artificial intelligence and the safety of information. In [19], Devedzic et al. develop automated educational processes using smart techniques, although the scheme suffers from several security issues. In [20], Wogu et al. discuss the consequences of artificial intelligence, intelligent classrooms, and online training systems for human development. In [21], Popenici et al. discuss the impact of artificial intelligence on the educational system. The authors also investigate the challenges confronting higher education institutions.

12.3 PRELIMINARIES

The basic concepts regarding ECC and bilinear pairing are discussed in this section. In addition, the entire system description of online pedagogy is also elucidated.

12.3.1 Elliptic curve cryptography

Elliptic curve cryptosystems [22] rely on an elliptic curve discrete logarithm problem (ECDLP) for security purposes. Since the solution to the ECDLP is totally exponential, elliptic curve cryptosystems have key sizes comparatively smaller than other key public systems (RSA, DSA) to ensure equivalent safeguards. The elliptic curve equation for the finite field F_p is given by $E: \beta^2 = \alpha^3 + p\alpha + q$, where $p, q \in F_p$ are the coefficients which satisfy the equation $4p^3 + 27q^2 \neq 0$. For addition of two different points X and Y on an elliptic curve $E(F_p)$, draw the tangent line l intersecting the elliptic curve at three points: X, Y and another point at Z. Then, Z point is reflected throughout the x-axis (i.e., -1 multiplies the y-coordinate of the point), such that $X + Y = Z'$. To add the point X to itself, draw the tangent line l that intersects the elliptic curve at two points, X and another point K. The point K is then reflected across the x-axis to produce a new point K', and $X + X = K'$. For any integer n, the point multiplication over E/F_p is denoted as $Y = nX + X + X\ldots + X(n \text{ times})$.

12.3.2 Bilinear pairing

Here, three cyclic additive group G_x, G_y and G_z of order a are considered. Let X, Y be the generators of G_x and G_y. Let ∂ be the isomorphism mapping from G_y to G_x such that $\partial(Y) = X$. The bilinear map is given by $e: G_x X G_y \rightarrow G_z$ and the bilinear pairing properties are as follows.

Bilinear: $e(X_1 + X_2, Y) = e(X_1, Y).e(X_2, Y), e(X, Y_1 + Y_2) = e(X, Y_1)$
$.e(X, Y_2)$ where $X_1, X_2, X \in G_x$ & $Y_1, Y_2, Y \in G_y$ and
$e(pX, qY) = e(X, Y)pq \forall p, q \in Z_a^*$
Non-degeneracy: $e(X, Y) \neq 1G_z$
Computability: There exists an efficient procedure to compute the bilinear map $e: G_x \times G_y \rightarrow G_z$.

12.3.3 System overview

In online teaching methodology, both instructor and learner play a key role. Table 12.1 shows the learner and instructor authentication phase of the proposed anonymous authentication scheme. Initially, if a learner wants to get an online teaching service from a particular instructor, that is, if the learner wishes to opt for a specific instructor online service, he/she sends the request

Table 12.1 Learner and instructor authentication phase of proposed scheme

---

Initialization phase

Point: $E\left(F_p\right)$

Private keys: $\theta, \varnothing \in Z_p^*$

Public key: $I_{pub} = \left(\theta + \varnothing\right)P$

Hash function: $H : \{0,1\} \rightarrow Z_p^*$

Public parameters: $I_{param} = \left(I_{pub}, P, E, H, p\right)$

Learner authentication

Learner	Instructor
	$RL_i, DL_i, f \in Z_p^*$
	$L_{pub} = \left(\theta + f\right)P$
	$L_{ack} = fP$
	$\left(RL_i, DL_i, L_{pub}, L_{ack}\right)$
$\longleftarrow$	$\left(RL_i, DL_i, f\right)$
$\left(RL_i, DL_i, f\right)$	
$Ck_i = H(DL_i \| L_{pub} \| i \| j \| k \| l)$	
$mess_i = (Ck_i \| L_{pub} \| i' \| j' \| k' \| l')$	
Instructor's authentication	
	$Ck'_i = H(DL_i \| L_{pub} \| a \| b \| c \| d)$
	$Ck_i = Ck'_i$
	Private key: g_i
	$\alpha = \dfrac{1}{\left(\theta + \varnothing + g_i\right)}P$
	$\beta = g_i P$
	$Ch_i = H\left(\alpha \| \beta \| u \| v \| w\right)$
$\longleftarrow$	$mess_i = (Ch_i \| \alpha \| \beta \| u \| v \| w)$
$Ch'_i = H\left(\alpha \| \beta \| u \| v \| w\right)$	
$Ch_i = Ch'_i$	
$e\left(v', \alpha\right) = e\left(P, P\right)$	
$B_i = \beta + fP$	
$C_i = H(DL_i \| B_i)$	
$L_{mess} = \left(DL_i \| B_i \| C_i\right)$	

demand to the instructor. Here, the instructor wants to check the authenticity of the particular learner. Moreover, the learner also authenticates the legitimacy of the instructor. After the initial registration process is completed, the learner generates the contender key, appends it with the message. and sends it to the instructor. Then, the instructor checks for the authenticity of that message after receiving the message from that learner. The instructor generates their contender key and matches it with the contender key of the learner. If both the keys match, then the message is accepted, and the learner is approved by the instructor to participate in the online mode. During the delivery of the online materials or online lectures, the content should not be modified. Moreover, the learner should be confident that he/she is receiving the content from the authenticated instructor. Therefore, the learner should authenticate the instructor. Here, initially the instructor generates the authentication key and provisional key to maintain the integrity of the online content.

In addition, the instructor generates the challenger key and appends it to its message and sends it to the learner. The learner on receiving the message calculates its challenger key and matches it with the challenger key of the instructor.

If both the keys match, then the learner accepts the content from the instructor. Here, by using the authentication key from the message, the learner checks the integrity of the instructor's online content. In addition to the message verification, the learner also generates the license message based on the badge calculation. Once the learner's license message is accepted by the instructor, the learner gets complete service from the instructor. Moreover, the license message comprises badge details. This will help to authenticate many learners at the same time that is, batch authentication can be performed with the help of these badges.

12.4 PROPOSED SCHEME

System initialization phase, learner authentication, and instructor authentication to enhance security features with the innovations in Industry 4.0 are described in this section. During the information exchange between the instructor and learner or vice versa, confidentiality is to be maintained. Here, mutual authentication takes place between the learner and the instructor in a secure way. Moreover, if the instructor wants to convey the information to a large number of learners, then a secure batch authentication scheme is also proposed for secure communication.

12.4.1 Initialization phase

The instructor selects an elliptic curve E with a prime order P. The base point in the elliptic curve E is represented as (F_p). The instructor selects two random numbers $\theta, \varnothing \in Z_p^*$ such that master key is θ and $\varnothing$ is the private key. Based on the private key, the instructor computes the public key $I_{pub} = (\theta + \varnothing)P$. Moreover, the cryptographic hash function is given as $H : \{0,1\} \rightarrow Z_p^*$ The instructor broadcasts the parameters $I_{param} = (I_{pub}, P, E, H, p)$ as public.

12.4.2 Learner authentication

In this proposed work, learner's authentication consists of the learner's registration process, key generation scheme, generation, and verification of the certificate.

12.4.2.1 Learner registration process

Learners are required to submit the important parameters like username, course-id, mode (part-time/full time), mail id, mobile number, among others to the instructor.

12.4.2.2 Key generation scheme

After the registration process, secret keys are generated by the instructor. The instructor first generates a random number $e_i \in Z_p^*$. Moreover, the real identity RL_l and dummy identity DL_l of the learner is also generated by the instructor. The dummy identity is calculated as $DL_l = e_i P$. In addition, instructor selects another random number for private key and is represented as $f \in Z_p^*$. Then, the public key for the learner is calculated as $L_{pub} = (\theta + f)P$. Similarly, the acknowledgement key for the learner is calculated as $L_{ack} = fP$. Once the required keys are calculated, instructor stores these $(RL_l, DL_l, L_{pub}, L_{ack})$ parameters secretly in his/her database. Moreover, the instructor secretly provides the public key L_{pub}, dummy identity of the learner DL_l, and the private key f in a secure way to the learner.

12.4.2.3 Learner's anonymous certificate generation

The learner randomly chooses $x, y, z \in Z_p^*$ and computes i, j, k and l such that $i = xP + L_{pub}, j = (y - z)P, k = (y + z)P$ and $l = (x + 2y)P$. Then the contender key is calculated by the learner as $Ck_l = H(DL_l \| L_{pub} \| i \| j \| k \| l)$. Once the contender key is computed, the learner also computes the dummy values as i', j', k' and l', such that $i' = (x + y + z)P, j' = -(y + z)P, k' = 2yP$ and $l' = -xP$. Finally, the learner sends the message to the instructor as $mess_l = (Ck_l \| L_{pub} \| i' \| j' \| k' \| l')$.

12.4.2.4 Learner's certificate verification

Once the message is received by the instructor, the instructor computes a, b, c and d to check the authenticity of the learner, where $= i' + j' + L_{ack} + \varnothing P$, $b = j' + k', c = i' + l'$ and $d = i' + j' + k'$. In addition, the instructor calculates its contender key as $Ck'_l = H(DL_l \| L_{pub} \| a \| b \| c \| d)$ and checks $Ck_l = Ck'_l$. If this holds, then the learner is accepted by the instructor to access the online teaching mode. Else, the learner is excluded from the instructor's online platform.

Proof of correctness

$$a = i' + j' + L_{ack} + \varnothing P$$
$$= (x+y+z)P - (y+z)P - (y+z)P + fP + \varnothing P$$
$$= xP + (f+\varnothing)P = xP + L_{pub} = i$$
$$b = j' + k'$$
$$= -(y+z)P + 2yP = (y-z)P = j$$
$$c = i' + l'$$
$$= (x+y+z)P - xP = (y+z)P = k$$
$$d = i' + j' + k'$$
$$= (x+y+z)P - (y+z)P + 2yP = xP + 2yP = l$$

12.4.3 Instructor's authentication

The learner must authenticate the instructor before communicating with each other.

12.4.3.1 Key generation scheme

The instructor first selects a short-time private key g_i from the set of random numbers as $g_1, g_2, g_3 \in Z_p^*$. Instructor computes the authentication key $\alpha = \dfrac{1}{(\theta + \varnothing + g_i)} P$ and the provisional $\beta = g_i P$.

12.4.3.2 Instructor's certificate generation

The instructor chooses two random numbers $r, t \in Z_a^*$ and calculates u, v and w, where $u = (g_i - \varnothing - f)P, v = (\varnothing + r + t)P$ and $w = -(r+t)P$. Based on these values, the instructor computes the challenger key $Ch_i = H(\alpha \| \beta \| u \| v \| w)$. Once the challenger key is computed, the instructor sends the message $mess_i = (Ch_i \| \alpha \| \beta \| u \| v \| w)$ to the learner.

12.4.3.3 Instructor's certificate verification

Once the message is received by the learner, the learner computes the challenger key $Ch'_i = H(\alpha \| \beta \| u \| v \| w)$. If $Ch_i = Ch'_i$, then the message is accepted by the learner, else rejected.

12.4.3.4 Integrity verification

The learner computes u' and v' such that $u' = u + v + w$ and $v' = u' + I_{pub} + fP$ and verifies $e(v', \alpha) = e(P, P)$. If this condition is satisfied, the learner accepts the instructor, else rejected.

Proof of correctness

$$v' = u' + I_{pub} + fP = u' + (\theta + \varnothing)P + fP$$
$$= u + v + w + (\theta + \varnothing)P + fP$$
$$= (g_i - \varnothing - f)P + (\varnothing + r + t)P + -(r + t)P + (\theta + \varnothing)P + fP$$
$$= g_i P + (\theta + \varnothing)P$$
$$e(v', \alpha) = e(g_i P + (\theta + \varnothing)P, \alpha)$$
$$= e((g_i + \theta + \varnothing)P, \frac{1}{(\theta + \varnothing + g_i)}P)$$
$$= e(P, P)$$

12.4.3.5 License generation

Once the instructor is successfully authenticated by the learner, the learner computes a badge for receiving the complete service from the instructor. The badge is calculated as $B_l = \beta + fP$. Based on the badge, the learner computes $C_l = H(DL_l \| B_l)$. Moreover, the learner sends the license message $L_{mess} = (DL_l \| B_l \| C_l)$ to the instructor.

12.4.3.6 License verification

Once the license is received by the instructor, the instructor computes $B_l' = \beta + L_{ack}$ and then calculates $C_l' = H(DL_l \| B_l')$. If both $C_l = C_l'$ then the license message is accepted by the instructor, else rejected.

12.4.4 Batch authentication

The batch authentication process is used to convey the same message to a number of authenticated users (learners) simultaneously. Due to the rapid growth of Industry 4.0, the number of learners should be benefited at the same time. Here, the number of learners is represented as p. If p requested online teaching mode at the same time, then the instructor computes γ and γ' such that, $\gamma = \sum_{i=1}^{p}(B_{li} - \beta_i)$ and $\gamma' = \frac{1}{\sum_{i=1}^{p} f}P$. Then, the instructor checks if $e(\gamma, \gamma') = e(P, P)$. If this condition is satisfied, the instructor schedules an efficient service to all the registered authenticated learners.

Proof of correctness

$$\gamma = \sum_{i=1}^{p}\left(B_{l_i} - \beta_i\right) = \sum_{i=1}^{p}\left(\left(\beta + fP\right)_i - \beta_i\right)$$

$$= \Sigma_{i=1}^{p}\left(\beta_i + \left(fP\right)_i - \beta_i\right) = \Sigma_{i=1}^{p}f_iP$$

$$e\left(\gamma,\gamma'\right) = e\left(\Sigma_{i=1}^{p}f_iP, \frac{1}{\Sigma_{i=1}^{p}}P\right)$$

$$= e\left(P,P\right)^{\Sigma_{i=1}^{p}fi \cdot \frac{1}{\Sigma_{i=1}^{p}f}} = e\left(P,P\right)\left(\text{by bilinear property}\right)$$

12.5 SECURITY ANALYSIS

Even though Industry 4.0 plays a significant role in the current scenario, several security threats [30–33] are to be addressed in online learning. In this section, important security attacks like impersonation attack, reply attack, message modification attack, fake message attack, non-repudiation, anonymity, and privacy preservation are discussed in detail.

12.5.1 Resistance to impersonation attack

To perform the impersonation attack, the intruder should impersonate a legitimate learner or instructor. This is impossible in this proposed scheme. The learner sends an authenticated message as $mess_l = (Ck_l \| L_{pub} \| i' \| j' \| k' \| l')$ to the instructor. To calculate Ck_l, the intruder wants to find the hashed value of DL_l, L_{pub}, i, j, k and l, where $Ck_l = H(DL_l \| L_{pub} \| i \| j \| k \| l)$. However, the values of i, j, k and l are calculated based on the random numbers generated by the learner. Further, to calculate DL_l, the intruder wants to find the value of e_i, where $DL_l = e_iP$ but the value of e_i is randomly chosen by the instructor and it is hard for the intruder to find its value. However, the value of i is calculated by the instructor as $a = i' + j' + L_{aut} + \varnothing P = i$. Therefore, the intruder wants to find the value of $\varnothing$ and L_{aut} to perform an impersonation attack. However, $\varnothing$ is the private key of the instructor which is difficult to find by the intruder. Moreover, L_{ack} is calculated as $L_{ack} = fP$ and is kept securely in the instructor database. Though $L_{pub} = (\theta + f)P$ has the parameter value f, it is hard for an intruder to calculate the value of f due to ECDLP. Therefore, an intruder can't calculate the contender key of the learner. To perform the impersonation attack from the learner side, the intruder should satisfy the condition $e(v',\alpha) = e(P,P)$. Here, v' and α are calculated based on the private keys of learner and instructor. So, an adversary can't find the private keys of both instructor and learner to perform an impersonation attack.

12.5.2 Resistance to message modification attack

The content of the message should be modified, to perform the message modification attack. If the message content is modified, then the integrity of the message is lost. Therefore, to preserve integrity, cryptographic hash functions are used in this proposed scheme. The learner, while sending the message, appends the contender key to the message. The contender key is calculated as $Ck_l = H(DL_l \| L_{pub} \| i \| j \| k \| l)$. Once the message is received by the instructor, the instructor calculates Ck'_l and checks $Ck_l = Ck'_l$. An intruder can't find the hashed value of the contender key of the learner to perform message modification. On the other hand, to perform this attack on the instructor's side, the intruder must find the value of $C_l = H(DL_l \| B_l)$. It is difficult for an intruder to calculate the value of the badge B_l, where $B_l = \beta + fP$. Here, the calculation of 'f' involves the difficulty of ECDLP.

12.5.3 Resistance to reply attack

To resist against reply attack, the timestamp is the basic solution. But, the time stamp requires time synchronization. So, in this proposed scheme, random numbers such as $x, y, z \in Z_p^*$ are chosen by the learner. So, the values of i, j, k and l are also changed randomly. Similarly, the instructor chooses short-time private key g_i from the set of random numbers as $g_1, g_2, g_3 \in Z_p^*$. Moreover, based on this private key, the authentication key and provisional keys are calculated as $\alpha = \dfrac{1}{(\theta + \varnothing + g_i)} P$ and $\beta = g_i P$. So, these key values are randomly changing with respect to time. Therefore, the proposed scheme is resistant to reply attack.

12.5.4 Resistance to fake message attack

To send a fake message to the instructor, the adversary wants to create a message similar to the message of the learner $mess_l = (Ck_l \| L_{pub} \| i' \| j' \| k' \| l')$. Although, if the intruder creates the same fake message as a learner, on receiving this fake message $mess_i = (Ck_l \| L_{pub} \| i' \| j' \| k' \| l')$ from the intruder, the instructor calculates a, b, c and d to check the authenticity of the intruder (fake learner), where $= i' + j' + L_{ack} + \varnothing P$. Here, L_{ack} is the acknowledgment key of the authenticated learner. This key is calculated by the instructor for each learner during the initial registration phase and is kept securely in a database. Therefore, if the learner is not registered in the online platform during the initial registration, then the authentication process fails. As a result, the instructor does not accept the message. Thus, the proposed scheme can withstand fake message attack.

12.5.5 Anonymity and privacy preservation

The learner sends the message $mess_l = (Ck_l \| L_{pub} \| i' \| j' \| k' \| l')$ to the instructor. Similarly, the instructor sends the message $mess_i = (Ck_i \| \alpha \| \beta \| u \| v \| w)$ to the learner. In either case, the real identity of the learner/

instructor is not revealed. Therefore, an adversary can't get the details regarding the authenticated learner/instructor. Moreover, the intruder gets only a zero-knowledge from the message. The private information of the learner/instructor is preserved using the proposed anonymous privacy-preserving authentication scheme.

12.5.6 Resistance against the non-repudiation attack

In the proposed scheme, the entities (learner/instructor) cannot repudiate after receiving information from the instructor/learner. While sending the information from the instructor to the learner, the authenticity of the learner is checked by the instructor using anonymous certificate verification. So, repudiation of the learner is not acceptable. Moreover, while sending the reply information to the instructor by the learner, the learner checks the authenticity of the instructor. So, an instructor can't repudiate after getting the reply information from the learner.

12.6 PERFORMANCE ANALYSIS

In this section, the suggested scheme's performance is analyzed in terms of computational cost, communication cost, and instructor serving capability.

12.6.1 Computational complexity

The proposed scheme's computational costs are compared with different existing schemes like Boneh et al. [23], Gong et al. [24], Yeh et al. [25] and Wang et al. [26]. During the calculation of computational cost, several operations such as bilinear pairing operation, hash function, one point multiplication, and one point addition are involved. Let T_{bp}, T_h, T_m and T_a be the representations used to perform bilinear pairing, hashing, one point multiplication, and one point addition operation. The proposed system is implemented using a 4-GHz PC hardware setup with 8-GB RAM and Cygwin 1.7.35–15 software with gcc version 4.9.2 [27]. For all the existing schemes and the proposed scheme, a maximum of 100 simulation runs are performed.

Figure 12.1 shows the graph plotted between the number of learners and the computational cost. The timing values for T_{bp}, T_h and T_m are 1.6 ms, 2.7 ms and 0.001 ms respectively. Here 'ms' represents milliseconds. The timing value for one point addition is very small and is taken as negligible. Table 12.2 shows the computational cost for different schemes.

12.6.2 Communication cost

Communication cost is demarcated as the number of bits required for the exchange of information between the authenticated learners and instructors. In this proposed scheme, the size of the contender key and challenger

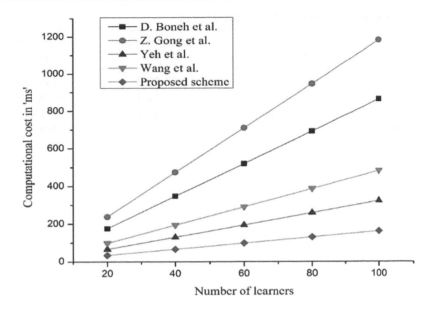

Figure 12.1 Computational cost for different schemes.

Table 12.2 Computational cost for various schemes

Schemes	For single authentication	For 'n' authentication
Boneh et al.	$4T_{bp} + 2T_h$	$(2 + 2n)T_{bp} + 2nT_h$
Gong et al.	$5T_{bp} + 2nT_h$	$(1 + 4n)T_{bp} + 2nT_h$
Yeh et al.	$3T_{bp} + 5T_m$	$(2n + 1)T_{bp} + 5nT_m$
Wang et al.	$4T_{bp} + 5T_m$	$(3n + 1)T_{bp} + (4n + 1)T_m$
Proposed scheme	$2T_{bp} + T_m$	$(1 + n)T_{bp} + nT_m$

key used in the message is 160 bits. Moreover, the size of the public keys, authentication key and provisional key are taken as 32 bits, since ECC is used. The total number of bits required for the information exchange in this proposed work is calculated as 640 bits. The proposed work is compared with different existing schemes such as Boneh et al. [23], Gong et al. [24], Zhang et al. [28], and Al-Riyami et al. [29]. Table 12.3 displays the communication cost and the number of messages used for different schemes. From the table, it is clear that the suggested scheme has lower communication cost than the existing schemes. Figure 12.2 shows the pictorial representation of communication cost for various schemes.

Table 12.3 Communication cost for various schemes

Schemes	Number of messages	For single verification (bits)	For 'n' verification (bits)
Boneh et al.	03	3842	3842n
Gong et al.	03	3582	3542n
Zhang et al.	02	2112	2112n
Al-Riyami et al.	02	1586	1586n
Proposed scheme	02	640	640n

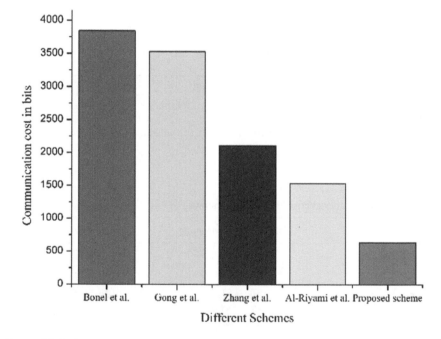

Figure 12.2 Communication cost for different schemes.

12.6.3 Instructor serving capability

Let there be N number of authenticated learners who required service from the instructor. Let $\wp$ represent the probability that the instructor can successfully provide the service to the authenticated learners. Let T_{total} represent the total computational time required for learner's anonymous authentication, instructor anonymous authentication, and license verification. The instructor serving capability is given by $I_{ser} = \dfrac{\wp}{N.T_{total}*N}$, where $T_{total} = 4T_{bp} + T_h + T_m$. The total computation time is calculated as 9.1 ms for a single learner.

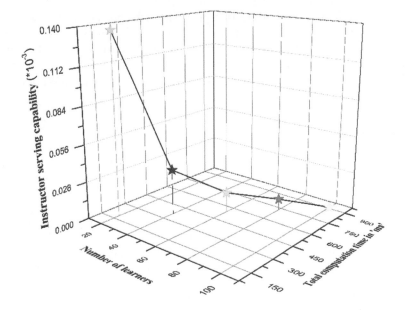

Figure 12.3 Instructor serving capability.

Figure 12.3 shows a graphical representation of the serving capability of the instructor with respect to the number of authenticated learners and computational time. The figure shows that the service-providing capability of the instructor is high when the number of learners and computing costs are low. As a result, the instructor authenticates 6,592 learners successfully in a single minute. Thus, the proposed scheme ensures a high serving ratio, when compared to the existing schemes as the number of learners approaching the instructor increases.

12.7 CONCLUSION

In this chapter, an efficient mutual and batch authentication scheme based on ECC for an online education system is proposed. Due to the impact of Industry 4.0, learners can enhance their skills with the emerging new technology. Here, the learner and the instructor will perform mutual authentication with each other in an anonymous way. The proposed scheme is free from several security threats like impersonation attack, message modification attack, fake message attack, and non-repudiation, among others. Since our proposed scheme is based on ECC, there is no exponential operation involved in the calculation of computational cost. Thus, the proposed scheme proves to be noteworthy when compared to the existing schemes in terms of computational cost. Moreover, the service-providing capability per minute for the authenticated learners is high in this proposed scheme. The future scope of this work can be extended to the incorporation of AI and soft computing techniques in anonymous authentication schemes. Further, with the emergence of Industry 4.0, augmented reality (AR) and Internet of Things (IoT) can be incorporated using software tools in the current online methodology.

REFERENCES

1. Adetoba, B. T., Awodele, O., and Kuyoro, S. O. (2016). E-learning security issues and challenges: A review. *Journal of Scientific Research and Studies*, 3(5), 96–100.
2. Lee, J., Bagheri, B., and Kao, H. (2015). A cyber-physical systems architecture for Industry 4.0-based manufacturing systems. *Manufacturing Letters*, 3, 18–23. doi: 10.1016/j.mfglet.2014.12.001.
3. Vijayakumar, P., Chang, V., Deborah, L. J., Balusamy, B., and Shynu, P. (2018). Computationally efficient privacy preserving anonymous mutual and batch authentication schemes for vehicular ad hoc networks. *Future Generation Computer Systems*, 78, 943–955. doi: 10.1016/j.future.2016.11.024.
4. Vijayakumar, P., Ganesh, S. M., Deborah, L. J., and Rawal, B. S. (2018). A new Smart SMS protocol for secure SMS communication in m-health environment. *Computers & Electrical Engineering*, 65, 265–281. doi: 10.1016/j.compeleceng.2016.11.016.
5. Iqbal, A., Rajasekaran, A. S., Nikhil, G. S., and Azees, M. (2021). A secure and decentralized blockchain based EV energy trading model using smart contract in V2G network. *IEEE Access*, 9, 75761–75777. doi: 10.1109/access.2021.3081506.
6. Subramani, J., Maria, A., Neelakandan, R. B., and Rajasekaran, A. S. (2021). Efficient anonymous authentication scheme for automatic dependent surveillance-broadcast system with batch verification. *IET Communications*, 15(9), 1187–1197. doi: 10.1049/cmu2.12152.
7. Kanda, G., Antwi, A. O., and Ryoo, K. (2018). Hardware architecture design of AES cryptosystem with 163-bit elliptic curve. *Lecture Notes in Electrical Engineering Advanced Multimedia and Ubiquitous Engineering*, 423–429. doi: 10.1007/978-981-13-1328-8_55.
8. Louw, J., Niezen, G., Ramotsoela, T. D., and Abu-Mahfouz, A. M. (2016). A key distribution scheme using elliptic curve cryptography in wireless sensor networks. In *2016 IEEE 14th International Conference on Industrial Informatics (INDIN)*. doi: 10.1109/indin.2016.7819342.
9. Koblitz, N. (1987). Elliptic curve cryptosystems. *Mathematics of Computation*, 48(177), 203–209.
10. Tiwari, H. D., and Kim, J. H. (2018). Novel method for DNA-based elliptic curve cryptography for IoT devices. *ETRI Journal*, 40(3), 396–409.
11. Singh, L. D., and Singh, K. M. (2015). Image encryption using elliptic curve cryptography. *Procedia Computer Science*, 54, 472–481.
12. Sengupta, A., and Ray, U. K. (2016). Message mapping and reverse mapping in elliptic curve cryptosystem. *Security and Communication Networks*, 9(18), 5363–5375.

13. Lee, Y., and Kim, H. (2013). Insider attack-resistant OTP based on bilinear maps. *International Journal of Computer Communication Engineeing*, 2(3), 304–308.
14. Ahmed, A. A., and Ahmed, W. A. (2019). An effective multifactor authentication mechanism based on combiners of hash function over internet of things. *Sensors*, 19(17), 3663. doi: 10.3390/s19173663.
15. Chen, Y., Wen, H., Son, H., Chen, S., Xie, F., Yang, Q., and Hu, L. (2018). Lightweight one-time password authentication scheme based on radio-frequency fingerprinting. *IET Communications*, 12(12), 1477–1484.
16. Shivraj, V. L., Rajan, M. A., Singh, M., and Balamuralidhar, P. (2015). One time password authentication scheme based on elliptic curves for Internet of Things (IoT). *2015 5th National Symposium on Information Technology: Towards New Smart World (NSITNSW)*. doi: 10.1109/nsitnsw.2015.7176384.
17. Amin, R., Islam, S., Biswas, G., Giri, D., Khan, M., and Kumar, N. (2016). A more secure and privacy-aware anonymous user authentication scheme for distributed mobile cloud computing environments. *Security and Communication Networks*, 9(17), 4650–4666.
18. Memon, I. Hussain, R. A., and Chen, G. (2014). Enhanced privacy and authentication: An efficient and secure anonymous communication for location based service using asymmetric cryptography scheme. *Wireless Personal Communications*, 84(2), 1487–1508.
19. Devedzic, V., and Debenham, J. (1998). An intelligent tutoring system for teaching formal languages. *Intelligent Tutoring Systems Lecture Notes in Computer Science*, 514–523. doi: 10.1007/3-540-68716-5_57.
20. Wogu, I. A., Misra, S., Assibong, P. A., Olu-Owolabi, E. F., Maskeliūnas, R., and Damasevicius, R. (2019). Artificial intelligence, smart classrooms and online education in the 21st century. *Journal of Cases on Information Technology*, 21(3), 66–79. doi: 10.4018/jcit.2019070105.
21. Popenici, S. A., and Kerr, S. (2017). Exploring the impact of artificial intelligence on teaching and learning in higher education. *Research and Practice in Technology Enhanced Learning*, 12(1), 22. doi: 10.1186/s41039-017-0062-8.
22. Harkanson, R., and Kim, Y. (2017). Applications of elliptic curve cryptography. In *Proceedings of the 12th Annual Conference on Cyber and Information Security Research*. doi: 10.1145/3064814.3064818.
23. Boneh, D., Lynn, B., and Shacham, H. (2004). Short signatures from the Weil pairing. *Journal of Cryptology*, 17(4, 297–319.
24. Gong, Z., Long, Y., Hong, X., and Chen, K. (2007). Two certificateless aggregate signatures from bilinear maps. In *Proceedings of 8th ACIS International Conference on Software Engineering, Artificial Intelligence, Networking and Parallel Distributed Computing (SNPD)*, vol. 3, pp. 188–193.
25. Yeh, L., and Tsaur, W. (2012). A secure and efficient authentication scheme for access control in mobile pay-TV systems. *IEEE Transactions on Multimedia*, 14(6), 1690–1693. doi: 10.1109/tmm.2012.2199290.
26. Wang, H., and Qin, B. (2012). Improved one-to-many authentication scheme for access control in pay-TV systems. *IET Information Security*, 6(4), 281–290. doi: 10.1049/iet-ifs.2011.0281.
27. Cygwin: Linux Environment Emulator for Windows. (n.d.) [Online]. Available: http://www.cygwin.com/.

28. Zhang, Z., Wong, D., Xu, J., and Feng, D. (2006). Certificateless public-key signature: Security model and efficient construction. In *Proceedings of ACNS 2006, LNCS* vol. 3989, Springer-Verlag, pp. 293–308.
29. Al-Riyami, S. S., and Paterson, K. G. (2003). Certificateless public key cryptography. In *Advances in Cryptology-Asiacrypt'03, LNCS* vol. 2894, Springer-Verlag, pp. 452–473.

Chapter 13

Sentiment Analysis

The beginning

C. Sindhu and G. Vadivu

SRM Institute of Science and Technology, Kattankulathur, Chennai, India

CONTENTS

DOI: 10.1201/9781003264538-13

With the explosion of new web technology, user generated content is all over the web and is accessible almost everywhere in the world. Such accessibility has paved way for an easier suggestion-seeking paradigm. In this fast-paced world, we humans find no time to stand and stare, which well suits this scenario, where we don't want to read through each and every review of a product or a service. Sentiment analysis is, thus an inevitable process, which helps every manufacturer and brand-owner to analyze the pros and cons of their own items and the competing products. Furthermore, be it any service or product, the experience shared about it is multi-dimensional with loads of emotions splashed into it. This chapter can help researchers explore further into the world of sentiment analysis.

13.1 INTRODUCTION

13.1.1 Motivation – the decision-making process

When it comes to the decision-making process, whatever the topic or product, it has always been our way to discuss with others before we finally decide. Before the internet revolution, we always relied on friends and relatives or consumer reports to help our decision making. With the advancement in web technology, we have various online platforms [1], such as blogs like *Google blogs* and *LiveJournal*; ecommerce sites like *Flipkart* and *Myntra*; review sites like *IMDb, Rotten Tomatoes*; discussion and so on, where we can get opinions on any particular topic or product. And these days we rarely ask our friends and relatives for such suggestions, because, rather than friends who would not have had any experience with the topic or product, we now have experts available online, who have done their research on it or who are working in that domain, or at least have purchased that product and used it. If we feel good about the topic, if we hate the product, or whatever feeling we might have experienced in relation to the topic or domain, the trend has become such that we tend to try to express it on the web. Such content generated by the user on web is called *user generated content* (UGC).

13.1.2 Sources of opinionated text

The web has provided several platforms which act as forums, where people share their ideas or experiences, create content, and also connect with one another. Online socializing platforms have evolved as a podium from where manufacturers and consumers can get enough feedback from the outside world. The most prominent sources of user generated content are listed as follows. *Twitter* [4] has been an official showcasing forum of one's participation, practice, beliefs, and actuality on diversified topics. It is also the largest microblogging platform on web. The unique feature of Twitter is that it only allows 140 characters maximum for a single post or 'tweet'. *Facebook* has been a powerful tool for connecting family, friends, and peers and also provides enough space for sharing text, image, and video data. More than 3 billion people from all around the whole world are free to share their ideas and thoughts on there. Also 180 million and more businesses have a presence on Facebook. *Blogs* [5], also called weblogs, usually act as informational websites. They are plotted in informal diary style, often written by an individual or a small group of people, and are open for people to respond with comments and suggestions. *YouTube* is a very popular video sharing platform, where over one billion hours of videos are watched every day. Any Google account user can upload their videos and people from all over the world can watch and comment on them. This is a rich source of user generated content. *Instagram* is an application platform for sharing images and videos with a wide range of viewers and also provides space for viewers' comments and texts. *Medium* is a technical content publishing platform with some social networking embedded in it.

Apart from these, *LinkedIn, Reddit, Sina Weibo* [6], *Pinterest, Telegram, Snapchat, WeChat, Tumblr, TikTok, Flickr,* and many more platforms are available for internet users to air their thoughts and, thus, user generated content is ever-growing. This user generated content usually does not follow formal syntactic or grammatical language structures.

13.1.3 Types of sentiment language structure

The language structure for reviews can be one amongst the following three types [3]: structured, semi-structured, and unstructured. Considering the structured format of reviews, they usually come with the formal reviews like reviewing a book or commenting on a work as the reviewer is likely to be from a professional background. In case of the semi-structured format of reviews, the negatives of the topic and the positives of the topic are given separately in an unstructured manner. This blend of partial structuring is termed as semi-structured sentiment structure. Finally, the unstructured sentiment structure includes free flow of text in an informal manner without any constraints. Here, the segregation of positives and negatives is not formally done.

13.1.4 Natural language processing

Now that we have all the information that we might require on a particular topic or domain, is that all? Thinking of it, we actually have so much, but it becomes really infeasible to read each and every online review as it might take a lot of time, and slow ingestion to bring out the essence of it. Hence it becomes essential to bring in the *Natural Language Processing* (NLP) techniques to speed up the process and also for efficient output. The techniques of NLP deal with the automatic processing and analysis of the natural free flow of user text; in this case, whatever content the user types online is just such natural language. There are several NLP techniques [4] like: *Named Entity Recognition* (NER*), Automatic Text Summarization, Aspect Mining, Topic Modelling, Speech Recognition, Machine Translation, Spam Identification, Automatic Questioning and Answering, Predictive Autotype Completion/Suggestion, and Sentiment Analysis* among others. In short, NLP makes the machine listen to speech or to read text, analyze it, estimate the sentiment present in the text, and also identify the significant factual or opinionated component of the text.

13.1.5 Sentiment Analysis

Analyzing opinionated text is an NLP task as it involves free flow of text as its input and it can also be considered as an information extraction task as its objective is to identify the writer's opinions and feelings given out as polarized comments, after incorporating all the inputs that they might have come across. This combinational task is called *Sentiment Analysis* [4]. As people are turning to various social media platforms, websites, and forums to express and seek opinions about any product, service, movie, or entity, sentiment analysis is a hot research topic these days. In general, sentiment analysis as a task, concentrates on identifying the attitude of the user from their free flow of text as speech or written text. This decade has seen an aggressive increase in web communication, which has been a driving force for the sharing of public opinion online, and in turn has driven the need for Sentiment Analysis. This public opinion sharing platform has made the web into a bigger repository of data, both structured and unstructured. Analyzing such data in order to extract the opinion of the public is an obvious challenge. Thus, Sentiment Analysis should be performed as a detailed three-step process.

13.1.5.1 Steps in Sentiment Analysis

Sentiment Analysis is a sub-task of *Data Mining*, which can be seen as a method of juicing out knowledge in the form of patterns from a huge amount of raw data. The seven prime steps [2] of data mining are: cleaning the data, integrating the data, reducing the dimensionality of data, transforming the data as required, mining knowledge, identifying patterns, and finally representing the knowledge thus acquired. Similarly, sentiment analysis has three prime steps. They are opinion mining, sentiment classification, and finally knowledge presentation, as in Figure 13.1.

a) *Opinion Mining* is the process of mining opinions or opinionated text for unanalyzed raw text and it usually feels like the pre-processing stage before the actual sentiment analysis stage. Opinion has five components to describe it. They are most commonly called a quintuple *(O, F, S, H, T)* [9] where

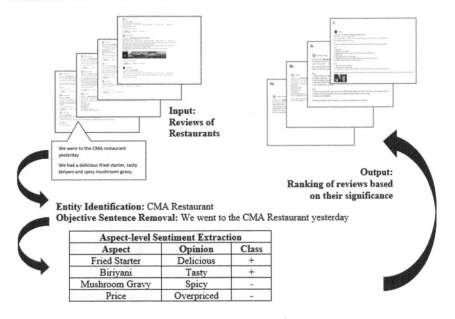

Figure 13.1 Sentiment Analysis with its three significant steps.

O denotes the object or the entity about which the sentiment is given.

F indicates the feature or the aspect of the object about which the sentiment is said.

S symbolizes the actual sentiment score of the opinion.

H denotes the opinion holder who gave the opinion.

T marks the time when the opinion was given.

Opinion Mining [10] is a two stepped process. The first step is *Web Crawling and Scraping*. Based on a keyword opinion search, several web pages maybe retrieved. All these web pages would be crawled, and the keyword matching texts would be scraped. The second step is extracting the opinionated sentences. The reviews that people write may be subjective (text with sentiments) or objective (text with facts). Consider the example given below, where the first statement is a fact, and the second statement is an opinionated sentence.

My dress was delivered yesterday. It's very beautiful.

b) *Sentiment Classification* [12] is the process of identifying and classifying the opinion given by the writer into one of the classes. It helps in analyzing what kind of sentiment the reviewer has expressed towards that product or domain. Sentiment Classification can be processed at various granularity levels.

c) *Knowledge Presentation* is the representation of the sentiment analyzed in the Opinion Mining and Sentiment Classification stages in a presentable

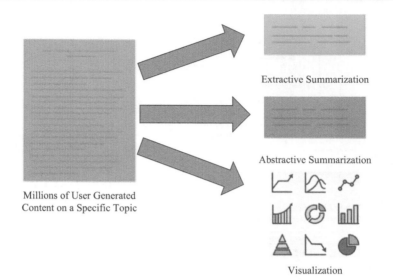

Figure 13.2 Conversion of user generated content to knowledge representation.

form. This presentable form can be in a ranked order, as a summarized output or in any visualized representation as in the Figure 13.2.

Ranked Presentation can be the ranking of the various aspects [53] of the entity or ranking the top '*n*' informative sentences or even ranking the top reviews.

Summarization [13], is the process of reducing the lengthy text into small, most informative pieces. It can be done in two ways.

    Extractive Summarization [77] is the process of extracting the significant sentences or parts of text for the final representation of the Sentiment Analysis.

    Abstractive Summarization is the process of extracting the significant text components from raw text and generating concise informative text from it.

Visualization can be thought of as the diagrammatic and graphical representation of the processed opinionated statements. There are several visualization tools available. Using these special tools, effective visual representation can be made exclusively for sentimentally analyzed data. A few such representations are given as follows.

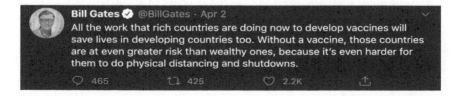

Figure 13.3 Tweet by Bill Gates, a sample input.

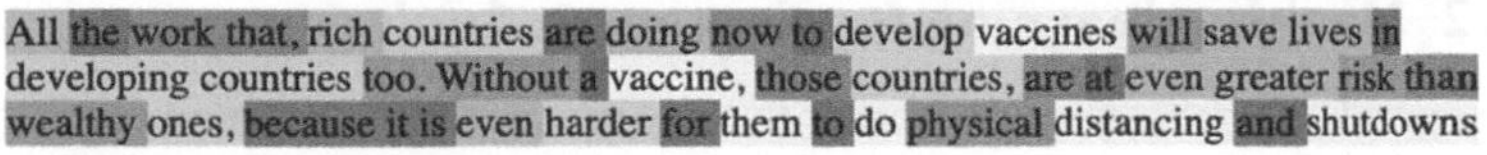

All the work that, rich countries are doing now to develop vaccines will save lives in developing countries too. Without a vaccine, those countries, are at even greater risk than wealthy ones, because it is even harder for them to do physical distancing and shutdowns

Figure 13.4 Illustration of text attention heatmap.

Consider a tweet as in Figure 13.3, where a celebrity has given some opinion on vaccines.

As the tweet is sentimentally analyzed, it could be better represented as a text attention heatmap as in Figure 13.4.

13.2 GRANULARITY LEVELS OF *SENTIMENT CLASSIFICATION*

Based on the granularity of analysis [4] and the focus on polarity, feelings, emotions (angry, happy, sad, and so on), and even on intentions (interested vs. not interested), Sentiment Classification can be done at three levels.

a) *Coarse-grained Classification*, which helps in identifying if the opinion is positive, negative, or neutral.
b) *Fine-grained Classification*, which identifies if the opinion expressed is very negative, negative, neutral, positive, or very positive. If polarity precision is important, consider expanding the polarity categories on a scale between 1 to 10 or so.
c) *Emotion Detection* [14, 15] is a classification process, which requires pre-defined emotion classes like happy, sad, excited, angry, fear, and disgust among others, for modelling it.

13.2.1 Levels of Sentiment Analysis

The old traditional approach *Word-level Sentiment Analysis* uses the *Bag of Words* (BOW) method. In this method, every word is tagged with a positive or negative label and then a logic like summation or standard deviation is applied, based on which the sentiment is determined. Here there is zero semantic consideration. The second method used for Sentiment Analysis is at document level [4], and is commonly termed as *Document-level Sentiment Analysis*. This is where a single topic or product's reviews are analyzed and a single dimensional report is produced. Here, the single dimensional report can be just denoting polarity or a sentence or even a summary. The next, finer level of analysis is at the sentence level, which is commonly known as *Sentence-level Sentiment Analysis*. In this approach, every sentence is classified into one of the labels, where the label can be neutral, negative, or positive or it can even denote an emotion. The fourth level of Sentiment Analysis is *Phrase-level Sentiment Analysis*, where every phrase of a sentence is identified and a polarity or an emotion is tagged to it. But this is not a successful method and is not widely used. Finally, the most used method is *Aspect-based Sentiment Analysis* [39].

13.2.2 Machine learning for *Sentiment Analysis*

The general workflow of Sentiment Analysis with the implementation of machine learning techniques [16, 17] is depicted in Figure 13.5. The first step is collection of data, which is usually based on any keyword. If the search keyword is 'XXYY mobile phone', then various webpages with the search word are crawled and the sentences with the keywords are retrieved. The web crawled and scraped data are stored in a file or database. The data is then fed into the pre-processing stage, where data cleaning is the prime task. Data cleaning [2] roughly includes removing the incomplete sentences, removing hashtags, removing the html tags, removing irrelevant sentences and so on. The cleaned data is split into 80% and 20% of data as training dataset and testing dataset respectively. The training dataset is then manually annotated with a panel of experts. Using the training dataset, a model is built, which can be a statistical or algorithmic methodology. Once the model is built, the testing data is used to check how the model responds to the unseen data, for which feature extraction is an inevitable step. Based on the extracted features, classification of the input text is carried out into one of the desired classes.

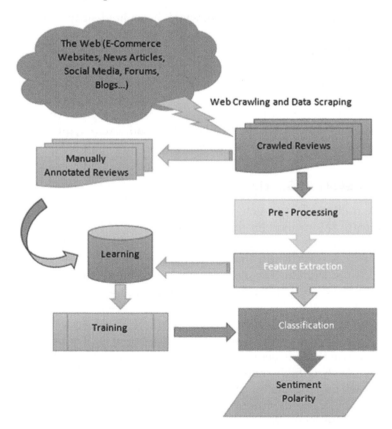

Figure 13.5 Analyzing the sentiment using a machine learning approach – a general workflow.

13.3 FEATURE EXTRACTION AND SELECTION TECHNIQUES

Engineering the features is a mandatory task [18–20] in order to process opinionated text to chunk out the sentiment. For such a process, converting the text into feature vectors helps in better and efficient processing using machine-learning methodologies. Here, in this section the most commonly used feature extraction techniques for sentiment analysis are discussed.

13.3.1 Term frequency

Word Frequency, also called Term Frequency (TF) is a traditional feature extraction method in text processing. Term Frequency, as the name suggests, is the frequency of occurrence of the term within a document. It can also be defined as the probability distribution of the frequency 'f' of token 't' in document 'd' normalized over the sum of the number of tokens in the document denoted as

$$\text{Term frequency} = \frac{f(t,d)}{\Sigma_{t' \in d} f(t',d)} \tag{13.1}$$

Another variation to this Term Frequency is the *Raw Count*, which is just the number of times a term 't' occurs in a document 'd' denoted by

$$\text{Raw Count}\_\text{Term Frequency} = f(t,d) \tag{13.2}$$

13.3.2 Term Presence

Term Presence is a more significant feature of Sentiment Analysis than Term Frequency [3]. Term Presence is also known as *Boolean Frequencies* or *Binary Weighing Method*. Here, the feature vectors are binary-valued, which actually indicates if a term is present (value 1) or not (value 0). In certain cases, even a single word's presence can totally change the polarity of a complete sentence. Another phenomenon, called the *Hapax Legomena* is to be noted here. **Hapax Legomena** is a case where a very rare word occurs and makes significant difference to the polarity of the text.

13.3.3 Term position

The position of words in a sentence and the placement of sentences in a paragraph means a lot. Certain placements can influence the polarity more than when it is placed elsewhere. In the case, of an *Information Retrieval* (IR) system, it can be very easily identified, where words appearing in titles, subtitles, or abstracts and so on are usually given more significance than the ones appearing in the body text. For example, 'I rode a 430 km beautiful stretch of highway with an unpredictable steering wheel', even though the sentence has positive words all along, the one key word 'unpredictable' decides the role of plotting the sentiment to that sentence. Hence, in general, sentences in a paragraph can be weighed as a strategy giving more significant importance to first 'n' sentences and the last 'm' sentences, than to the sentences appearing elsewhere.

13.3.4 Log Normalization

Log Normalization aids in big feature set scenarios, and is calculated by taking log transformation over the frequency 'f' of the token 't' in the document 'd' denoted as

$$\log \text{Normalization}\big(tf\,(t,d)\big) = \log\big(1 + f\,(t,d)\big) \tag{13.3}$$

13.3.5 Inverse Document Frequency

Inverse Document Frequency (IDF) is a metric that decides how informative a particular word is to a document, based on its occurrence, across all the other documents. Its occurrence could be more frequent or very rare. It is calculated by taking the logarithm of the ratio between 'D', which is the sum of the number of all documents in the given text to 'Dt', the total number of documents that contain the word. The Inverse Document Frequency can be calculated using the formula,

$$\text{Inverse Document Frequency}\,(t,D) = \left(\log \frac{D}{1+Dt}\right) \tag{13.4}$$

where, 'D' indicates the number of documents in the given text

'Dt' suggests the total number of documents in the corpus with the word 't', when $Dt \neq 0$

In case, if the word 't' is not present in the given text, then it would lead to a division by zero, hence a common adjustment is made by adding a 1 to the denominator.

13.3.6 Term Frequency-Inverse Document Frequency

Term Frequency-Inverse Document Frequency, popularly known as TF-IDF [21] is one of the most prevalently used feature selection method, which combines the concepts of both Term Frequency and Inverse Document Frequency. The value of TF-IDF is high when TF is high in the given text and document frequency of the term in the entire collection of documents 'D' is low. TF-IDF can be employed to replace counter functions. The result is also normalized row wise when divided by L2 normalization. Infrequent words will be given greater weight than recurrent words among medium frequency words. For example, stop words like '.' show up more than the verb 'eat' in a document. TF-IDF cuts down the impact of stop words. The formula for

TF-IDF of a term 't' appearing in a document 'd' belonging to the corpus 'D' can be calculated as given in Equation 13.5.

$$tf\_idf(t,d,D) = tf(t,d)^* idf(t,D) \tag{13.5}$$

13.3.7 Bag of Words

In order to use Bag of Words (BOW) [4] as a feature selection method, the text is tokenized and tabulated with its tokens occupying separate columns. Likewise, all the reviews are recorded in the rows of the table. This is called text vectorization. However, the order of the sequence is not maintained and thereby known as a BOW.

There are too many features in BOW which becomes overwhelming for the model. In Uni-gram, Bi-gram and other N-grams, this order is preserved. Features are reduced through N-grams based on the frequency of occurrence in a document of a corpus. Stop words are the ones with high frequency. On the other hand, typos, and rare phrases like 'don't need else 1l overfit' are of low frequency. A mid-range N-gram is suggested for good results. There are many approaches to resolve this. After assessing the nuances of the application, one can filter a suitable approach. These may be frequency or ranking motivated.

13.3.8 N-gram features

N-grams are significant features which helps in the capture of context to a better extent, hence are commonly used for sentiment analysis tasks. In [3], the authors have identified that the unigrams report sentiment better than the bigrams during the sentiment classification of movie reviews, but [22] proved that in most cases, bigrams and trigrams perform better than the unigrams.

N-gram is key in linguistics. In N-gram, N can be a value equal to 1 or 2 or 3 or 4 or n. N denotes the number of words or letters or syllables to be grouped in text. N-gram calculates the likelihood of the next item given that it has already seen past items. Variations of N-gram are Unigram, Bi-gram, Tri-gram, and so on. It naturally arranges all the items into sets of co-existing features. As the value of 'N' increases, whether it would give significant features is still under research.

13.3.9 Emoticon dictionary

Emojis or emoticons [14] are a large portion of the data generated every day on Twitter, Instagram, and other such platforms. Feeding the program with an emoticon dictionary will make it able to recognize sentiment in new data. So, knowledge otherwise squandered will instead augment and elucidate the intention of the user. Since the rise in smartphones and high-speed mobile data, social media platforms have prevailed much more than they were able to up until a few years ago. Emojis are the most efficacious medium for expressing emotions. If the code is unable to derive facts from these emojis, a huge chunk of data is unharnessed. Emoticon dictionaries direct the code to harness facts from emojis which immensely benefits Sentiment Analysis.

13.3.10 Topic-based features

Apart from using BOW and phrases as features, significant topics can be derived to be used as features. But individual phrase values have no correlation with overall text sentiment in many domains. In the Sentiment Analysis of a text, a challenge is to manipulate certain elements of the text that are in some way indicative of the whole text's tone. To strengthen emotions, often deceptive phrases and thwarted hopes are used. It would not be possible to differentiate between what is said locally in phrases [23] and what is said internationally throughout the text by using BOW or individual phrases, such as making parallels between the examined entity and other entities, sarcasm, understatement, and digressions, all of which are used in abundance in many realms of discourse. These features were developed by Turney [1]

13.3.11 Parts of speech

Knowledge of parts of speech (POS) is most widely used in all NLP tasks. One of the most significant explanations is that they offer a crude means of disambiguation of word meaning. Though there are several POS tags, adjective, verb and adverb plays the most vital role in Sentiment Analysis [27].

Of all parts of speech, adjectives are most commonly used as characteristics for sentiment detection [24–26]. A strong correlation has been found between adjectives and subjectivity. Although all the parts of speech are significant, all the works focusing on only adjectives for feature generation have recorded adjectives as a very commonly used component to depict most of the emotions and with high precision. [3] inferred about 82.8% accuracy in film review domains using only adjectives.

Mostly, adverbs have no previous polarity. But when they happen with adjectives carrying sentiment, they may play a major role in deciding a sentence's sentiment. [25] have shown how the adverbs modify the adjective's sentiment value in which they are used. Adverbs of degree are graded as follows on the basis of the degree to which they change their sentiment meaning.

i. Affirmative adverbs like 'certainly' and 'totally'
ii. Adverbs of doubt like 'maybe' and 'probably'
iii. Adverbs of strong intensity like 'exceedingly' and 'immensely'
iv. Adverbs of weak intensity like 'barely' and 'slightly'
v. Adverbs of negation and minimizers like 'never'

13.3.12 Removal of non-alphabetic characters

Depending on the aim of analysis, brooming out uninformative content from the text impacts Sentiment Analysis. All terms that do not carry any sort of sentiment with them, even around other terms, are removed. Numbers, links, Hypertext Markup Language (HTML) Tags, characters that are not from the English language like return characters, special characters, and stop words are discarded. For example, '\n', ';', '<Head>', and '9'.

13.3.13 Negation handling

A negation lexicon is similar to the emoticon dictionary. From observation, there are more negative comments out there than positive comments [28]. A massive issue faced by people who process text is that they do not pay attention to negation handling. A negation lexicon will put across how negative comments take form which allows the system to identify the same.

Negative words are mostly written informally like 'can't, 'won't', and 'doesn't'. These are contracted forms of 'cannot', 'will not', and 'does not' respectively. Overlooking these words and misinterpreting them as nonnegative will mislead the model. Hence, they are changed to their formal forms.

13.3.14 Short form expansion

In the current internet times, short forms are very common. Besides, there are abbreviations and acronyms which are also short forms of long names. For example, 'IDC' is used instead of 'I don't care'. Unless there is a dictionary which teaches the program all of these, it is unlikely that it will recognize them correctly. Therefore, expansion of the short forms will minimize loss of information.

13.3.15 Sentiment polarity score

The polarity score of sentiment gives text a score ranging from overwhelmingly positive to strongly negative [21]. With neutral in the center, it is a scale of intense feelings and everything in between. Until fitting them to an algorithm, tagging text with scores will boost the methodology. Two lexicons, namely AFINN [29] and SentiWordNet [30], are usually used to do this.

13.3.16 Number of hashtags

Hashtags are the new trend that sits well with the young population. Hashtag is a means of following all the posts related to the name of the hashtag. For example, #womensday is a hashtag where people following that particular hashtag will be shown all the posts about Women's Day put up by others using it. Incorporating hashtag features assists the model to keep track of what the general population enjoy consuming.

Despite the availability of these rich feature engineering methods, Sentiment Analysis faces several challenges, which might require attention. So, next comes the challenges in sentiment analysis.

13.4 CHALLENGES IN SENTIMENT ANALYSIS

In our day-to-day life, we come across zillion data in the web, most of which might be totally irrelevant to us. Every second, people keep updating their life stories, experiences, and thoughts on the web. With the increase in such data, the complexity of natural language text processing and automated analysis also increases. Irrespective of whether the statement is grammatically correct or not, natural language needs to be processed to extract the emotion and sentiment of the writer. Challenges in the field of Sentiment Analysis are umpteen. Some of the momentous challenges are discussed herewith

Objective Statement Identification also termed as *Subjectivity Detection* [11, 31, 32] is a prime task and is very significant with respect to Sentiment Analysis, because only subjective statements play a role in Sentiment Classification. Hence, it becomes important to identify and eliminate the objective statements [33]. This can also be considered as a pre-processing step for Sentiment Analysis. Consider the examples below, where despite the fact that both of them contain the polarity word, favorite, the first statement is objective whereas the second statement is subjective.

My favorite pair of sneakers are not in stock.
My favorite vegetable is the awesome tasting carrot.

Aspect Polarity Mapping [39] is the problem of identifying which aspect is to be mapped with which polarity word when a single statement carries multiple aspects and polarity words. Primarily, identifying the aspects itself is a challenge. Consider the examples below, where the opinion on the aspect 'food' is positive but the sentiment on the aspect 'time' (i.e., the time taken to serve food) is negative. Even though it looks easy, making a model, which could be automated to perform the aspect polarity mapping is quite difficult.

The food was delicious, but on an empty stomach, don't come here.

Contradiction Analysis is a slightly modified form of the aspect-polarity mapping task, where a single aspect gets more than one polarity. In certain cases, the overall polarity and a specific aspect polarity which is closer to the overall polarity gets a directly conflicting polarity from the same reviewer. Such an analysis is also called a *conflicting sentiment analysis* or *thwarted expectation analysis*. In the example given below, the overall review of the phone is positive, but a particular aspect is marked negative by the reviewer.

Great phone but it doesn't support playing audio when on call.

Entity Identification [43] can be thought of as another dimension to the aspect identification task, where, generally when comparative sentences appear, it is hard to map the polarity with more than one entity available. In the example given below, whether positive polarity is to be given to the first entity (Samsung) or the second entity (Blackberry) is a challenging task, when we have even complex sentences.

Samsung is much better than Blackberry.

Word Sense Disambiguation (WSD) [34] is where one word acts differently in different places. In the example given below, the same word 'bank' means a riverbank in the first statement and a money bank in the second statement. It is challenging to make a machine understand the context of the word 'bank' using the other words in the statement.

The river overflowed its bank.
The customers are overflowing the bank.

Domain Dependency, is another dimension to Word Sense Disambiguation, where the same word works differently for different domains as in the examples depicted below. The first statement implies a negative impact and, the second statement implies a positive impact. One major polarity changer in these examples is the word 'cold' apart from the domain keywords, pizza, and coke.

They delivered a cold pizza.
They served cold Coke.

Automating Negation Identification [8, 28] is difficult when 'no', 'never', 'not' and other negation words are not handled properly. Let's consider three examples for this scenario, given below. In the first statement, with a single negation word 'none' the complete statement is negated. In the second statement, even though it has two negated words, it only gives an emphasis on the negation. The third example is a grammatically incorrect statement which actually conveys 'There isn't a problem' but with natural language processing, we could only expect the conventional flow of text.

None of us liked the movie.
I didn't steal nothing.
There isn't no problem.

Sarcasm Detection [36, 52] is hard to handle unless several features are taken into account. One such compelling feature is the analysis of the presence and significance of numbers in a sarcastic statement.

For example, consider these three statements, where the presence of numbers, brings out the sarcastic effect aftermath.

This brand-new mobile phone has an outstanding battery backup.

(Non-sarcastic)

This brand-new mobile phone has an outstanding battery backup of two hours.

(Sarcastic)

This brand-new mobile phone has an outstanding battery backup of 24 hours.

(Non-sarcastic)

Spam Detection [35] is yet another challenge, where companies spread good opinions about themselves, and negative opinions about their competitors. These fake reviews are most popularly called 'bogus reviews'. Most of the work so far on spam detection has been conducted using supervised machine learning methods with the help of various features. The most compelling features are the lexical features like the n-grams and parts-of-speech, the content similarity, the spammer's writing pattern similarity, and, of course, the abnormal behavior of the spammer.

Internet Slang keeps changing daily and these days we see many new open words. In the example given below, 'gud' and 'lit' is how the reviewer has written 'good' and 'light'. It is important to include these sentences for processing rather than discarding these sentences during pre-processing.

The phone is really gud and the camera quality is lit.

Use of *transliterated words* has always been frequent while commenting on the web, and its use is increasing day-by-day. In India, the most common language is Hindi, as three-fourths of Indian web users use this language prevalently. Apart from that, local regional languages are also found. In the example given below, the Thamizh language is transliterated into English by the writer, which actually means, 'this offer is so good, hence is must buy'.

Intha deal romba nalla iruku, must buy.

Dialects and Regional Influences also considerably impact Sentiment Analysis, as is given in the example below. It is said that America and Britain are 'two nations divided by a common language'. 'Cookie' and 'biscuit' mean the same. Similarly, 'vacation' and 'holiday' mean the same, just that the first word is American and second word is British, respectively. Making a machine understand all such variations is a real challenge.

The cookie topping on the ice cake was yummy.
This book kept me occupied during the vacation.

Emoticons and Emojis [14] are prevalently used while expressing one's sentiment. Traditionally, punctuation was removed as a part of pre-processing. These days with the usage of emojis and emoticons for expressing sentiment, it has become mandatory to process these emojis and emoticons. There are two particularly popular styles of emoticons. They are the *Western-styled* and *Eastern-styled* emoticons. The Western Style is encoded in only one or two characters as in :D, :) and so on. The Eastern Style is a longer combination of characters as in ¯_(ツ)_/¯

World Knowledge has become an important component, that should be fused into the machine learning system to detect sentiments accurately. Consider the two statements given below, where the first statement gives a negative sense, and second statement gives a positive sense. To identify the sentiment, it is vital to know, who or what are Frankenstein and leprechauns.

He is a Frankenstein.
He is a Leprechaun.

Pragmatics deals with understanding the sentences beyond the literal meaning of the statement. In the examples given below, words like 'brains' and 'hand' are not to be taken literally. Given certain scenarios and states, we humans can easily understand the context, but making the machine understand where to take the literal meaning and where not to, is definitely a greater challenge.

Using this product really gave me some brains.
Can you give me a hand? I really find it difficult to operate this product.

Implicit Sentiment [41] is where aspect words or sometimes entity words are not explicitly found in the review, but are implicitly embedded. To build a model which can interpret implicit sentiment is an indefinite challenge. In the examples given below, 'weight' is the aspect discussed but it is not explicitly used.

It weighs a lot.
Too heavy.

All the challenges discussed so far are just a handful of them, but as we start experimenting with them, indefinite issues start to emerge. The willingness to facing these issues intensifies as the applications and scope of Sentiment Analysis outweighs the challenges.

13.5 RESEARCH CHALLENGE ACCURACY

All the research challenges in the field of Sentiment Analysis have been addressed over the years and the current scenario of research innovation level can be understood from the percentage of accuracy reached so far. Table 13.1 gives the percentage of accuracy achieved so far in various sentiment analysis challenges like spam detection, sarcasm detection, cross domain sentiment analysis [50], topic-level sentiment classification, inter aspect relations, sentiment lexicon construction, implicit sentiment analysis, semantic disambiguation, entity-level sentiment classification and multi-class sentiment analysis. It is also depicted in Figure 13.6. From Table 13.1, we can understand that still there is a lot of scope for study in the field of analyzing sentiments.

Table 13.1 Research challenges in Sentiment Analysis and the recent % of accuracy

Sentiment Analysis challenges	% of accuracy
Spam detection [35]	90.06
Sarcasm detection [36]	97.87
Cross domain Sentiment Analysis [37]	83.50
Topic-level sentiment classification [38]	92
Inter aspect relations [39]	81.38
Sentiment lexicon construction [40]	84.32
Implicit Sentiment Analysis [41]	80.55
Semantic disambiguation [42]	82
Entity-level sentiment classification [43]	71.36
Multi-class Sentiment Analysis [44]	60.2

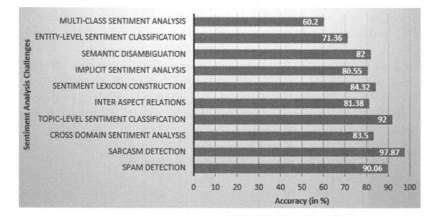

Figure 13.6 Research challenges in Sentiment Analysis and the accuracies obtained so far.

13.6 APPLICATIONS AND SCOPE OF SENTIMENT ANALYSIS

Sentiment Analysis has become the need of the hour, because with the eruption of the social media network and e-commerce platforms, and the limited time that the users have, it is pretty time consuming to read all the comments and interpret their essence. Hence, a sentimentally analyzed abstract in a summarized form or a visualizable representation can reduce frustration when skimming through these websites.

Word of Mouth (WOM) is the method of transmitting data from person to person and plays a major role in the purchase decisions of consumers. WOM includes customers exchanging attitudes, beliefs, or reactions with other people regarding companies, goods, or services in commercial situations. The functions of WOM communication are focused on social networking and trust. People in their social networks rely on families, acquaintances, and others. Research also shows that individuals tend to trust apparently disinterested opinions, such as online reviews, from individuals outside their immediate social network. This is where sentiment analysis comes into play. The 'decision-making process' has become simpler for us by the increasing availability of opinion-rich tools such as online review sites [45], blogs, and social networking sites. Consumers have a soapbox of unparalleled breadth and influence with the proliferation of Web 2.0 sites from which they can express opinions. Major businesses have recognized that these user voices control the shaping of other customers' voices.

The other dimension with respect to e-commerce sites is that Sentiment Analysis can help in *recommendation suggestions* [45]. Based on the user's purchase history, transaction logs, browsing links, and commonly searched items, the current day e-commerce purchase sites provide the users with ample recommendation. With the analyzed feedback of previous consumers, an item can either be recommended or be discarded by the trained model. This commendation system can also be useful not only in product suggestions but also in services. Product producers always try to improve their products and services, for which they could make a great deal from the reviews posted by the end-user customers. But just the raw reviews would be tedious to work with. Thus, Sentiment Analysis would be of great use to such producers and manufacturers. On the other hand, new customers would also identify the positives or negatives of various features of the products, and would make a more refined purchase decision.

Classifying emails into spam and not spam, based on heated language, is also a common task [35]. Identifying unfriendly terms and the history of the phone number blocking a number is also very prevalent. Spam Detection is not only useful in email classification, but is also becoming popular in review classification and other textual conversations these days. Sentiment Analysis also plays a vital role in context-sensitive information detection and analysis.

Sentiment Classification is used for various purposes. One such purpose is for analyzing and tracking the literary reputation of authors [46]. The input reviews are drawn from literary reviews, letters to the editor, journal articles, and critical and academic publications for such an examination. When it comes to question and answering sessions [51] on many websites, Sentiment Analysis can play a vital role. Based on the user's question and other transactional details, answers can be automated with a positive or a negative polarity touch.

Another prime use of sentiment analysis is in analyzing public opinion of political leaders regionally, nationally, and worldwide [47]. Public opinion [48] can be analyzed with respect to the rules, regulations, and other implementations by the government as well.

Sentiment Analysis can be useful in several Data Mining applications. It also plays a significant role in Information Retrieval. In addition, without using such data, applications such as ranking films based on online film reviews [5] could not arise. Sentiment Analysis thus finds its use for product reviews in the consumer market, marketing to understand consumer perceptions and patterns, social media to find general opinions on recent hot topics in the region, and film to find out whether a newly released film is a hit [49]. [20] broadly classifies the applications into the following categories.

13.7 MULTILINGUAL SENTIMENT ANALYSIS

Every language has its own way of expression in its free natural language form. In India, more than 20 languages are used prevalently for speaking, reading, and writing. And many languages are derived from several other languages.

13.7.1 Thamizh text Sentiment Analysis

Thamizh, most popularly written as Tamil, is the most ancient language. Very similar to the way English is used for Sentiment Analysis, Thamizh text Sentiment Analysis is also performed widely. Thamizh movie reviews using Thamizh tweets were used for predicting the polarity of the reviews [54]. Thamizh Twitter data was used to perform rule-based Sentiment Classification [55]. Word Sense Disambiguation was also addressed in Thamizh using path length similarity [56]. SentiWordNet and WordNet for Thamizh is also being prepared by various researchers in various phases [57, 58].

13.7.2 Chinese text Sentiment Analysis

Sentiment Analysis is a very popular task, that it has been explored in several languages. English is the most researched language with respect to Sentiment Analysis. The next most predominant language in Sentiment Analysis is Chinese. In Chinese language, just like English, almost all the Sentiment

Analysis tasks have been explored. Chinese sentiment dictionaries [59, 60] have been created explicitly for micro-blogging services. Chinese product reviews for e-commerce websites [61] were explored using sentiment lexicon and deep learning techniques. Herd behavior [62] in the Chinese stock market was also explored. Topic-level Chinese Sentiment Analysis has been done using spectral clustering [63].

13.7.3 Arabic text Sentiment Analysis

Sentiment Analysis is becoming quite popular with Arabic text also. Using surface and deep feature ensembles, Sentiment Analysis was explored very recently [64]. Convolutional Neural Networks were used to exploit Arabic dialect-oriented sentiment polarity analysis [65]. Arabic Sentiment Analysis has also been performed with multi-level parallel attention neural models designed for better performance [66].

13.7.4 Urdu text Sentiment Analysis

Urdu is a very popular language derived from several languages like Arabic, Sanskrit, and Persian. Sentiment Analysis has been performed on Roman influenced Urdu in a few works [67, 68].

13.7.5 Spanish text Sentiment Analysis

In the Spanish language, Twitter data is most commonly used for Sentiment Analysis. Social bots were identified in the Spanish election from Twitter using political Sentiment Analysis [69]. Negation identification was performed in Spanish Twitter data [70]. Both supervised and unsupervised machine learning methods were used to classify polarity-based Spanish reviews [71].

Sentiment Analysis in Russian [72], Malay [73], and Hindi [74] has also started to be explored with the necessary sentiment lexicon collections.

13.8 PERFORMANCE METRICS

As Sentiment Analysis is performed, it is obvious that every review or every sentence in the review is classified into one of the desired classes. Eventually, it is important to analyze the model that was developed. The efficiency of every algorithm can be evaluated using some metrics. In the process of evaluating the Sentiment Analysis model, four metrics are most popularly used. They are precision, recall, f1 score, and accuracy. Other metrics include ranking loss, mean squared error, least absolute error, discounted cumulative gain, and mean absolute error [75].

Precision is the measure of how often a sentiment rating was correct. Accuracy records how many of those who were rated to have tonality were rated correctly for documents with tonality. The formula given in Equation 13.6, can be used to measure precision, where TP is True Positive and FP is False Positive.

$$\text{Precision} = \frac{\text{TP}}{\text{TP} + \text{FP}} \tag{13.6}$$

Recall is the measure of how many documents with sentiment were rated as sentimental. This could be seen as how the method defines neutrality correctly. Generally, in tests of broad subject matter, high recall scores are very difficult, as the machine is expected to grasp ever-larger sets of words and language. With the formula given in Equation 13.7, where TP stands for True Positive and FN stands for False Negative, recall can be determined.

$$\text{Recall} = \frac{\text{TP}}{\text{TP} + \text{FP}} \tag{13.7}$$

F1 score is also known as *F-Score* or *F-Measure*, which is a combination of precision and recall. F1 Score impacts both faulty positives and faulty negatives. Though precision is more direct than F1 score, F1 score is proven to be more helpful than precision. Precision effects most if the faulty positives and faulty negatives have a relative cost. If the expense of defective positives and faulty negatives is distinct and varied, it is more useful to look at both Accuracy and Recall values. The score is in the 0.0–1.0 range, where 1.0 will be fine. The F1 score is very useful, as it gives us a single metric that rates both the accuracy and recall of a device. As such, it is widely used in the fields of linguistics and natural language processing by experts and researchers to simply characterize the output of such systems. The F1 score can be calculated using the formula given in Equation 13.8.

$$\text{F1 score} = \frac{2 * \text{Precision} * \text{Recall}}{\text{Precision} + \text{Recall}} \tag{13.8}$$

Accuracy is the most widely used execution measure in Sentiment Analysis. Accuracy can be determined using the formula given in Equation 13.13.9, where TP denotes True Positive, TN denotes True Negative, FP denotes False Positive, and FN denotes False Negative.

$$\text{Accuracy} = \frac{\text{TP} + \text{TN}}{\text{TP} + \text{TN} + \text{FP} + \text{FN}} \tag{13.9}$$

Ranking Loss [76] is the measure used to calculate the average distance between the predicted rank value and the actual rank value. It can also be represented as in the formula given in Equation 13.10, where it is depicted as the average deviation between the actual sentiment score of the entity 'as' and the predicted sentiment score 'ps' of the same entity, with 'C' sentiment classes and 'N' rows of data.

$$\text{Ranking Loss} = \sum_{i=1}^{N} \frac{|as_i - ps_i|}{C * N} \tag{13.10}$$

Mean Squared Error (MSE) [78] is also popularly called *Mean L2 Error*. MSE is used to evaluate the prediction error of the model being evaluated. This evaluation metric is most commonly used for regression analysis. MSE can be computed using the formula given in Equation 13.11, where 't_i' is the vector representation of 'N' sentiment class prediction and 'p_i' is the vector representation of true sentiment class values.

$$\text{Mean Squared Error} = \frac{1}{N} \sum_{i=1}^{N} (t_i - p_i)^2 \tag{13.11}$$

Least Absolute Error (LAE) [79] is also popularly known as *Mean L1 Error*. LAE is used to evaluate the sentiment class classification error. LAE can be calculated using the formula given in Equation 13.12, where 't_i' is the vector representation of 'N' sentiment class prediction and 'p_i' is the vector representation of true sentiment class values.

$$\text{Least Absolute Error} = \sum_{i=1}^{N} |t_i - p_i| \tag{13.12}$$

The normalized *Discounted Cumulative Gain* (DCG) [78, 80] is also used in few works and is identified as more useful in computing the most relevant aspects of the entities. This relevance factor is not essentially a binary value. The DCG can be calculated using the formula given in Equation 13.13, where 'k' is the top-rated aspects and 'relevance (i)' is the relevance score of the aspect 'i'.

$$\text{Discounted Cumulative Gain} = \sum_{i=1}^{k} \frac{2^{\text{relevance}(i)} - 1}{\log_2(i+1)} \tag{13.13}$$

In order to normalize the DCG value thus obtained, it is necessary to implement cross-query evaluation, where this DCG value is divided by the ideal DCG value.

13.9 CONCLUSION

Sentiment Analysis can be considered as the precise interpretation of the reviews that any service has received, classifying them into groups and categories for easy navigation and construal. The customers can thus navigate these categories to search for whatever they require. This makes the task for the consumer much more convenient as they do not have to go through and break down each and every review for a product or a service they wish to purchase. Instead, they can look up the aspects they desire and find the features, opinions, and pros and cons in a remarkably simpler fashion in order make a self-suited decision. The level of this polarity analysis is myriad, ranging from a single sentence, involving a whole paragraph, or a whole document. Sentiment Analysis is a budding area of research and needs more attention. Thus, this chapter helps a beginner or a naïve researcher of this domain get better clarity on where and what to start with in anything related to Sentiment Analysis.

REFERENCES

1. Peter D. Turney, 2002, "Thumbs Up or Thumbs Down? Semantic Orientation Applied to Unsupervised Classification of Reviews", *Proceedings of the 40th Annual Meeting of the Association for Computational Linguistics (ACL)*, pp. 417–424.
2. Jiawei Han, Micheline Kamber, and Jian Pei, 2012, *Data Mining: Concepts and Techniques*. 3rd ed. Waltham, MA: Morgan Kaufmann Publishers.
3. Bo Pang, Lillian Lee, and Shivakumar Vaithyanathan, 2002, "Thumbs Up? Sentiment Classification Using Machine Learning Techniques", *EMNLP-2002*, pp. 79–86.
4. Bo Pang and Lillian Lee, 2008, "Opinion Mining and Sentiment Analysis", *Foundations and Trends in Information Retrieval*, vol. 2, no 1–2, pp. 1–135.
5. Alexander Pak and Patrick Paroubek, 2010, "Twitter as a Corpus for Sentiment Analysis and Opinion Mining", *Proceedings of the Seventh conference on International Language Resources and Evaluation*, pp. 1320–1326.
6. Sien Chen, Yinghua Huang, and Wen-Ter Huang, 2016, "Big Data Analytics on Aviation Social Media: The Case of China Southern Airlines on Sina Weibo", *2016 IEEE Second International Conference on Big Data Computing Service and Applications* (Big Data Service), Oxford, UK, pp. 152–155.
7. Ari Firmanto Suhariyanto, and R. Sarno, "Prediction of Movie Sentiment Based on Reviews and Score on Rotten Tomatoes Using Senti Wordnet", *2018 International Seminar on Application for Technology of Information and Communication*, Semarang, Indonesia, pp. 202–206, 2018.
8. Saluk Maria Jimenez Zafra, Maria Teresa Martin Valdivia, Eugenio Martinez Camara, and L. Alfonso Urena Lopez, 2019, "Studying the Scope of Negation for Spanish Sentiment Analysis on Twitter", *IEEE Transactions on Affective Computing*, vol. 10, no. 1, pp. 129–141.
9. Bing Liu, 2010, "Sentiment Analysis and Subjectivity", *Handbook of Natural Language Processing*.

10. Hsinchun Chen and David Zimbra, 2010, "AI and Opinion Mining", *IEEE Intelligent Systems*, vol. 25, no. 3, pp. 74–80.

11. C. Sindhu, Binoy Sasmal, Rahul Gupta, and J. Prathipa, (2021), "Subjectivity Detection for Sentiment Analysis on Twitter Data", In: Hemanth, D., Vadivu, G., Sangeetha, M., and Balas, V. (eds) *Artificial Intelligence Techniques for Advanced Computing Applications. Lecture Notes in Networks and Systems*, vol 130. Singapore: Springer. https://doi.org/10.1007/978-981-15-5329-5_43

12. Ahmed Abbasi, Stephen France, Zhu Zhang, and Hsinchun Chen, 2011, "Selecting Attributes for Sentiment Classification Using Feature Relation Networks", *IEEE Transactions on Knowledge and Data Engineering*, vol. 23, no. 3, pp. 447–462.

13. Kethan Pabbi, C., Sindhu, Isukapalli Sainath Reddy, and Bhumireddy Naga Sai Abhijit, 2021, "The Use of Transformer Model in Opinion Summarisation", *Webology*, vol 18, pp. 1084–1095.

14. Paul Ekman, 1972, *Emotion in the Human Face*, in Pergamon General Psychology Series, (11) https://doi.org/10.1016/C2013-0-02458-91972.

15. Jackson Liscombe, Giuseppe Riccardi, and Dilek Hakkani Tür, 2005, "Using Context to Improve Emotion Detection in Spoken Dialog Systems", *Interspeech*, pp. 1845–1848.

16. George Forman, 2004, "An Extensive Empirical Study of Feature Selection Metrics for Text Classification", *Journal of Machine Learning Research*, vol. 3, pp. 1289–1305.

17. Ahmed Abbasi, Hsinchun Chen, and Aran Salem, 2008, "Sentiment Analysis in Multiple Languages: Feature Selection for Opinion Classification in Web Forums", *ACM Transactions on Information Systems*, vol. 26, no. 3, Article No. 12.

18. Yuming Lin, Jingwei Zhang, Xiaoling Wang, and Aoying Zhou, 2012, "Sentiment Classification via Integrating Multiple Feature Presentations", WWW 2012 – Poster Presentation, pp. 569–570. https://citeseerx.ist.psu.edu/document?repid=rep1&type=pdf&doi=de5866317ba83615cc995ae504e083e8112ed1a5

19. Mark A. Hall and Lloyd A. Smith, 1997, "Feature Subset Selection: A Correlation Based Filter Approach", *Proceedings of the Fourth International Conference on Neural Information Processing and Intelligent Information Systems*, pp. 855–858.

20. Suge Wang, Deyu Li, Xiaolei Song, Yingjie Wei, and Hongxia Li, 2011, "A Feature Selection Method Based on Improved Fisher's Discriminant Ratio for Text Sentiment Classification", *Expert Systems with Applications*, vol. 38, no. 7, pp. 8696–8702.

21. Shitanshu Verma and Pushpak Bhattacharyya, 2009, "Incorporating Semantic Knowledge for Sentiment Analysis", *Proceedings of International Conference on Natural Language Processing. International Conference on NLP (ICON 2009)*, Hyderabad, Dec, 2009. https://www.cse.iitb.ac.in/~pb/pubs-yearwise.html

22. Kushal Dave, Steve Lawrence, and David M. Pennock, 2003, "Mining the Peanut Gallery: Opinion Extraction and Semantic Classification of Product Reviews", In *Proceedings of the 12th international conference on World Wide Web (WWW '03)*. Association for Computing Machinery, New York, NY, USA, pp. 519–528. https://doi.org/10.1145/775152.775226

23. Chenghua Lin, Yulan He, R. Everson, and S. Ruger, 2012, "Weakly Supervised Joint Sentiment-Topic Detection from Text", *IEEE Transactions on Knowledge and Data Engineering*, vol. 24, no. 6. pp. 1134–1145.
24. Vasileios Hatzivassiloglou and Kathleen McKeown, 1997, "Predicting the semantic orientation of adjectives", *Proceedings of the 35th Association for Computational Linguistics and 8th Conference of the European Chapter of the Association for Computational Linguistics*, pp. 174–181.
25. Farah Benamara, Carmine Cesarano, Antonio Picariello, Diego Reforgiato, and VS Subrahmanian, 2007, "Sentiment Analysis: Adjectives and Adverbs are better than Adjectives Alone", *Proceedings of the International Conference on Weblogs and Social Media*, Boulder, CO, USA, pp. 1–4.
26. Vasileios Hatzivassiloglou and Janyce Wiebe, 2000, "Effects of Adjective Orientation and Gradability on Sentence Subjectivity", *Proceedings of the 18th Conference on Computational Linguistic*, vol. 1, pp. 299–305.
27. Sindhu Chandra Sekharan and G Vadivu, 2020, "Effects of Adjective Verb Adverb on Sentiment Classification Using Support Vector Machine for Green Communication", *Journal of Green Engineering*, vol 10, pp. 91–102.
28. Michael Wiegand and Alexandra Balahur, 2010, "A Survey on the Role of Negation in Sentiment Analysis", *Proceedings of the Workshop on Negation and Speculation in Natural Language Processing*. https://aclanthology.org/W10-3111/
29. Finn rup Nielsen, 2011, "A new ANEW: Evaluation of a word list for sentiment analysis in microblogs". https://www.semanticscholar.org/paper/A-New-ANEW%3A-Evaluation-of-a-Word-List-for-Sentiment-Nielsen/d38763b4b0bbf1ed91b55107c658fcc96f8ef82d
30. Esuli and Sebastiani, 2006, "SentiWordNet: A Publicly Available Lexical Resource for Opinion Mining", *International Conference on Language Resources and Evaluation (LREC)*, pp. 417–422.
31. Ellen Riloff and Janyce Wiebe, 2003, "Learning Extraction Patterns for Subjective Expressions", *Proceedings of the Conference on Empirical Methods in Natural Language Processing*. Association for Computational Linguistics, USA, pp. 105–112. https://doi.org/10.3115/1119355.1119369 https://dl.acm.org/doi/10.3115/1119355.1119369 https://aclanthology.org/W10-3111/
32. Ellen Riloff, Janyce Wiebe, and William Phillips, 2005, "Exploiting Subjectivity Classification to Improve Information Extraction", *Proceedings of Association for the Advancement of Artificial Intelligence*, pp. 1106–1111.
33. Janyce Wiebe and Ellen Riloff, 2011, "Finding Mutual Benefit between Subjectivity Analysis and Information Extraction", *IEEE Transactions on Affective Computing*, vol. 2, no. 4, pp. 175–191.
34. C. Sindhu, Rajkakati D., and Shelukar C, 2021, "Context-Based Sentiment Analysis on Amazon Product Customer Feedback Data", In: Hemanth, D., Vadivu, G., Sangeetha, M., and Balas, V. (eds) *Artificial Intelligence Techniques for Advanced Computing Applications, Lecture Notes in Networks and Systems*, vol 130, Singapore: Springer.
35. Sindhu Chandra Sekharan, G. Vadivu, Anirudh Singh, and Rahil Patel, 2018, "Methods and Approaches on Spam Review Detection for Sentiment Analysis", *International Journal of Pure and Applied Mathematics*, vol. 118, no. 22 B, Special Issue, pp. 683–690.

36. Mandala Vishal Rao and Sindhu Chandra Sekharan, 2021, "Detection of Sarcasm on Amazon Product Reviews using Machine Learning Algorithms under Sentiment Analysis", *2021 Sixth International Conference on Wireless Communications, Signal Processing and Networking (WiSPNET)*, pp. 196–199, https://doi.org/10.1109/WiSPNET51692.2021.9419432.

37. Yanbin Hao, Tingting Mu, Richang Hong, Meng Wang, Xueliang Liu, and John Y. Goulermas, 2020, "Cross-Domain Sentiment Encoding through Stochastic Word Embedding", *IEEE Transactions on Knowledge and Data Engineering*, vol. 32, no. 10, pp. 1909–1922.

38. Huizhi Liang, Umarani Ganeshbabu, and Thomas Thorne, 2020, "A Dynamic Bayesian Network Approach for Analysing Topic-Sentiment Evolution", *IEEE Access*, vol. 8, pp. 54164–54174.

39. Sindhu Chandra Sekharan and G. Vadivu, 2021, "Fine Grained Sentiment Polarity Classification Using Augmented Knowledge Sequence-Attention Mechanism", *Journal of Microprocessors and Microsystems*, vol 81. https://doi.org/10.1016/j.micpro.2020.103365.

40. Dong Deng, Liping Jing, Jian Yu and Shaolong Sun, 2019, "Sparse Self-Attention LSTM for Sentiment Lexicon Construction", *IEEE/ACM Transactions on Audio, Speech, and Language Processing*, vol. 27, no. 11, pp. 1777–1790.

41. Enguang Zuo, Hui Zhao, Bo Chen, and Qiuchang Chen, 2020, "Context-Specific Heterogeneous Graph Convolutional Network for Implicit Sentiment Analysis", *IEEE Access*, vol. 8, pp. 37967–37975.

42. Fulian Yin, Yanyan Wang, Jianbo Liu, and Lisha Lin, 2020, "The Construction of Sentiment Lexicon Based on Context-Dependent Part-of-Speech Chunks for Semantic Disambiguation", *IEEE Access*, vol. 8, pp. 63359–63367.

43. Jianfei Yu, Jing Jiang, and Rui Xia, 2020, "Entity-Sensitive Attention and Fusion Network for Entity-Level Multimodal Sentiment Classification", *IEEE/ACM Transactions on Audio, Speech, and Language Processing*, vol. 28, pp. 429–439.

44. Mondher Bouazizi and Tomoaki Ohtsuki, 2019, "Multi-Class Sentiment Analysis on twitter: Classification Performance and Challenges", *Big Data Mining and Analytics*, vol. 2, no. 3, pp. 181–194.

45. Zhu Zhang, 2008, "Weighing Stars: Aggregating Online Product Reviews for Intelligent E-Commerce Applications", *IEEE Intelligent Systems*, vol. 23, no. 5, pp. 42–49.

46. Maite Taboada, Mary Ann Gillies, and Paul McFetridge, 2006, "Sentiment classification techniques for tracking literary reputation", *Language Resources and Evaluation Workshop: Towards Computational Models of Literary Analysis*, pp. 36–43.

47. Matt Thomas, Bo Pang, and Lillian Lee, 2006, "Get Out the Vote: Determining Support or Opposition from Congressional Floor-Debate Transcripts", *Proceedings of the Conference on Empirical Methods in Natural Language Processing*, pp. 327–335.

48. George Stylios, Dimitris Christodoulakis, Jeries Besharat, Maria-Alexandra Vonitsanou, Ioanis Kotrotsos, Athanasia Koumpouri, and Sofia Stamou, 2010, "Public Opinion Mining for Governmental Decisions", *Electronic Journal of eGovernment*, vol. 8, no. 2, pp. 203–214.

49. Junichi Tatemura, 2000, "Virtual reviewers for collaborative exploration of movie reviews", *Proceedings of Intelligent User Interfaces*, pp. 272–275.

50. Danushka Bollegala, David Weir, and John Carroll, 2013, "Cross-Domain Sentiment Classification using a Sentiment Sensitive Thesaurus", *IEEE Transactions on Knowledge and Data Engineering*, vol. 25, no. 8, pp. 1719–1731.
51. Lucian Vlad Lita, Andrew Hazen Schlaikjer, Wei Chang Hong, and Eric Nyberg, 2005, "Qualitative Dimensions in Question Answering: Extending the Definitional QA task", *Proceedings of Association for the Advancement of Artificial Intelligence*, pp. 1616–1617.
52. C. Sindhu, Isukapalli Sainath Reddy, and Settipalle C. Sai Pavan Kumar Reddy, 2021, "Consolidating Pattern-Based Approach for Detecting Sarcasm in Numerical Portions of the Text", *2021 Sixth International Conference on Wireless Communications, Signal Processing and Networking (WiSPNET)*, pp. 230–234, https://doi.org/10.1109/WiSPNET51692.2021.9419430.
53. C. Sindhu and Asha Gutlapalli, 2019, "A Comprehensive Study on Aspect Based Sentimental Analysis Framework and its Techniques", *Emerging Trends in Artificial Intelligence for Internet of Things*, vol. 1, pp. 21–40.
54. Vallikannu Ramanathan, Meyyappan Thiunavukkarasu, and S. M. Thamarai, 2019, "Predicting Tamil Movies Sentimental Reviews Using Tamil Tweets", *Journal of Computer Science*, vol. 15, no. (11), pp. 1638–1647.
55. Nandana Ravishankar and R. Shriram, 2018, "Grammar Rule-Based Sentiment Categorisation Model for Classification of Tamil Tweets", *International Journal of Intelligent System Technology Application*, vol. 17, pp. 89–96.
56. N. Kausikaa and V. Uma, 2016, "Sentiment Analysis of English and Tamil Tweets Using Path Length Similarity-Based Word Sense Disambiguation", *IOSR Journal of Computer Engineering*, vol. 18, pp. 82–89.
57. A. Kannan, G. Mohanty, and R. Mamidi, 2016, "Towards Building a SentiWordNet for Tamil", *Proceedings of the 13th International Conference on Natural Language Processing, (NLP' 16), ACL*, Varanasi, India, pp. 30–35.
58. Sankaravelayuthan Rajendran, Selvaraj Arulmozi, B. Kumara Shanmugam, S. Baskaran, and S. Thiagarajan, 2002, "Tamil wordnet", *International Global Word Net Conference Mysore*, vol. 152, pp. 271–274.
59. Jiesheng Wu, Kui Lu, Shuzhi Su, and Shibing Wang, 2019, "Chinese Micro-Blog Sentiment Analysis Based on Multiple Sentiment Dictionaries and Semantic Rule Sets", *IEEE Access*, vol. 7, pp. 183924–183939.
60. Guixian Xu, Ziheng Yu, Haishen Yao, Fan Li, Yueting Meng, and Xu Wu, 2019, "Chinese Text Sentiment Analysis Based on Extended Sentiment Dictionary", *IEEE Access*, vol. 7, pp. 43749–43762.
61. Li Yang, Ying Li, Jin Wang, and R. Simon Sherratt, 2020, "Sentiment Analysis for E-Commerce Product Reviews in Chinese Based on Sentiment Lexicon and Deep Learning", *IEEE Access*, vol. 8, pp. 23522–23530.
62. Rui Ren and Desheng Wu, 2020, "An Innovative Sentiment Analysis to Measure Herd Behavior", *IEEE Transactions on Systems, Man, and Cybernetics: Systems*, vol. 50, no. 10, pp. 3841–3851.
63. Bo Zhang, Duo Xu, Huan Zhang, and Meizi Li, 2019, "STCS Lexicon: Spectral-Clustering-Based Topic-Specific Chinese Sentiment Lexicon Construction for Social Networks", *IEEE Transactions on Computational Social Systems*, vol. 6, no. 6, pp. 1180–1189.
64. Nora Al-Twairesh and Hadeel Al-Negheimish, 2019, "Surface and Deep Features Ensemble for Sentiment Analysis of Arabic Tweets", *IEEE Access*, vol. 7, pp. 84122–84131.

65. Muath Alali, Nurfadhlina Mohd Sharef, Masrah Azrifah Azmi Murad, Hazlina Hamdan, and Nor Azura Husin, 2019, "Narrow Convolutional Neural Network for Arabic Dialects Polarity Classification", *IEEE Access*, vol. 7, pp. 96272–96283.

66. Mohammed A. El-Affendi, Khawla Alrajhi, and Amir Hussain, 2021, "A Novel Deep Learning-Based Multilevel Parallel Attention Neural (MPAN) Model for Multidomain Arabic Sentiment Analysis", *IEEE Access*, vol. 9, pp. 7508–7518.

67. Faiza Mehmood, Muhammad Usman Ghani Khan, Mini Xian, Rehab Shahzadi, Waqar Mahmood, and Muhammad Nabeel Asim, 2020, "A Precisely Xtreme-Multi Channel Hybrid Approach for Roman Urdu Sentiment Analysis", *IEEE Access*, vol. 8, pp. 192740–192759.

68. Khawar Mehmood, Daryl Essam, Kamran Shafi, and Muhammad Kamran Malik, 2019, "Discriminative Feature Spamming Technique for Roman Urdu Sentiment Analysis", *IEEE Access*, vol. 7, pp. 47991–48002.

69. Javier Pastor-Galindo, Mattia Zago, Pantaleone Nespoli, Sergio López Bernal, Alberto Huertas, Mauel Gil Pérez, José A. Ruipérez-Veliente, Gregorio Martinez Perez, and Felix Gomez Marmol, 2020, "Spotting Political Social Bots in Twitter: A Use Case of the 2019 Spanish General Election", *IEEE Transactions on Network and Service Management*, vol. 17, no. 4, pp. 2156–2170.

70. Salud Maria Jimenez Zafra, Maria Teresa. Martin Valdivia, Eugenio Martinez Camara, and L. Alfonso Urena Lopez, 2019, "Studying the Scope of for Spanish Sentiment Analysis on Twitter", *IEEE Transactions on Affective Computing*, vol. 10, no. 1, pp. 129–141.

71. María-Teresa Martín Valdivia, Eugenio Martínez-Cámara, Jose M. Perea-Ortega, and L. Alfonso Ureña-López, 2013, "Sentiment Polarity Detection in Spanish Reviews Combining Supervised and Unsupervised Approaches", *Expert Systems with Applications*, vol 40, no. 10, pp. 3934–3942.

72. Sergey Smetanin, 2020, "The Applications of Sentiment Analysis for Russian Language Texts: Current Challenges and Future Perspectives", *IEEE Access*, vol. 8, pp. 110693–110719.

73. Muhammad Fakhrur Razi Abu Bakar, Norisma Idris, Liyana Shuib, and Norazlina Khamis, 2020, "Sentiment Analysis of Noisy Malay Text: State of Art, Challenges and Future Work", *IEEE Access*, vol. 8, pp. 24687–24696.

74. Sindhu C, Shilpi Adak, and Soumya Celina Tigga, 2021, "Opinionated Text Classification For Hindi Tweets Using Deep Learning", *2021 5th International Conference on Computing Methodologies and Communication (ICCMC)*, pp. 1217–1222, doi: 10.1109/ICCMC51019.2021.9418361.

75. Kim Schouten and Flavius Frasincar, 2016, "Survey on Aspect-Level Sentiment Analysis", *IEEE Transactions on Knowledge and Data Engineering*, vol. 28, no. 3, pp. 813–830.

76. Koby Crammer and Yoram Singer, 2001, "Pranking with Ranking", *Proceedings of Advances in Neural Information Processing Systems*, vol. 14, pp. 641–647.

77. Sindhu Chandra Sekharan and G. Vadivu, 2021, "ExOpSum: An Extractive Opinion Summarization Methodology based on Aspect-Sentence-Review Ranking", *International Conference on Artificial Intelligence and Machine Vision (AIMV)*, 2021, pp. 1–5, doi: 10.1109/AIMV53313.2021.9670917.

78. H. Wang, Y. Lu, and C. Zhai, 2011, "Latent Aspect Rating Analysis Without Aspect Keyword Supervision", *Proceedings of 17th ACM SIGKDD International Conference on Knowledge Discovery in Data Mining*, pp. 618–626.

79. Bin Lu, Myle Ott, Claire Cardie, and Benjamin K. Tsou, 2011, "Multi-Aspect Sentiment Analysis with Topic Models", *Proceedings of the IEEE 11th International Conference on Data Mining*, pp. 81–88.
80. Kalervo Jarvelin and Jaana Kekalainen, 2002, "Cumulated Gain-Based Evaluation of IR Techniques", *ACM Transactions on Information Systems*, vol. 20, no. 4, pp. 422–446.

Index

Pages in *italics* refer figures, **bold** refer tables.